Cultural Activisms

Cultural Activisms

Poetic Voices, Political Voices

edited by

Gertrude M. James Gonzalez

and

Anne JM Mamary

State University of New York Press

Production by Ruth Fisher
Marketing by Dana E. Yanulavich

Published by
State University of New York Press, Albany

© 1999 State University of New York

For information, address the State University of New York Press,
State University Plaza, Albany, NY 12246

Library of Congress Cataloging-in-Publication Data

Cultural activisms : poetic voices, political voices / edited by
Gertrude M. James Gonzalez and Anne J.M. Mamary.
    p. cm.
    Includes index.
    ISBN 0-7914-3965-8 (alk. paper)
    ISBN 0-7914-3966-6 (pbk. : alk. paper)
    1. American literature—Minority authors. 2. American
literature—20th century. 3. Commonwealth literature (English).
4. Culture—Political aspects. 5. Art—Political aspects. 6. Feminist
theory. I. Gonzalez, Gertrude M. James, 1967– . II. Mamary, Anne
J.M., 1964– .
  PS508.M54C85 1998
  810.8'0920693—dc21   98-13727
                                               CIP

10 9 8 7 6 5 4 3 2 1

In memory of
Ana M. Gonzalez Acosta de James
(1937–1996), my mother and my friend.

Contents

Acknowledgments

A number of Universities, colleagues, friends, and family have been supportive and encouraging throughout the four years in which this anthology developed. We greatly appreciate their interest in the unfolding of the book.

First we recognize the efforts of Greg Thomas and Pam Weems, our colleagues and friends with whom we not only began this project as a conference but with whom we also worked during the early stages of the anthology's inception and growth; they have since moved on to other projects, but we are happy to have received their input, ideas, and revolutionary spirit.

St. Lawrence University supported this anthology with a generous research grant. Binghamton University of the State University of New York, and Cortland College of the State University of New York also assisted our work both technically and financially.

We especially thank Lois Patton at SUNY Press for her encouragement and support. Professors Jeffner Allen and Nkiru Nzegwu have been our mentors, offering us invaluable guidance at every stage of the project's development. Peter Klosky and Roberta Wackett designed Ronald Gonzalez's "Devil Things." The illustrations between sections are by Gertrude M. James Gonzalez. We also offer special thanks to Jeanne Constable, Anne Csete, Amy Burtner, Jean Deese, Mary Haught, Peter Klosky, Helene Shulman Lorenz, Janet Manbeck, PJ McGann, Michelle Meyers, Joanne G. Passaro, Patrick Rivers, Cami Townsend, Maria Wackett, Roberta Wackett, and Amy Wieber, who helped us in various ways.

Introduction

The poets, installation artists, essayists, sculptors, sketch artists, fiction writers, performance artists, muralists, and experimental writers who contribute to *Cultural Activisms: Poetic Voices, Political Voices* are as diverse in cultural origins as they are in their forms of expression. Drawing on her or his own cultural and creative wellsprings, each artist offers a particular understanding of culture, activism, poetry, voicing, and politics. The strands the artists and writers have spun are of varied tones, textures, and colors. These strands do not easily lend themselves to being woven into one common fabric or collective language and we have purposefully tried to resist any temptation to force a single unifying theme. As a result, we feel a particular challenge trying to introduce this book and its authors. A history of the project might be helpful. . . .

This anthology had its beginnings in a conference we organized with Greg Thomas and Pam Weems at the State University of New York at Binghamton in 1992. In different ways each of us felt ignored, threatened, erased, misunderstood, undermined, and deadened as a result of racist, sexist, heterosexist, classist, and other oppressive forces both in and out of academia. The conference was, in part, an attempt to resist and bend the narrow confines in which we found ourselves. But this was not the most important part of our work on the conference or on this anthology.

There were some who described the conference as "anti-academic" or "anti-mainstream" or "anti-hegemonic." While resistance was part of our work, we refused to allow ourselves to be defined once again by the very people who were making our lives difficult in the first place. True enough, everyone who participated in the conference stood in one way or another apart from dominant culture(s) and power(s), but the plural creative energy the event generated helped to make it clear that neither the four of us nor any of the panelists and performers could be easily defined as one undifferentiated "other," or monolithic mass of "difference." We resisted the re-channelling of our energy and the wonderful creativity of the conference participants into an energyless and non-creative place.

And furthermore, we hoped that it was not only shared feelings of frustration that drew us together nor resistance to injustice which defined our creative and political work. As we brought four very different voices to the project, we tried to notice when we were connecting and when we could not. We moved in different ways and spoke in different languages as we strove to create spaces for all sorts of conversations, even when some of us couldn't or wouldn't occupy those spaces. We certainly were not asking for those dominant forces to "give" us space. But we *were* adamant about taking and making space for ourselves, our art, our many cultures and languages. And so our work on the conference left us feeling a little like bandits, stealing around the edges of our department, and banshees, wailing in languages incomprehensible to many who move in dominant worlds and tongues.

Claiming space for our lives and projects, the conference, and this book, is about taking very seriously our selves and cultures. We think about culture in broad terms—cultures of ethnicity, race, gender, class, sexuality, age, ability, spirituality, cultures of art and writing—the ways in which our lives are shaped and in which we shape our own and others' lives. Cultural activisms grow out of our cultures. Cultural activisms rework, revisit, recite, and re-site our cultures of origin, our cultures of choice, our hoped-for cultures and the overlappings of these cultures. We live and write and think and play and paint and draw and dance and sculpt and desire and cry and scream and hope and pray not only to undermine oppressive foundations but also to create and nurture living, exciting, sometimes unforeseen realities. And so, this book, like the conference, opens into wide, rich, and varied terrains for multiple expressions of cultural creation, and activism.

As four organizers became two editors, we knew that we weren't the only ones engaged in such cultural and political expression, and we were eager to see what kind of work others were doing. We certainly never could have anticipated the roads down which the project has taken us and the creative, funny, insightful, serious, wonderful writers and artists we have met along the way. We spent fascinating days voyaging through journals at the Cornell University and SUNY Binghamton libraries, exploring books in stores, friends' houses, and in reviews. We visited bookstores, cafes, and artists' studios seeking out contributions, and we handed out fliers at poetry readings, open mic nights, and at academic conferences of many sorts. We approached cousins, strangers, friends, and friends of friends about sharing their words and work with us. And then there was the excitement of envelopes arriving in the mail, some spilling photographs and others splashing words like spring raindrops onto our tables.

A gathering of these offerings, *Cultural Activisms: Poetic Voices, Political Voices* has grown into a multi-genred mosaic, which offers multiple resistances to oppression through a variety of styles. Rather than exclusively theorizing about how art and writing might be political, this text presents art and writing that is political. The wide array of voices and styles in the text is one of the book's strengths as it not only offers a multifaceted approach toward activism and positive change, but also offers a range of emotions, including anger, passion, joy, fear, and courage. In addition, this book claims space for the humor and hope that can come even in the face of violence and despair. The organization of the pieces and some of the contributions themselves may seem unconventional and sometimes unsettling. For example, from one chapter to the next, or even within one chapter, there can be a strong shift of emotion or passion. We find these shifts, although sometimes jarring, to be the sorts of feelings and, at times, rapidly shifting feelings, we encounter in our everyday lives and work.

And so, we have learned about working together over several years and many miles, and about how hard it can be to write together when we have different politics, different cultural backgrounds, different ways of working with language, and different ways of conceptualizing similar ideas. We've discovered that the two of us, along with each of the contributors to the anthology, do not stand on the "same" ground, even if we slide together across the same snow-covered field in Upstate New York or splash through the same turquoise-clear water in Southern Florida. But, in the spaces stolen, bandit-like, we hope that this collection of pages "works" together to sustain poetic cultural activism—unconstrained by a solitary vision or a firm, unchanging landscape.

☙❧

"Winged Tongues," this book's first section, addresses questions of language, both literal and figurative/cultural; cultural appropriations; colonization; and the commodification of cultures. In addition to naming multiple silences, the contributors to this section also pronounce the richness of their various languages. These tongues often connect an author to his or her cultures, while offering tools of resistance and creativity.

The second section of this book invokes the many senses of the word, "Passages": lines of text, the shape of a maze or passageway, a journey or migration, a shift or translation. The movements may be within a particular cultural setting or across languages or cultural barriers. Some of the authors recount forced crossings and some map passages into places of greater freedom, either present or hoped-for; each author makes note of the toll her or his passage exacts on the body and spirit or on the telling of the story.

"Spinning Memories," the next section of this book, explores silences in official histories and excavates and retells buried stories—spinning meaning out of fragmented history, gaps in dominant texts, and stories passed along from generation to generation and spinning off in new directions, reclaiming desire, meaning, magic, possibility. Although myriad stories and voices weave in and among the chapters in this section, a position of utter relativism or "any story goes" would silence many of the voices gathered here. The authors in this section work against both forgetting and refusing to know—some examining and evaluating locations of privilege and others reclaiming and reinventing historically stifled voices.

The fourth section of this book, "Bones and Shadow," invokes life and life-sustaining connection in the face of despair, evil, and death. The pieces in this section gather many ways in which life is/lives are embodied. Physical attack, torture, violence, fear are not abstractions—it is a particular woman or man who suffers pain in her or his own body, heart, soul. Memories, stories, rituals of everyday life, incantations, intimacy, passion, sweet joy, desire proclaimed in codes of body and dress, some memories so painful they are hidden away until strength is gathered. In this section there is a sense of mourning for loved ones who have died and of prayer to stave off the deaths of those still living. Invoking both horror and tenderness, this section suggests the tenacity and fragility of human connection, sometimes across differences of geography and culture.

Fragile and tenacious connections weave also through "Night Blossoms," the final section of *Cultural Activisms: Poetic Voices, Political Voices*. Night blossoms—a midnight fragrance, song, glance, connections made in codes of language across taped telephone lines—summon friendship, gentleness, passion, and hope. One of the themes of this section is careful attention—to friends' pain, to friends' joy, to differences among people and the strength in these differences. Life is embraced on the edge of death, in the stories and poems of those already gone—night blossoms into a wider array of possibilities than anyone could have foretold.

☙❧

The process of editing this collection has been a cultural activism of its own. As we discussed the project and particular pieces with friends, we discovered that often several people who read the same piece were moved in very different ways. These diverse perspectives and responses often highlighted and added to the richness of the essay or poem or artwork. Sometimes a selection rearranged the conceptual ground on which one or both of us stood, making us see that selection and others in wholly new lights. As we read and edited and faxed and wrote and e-mailed and phoned contributors and each other, our own frames of reference sometimes changed shape. And so we hesitate to frame the sections of and contributors to this book too specifically precisely to leave room for readers to bring their own voices, cultures, perspectives, and creativities to the text—knowing that readers will bring layers of richness and changing perspective.

Perhaps it will become possible, when such shifts in perspective are attempted, to listen more closely to the "incoherent" wailing of banshees. If one re-tunes one's ears away from standards of dominant tongues, the banshees may sound wise not deranged, oracular not incoherent. For banshees are female spirits believed to presage a death in the family by wailing outside the house. *Cultural Activisms: Poetic Voices, Political Voices* suggests that space is taken, oracles revealed, even if no one but the bandit or the banshee attends. However your ear is pitched, whatever the terrain under your feet, it is our wish that the selections in the book invite you to revel in the undercover work of bandits and to find great promise in the wailing of banshees.

winged tongues

Bird Lessons

        "You will find it in the soup"
    the bowl with steam turning to clouds
into shapes   My friends cringe as they fish
with their spoon net
   but no petals of flesh are caught
       only pilaf noodles that narrow on each end
"We call them bird's tongue because of the shape
you will find them in the soup"
Their eyes look down
   they had expected something exotic
     and would have preferred pink flesh

but it is I who cringe
     we are not savages   I am blind
by pink tongues flapping in my broth

pink tongues flapping in my broth they paddle to stay alive
propel from one side to the other what if they jump and flap a
slap across my face? tongues would never do that I put them in
boiling broth expand them to their greatest potential they are
noodles and I am obsessed with their name why should pasta
tamer than alphabets have such a vicious name the bird left
with gaping hoarse beak put up your fists you phrase maker
we have letters to settle I grew up with my grandmother

3

putting them in my vegetable soup my mother in chicken
soup and I in clear broth how dare you give a name with
color shall giants cut my tongue to flavor their soup and do
men who turn cannibal eat the round soft point you touch to
the tip of your nose? what kind of tongue do the dead have
thin flat or with zigzag cuts like my last lover? how to treat
these noodles in my broth will they grow to giants *lesan el
asfour lesan* tongue *el* of *asfour* bird a tiny bird forced to put in
my soup explain to dinner guests what is in their bowls or
when I send a stranger to shop no other translation and I am
blind with birds flapping in my broth.

"I love your shirt.
I love Egyptian!
I love it!!!"

The pharaohs on my shirt
must have struck
him eloquent.
This youth bounding through CVS
without losing a step
announced his views on my native land.
Inspired by Isis
her winged arms outstretched in a gesture
                                    He felt
                                    he must
                                         declare. . .

Love
      the old city of Cairo a bare foot boy in white shorts
races with a stick tapping a bicycle tire
a man, his face obscured in a steam of hot clouds, pushes a cart
full of roasting peanuts   "5 piasters" each soiled brown bag

      a walk on the corniche   turquoise Nile glass blue
as the sun drowns its rays
and the last taxi honks

Shall I say I love your Plymouth Rock and Salem Harbor shirt
      and by such I love American?

sea legs balancing on rock
first crop stagnant in the earth

the deliquescence from your lips this melting pot
compressed image on my back

> *"That's why I want to learn*
> *to speak the English . . . so*
> *people will think I'm white."*
> Zakia, an Ethiopian refugee
> hoping to come to the U.S.

gone astray the morning how
landed in sunshine, a dog barked the night
fear mixes slowly like butter and sugar
shaped flat ground into "but your English is so good"
> tongues wounding around loose leaf tepee
> Babel is nonsensical if you're monolingual
> while others gossip about passersby

The Egyptian driver lassoed by his own tongue's swear
when the other boomeranged back the same dialect

> caught by surprise
a stranglehold that tips us to precarious balance
such a pleasant conversation—slipped out, pulled beneath
unawares the "but you speak English so well"
> like a native—stutter the letters
> sound out the microphone—
a cutthroat tongue frantic

As a child I made up my own language with fingers
tapping the rhythm of syllables
> combining sounds . . .
We create a tug *tafrazeehea tagragehea*
syntax askew: fingertips play thumb piano melodies
> strutting the harmony alone

Please state your native tongue: misplaced the original
> replaced by one non-native

My English so well learned in my own country
chattering sounds in one alphabet close
the vowels of your misconstrued remark.

gameboy

he buys me a glass
of bass draft
& asks
if I am japanese

his remarks:
you are the perfect
combination of boy & man

are you the hip hot hung
  9 inches of fun
  seeking the slim,
  smooth, smiling
  authentically
  thai-tasting
  geisha-guy
  on the side
  macho dancer
  looking for his lord & master
  m. butterfly-wedding
  banquet-joy fuck club

I am not a korean dragon lady
running down avenue a
with a tea pot between my legs

shouting
  where's my tip-
  gimme my trophy
you wanna play with me?
you can just quit orientalizin'
cuz I ain't gonna
change my
cotton-knit calvins
for you or my mother

if I lose

I ain't gonna fry you an emperor's meal
or throw you eurasia
or butterfly you an opera

I'm thru givin' sex tours of unicef countries
3rd world is for hunger & sally struthers

I've long been the "it"
in a rice queen phenomenon
that's burned faster than gin bottles
thrown at the black of my skillet

games so old as jason & hercules
men fucking my body
like fresh golden fleeces

they ride my boyhood on bikes
in the woods
then rape it & kill it
with leashes spit words
in personal ads
(those clever written puzzles)
for fun
they blood-brother baptize
my emotions
then martyr my sisters
in the backroom basements

I'm thru with charades
I'm thru with your malice
& your riots like hopskotch
I'm not gonna fight it

I am beyond being
poker-faced/mysterious/submissive
wanted by you
or a being who's glossy
& g.q. queen gorgeous

you wanna play freeze tag
I'm frozen already
touch me
you'll swear I'm the iceman's ice monkey

hit me
& watch where the mah jong chips land

lust me
I'll soon feel the back of your hand

play with me then
if you think the sweet that's left
to the taste in my tongue
is enough & not bitter

love me for this
I forfeit the game
remove my make-up

& call you the winner

three forty-seven A.M.
Last call for drinks
I stumble to his
motorcycle
Ride the wind
behind his back
My hair plays—
Born to be Wild

four A.M.
Inside his apartment
is an enourmous
—tank of goldfish
anthropology books—
spill over a desk
(I'm glad there are
no dogs)

four twenty-one A.M.
He unbuttons my shirt
licks my tit
slams me eagle
on the mattress

five-thirty A.M.
I stare at his body
with my stain on his chest
"You're my best geisha-boy!"
He whispers, turning the halogen off

six thirty-three A.M.
The sky turns from purple to orange
as I walk home from the East to the West
and roll back on my bed

seven-ten P.M.

He doesn't know that I compose poems on a keyboard
that I wear eye glasses to work   that I spell my name
with one "g"   that I am allergic to cut grass

this is the vanishing act of the year

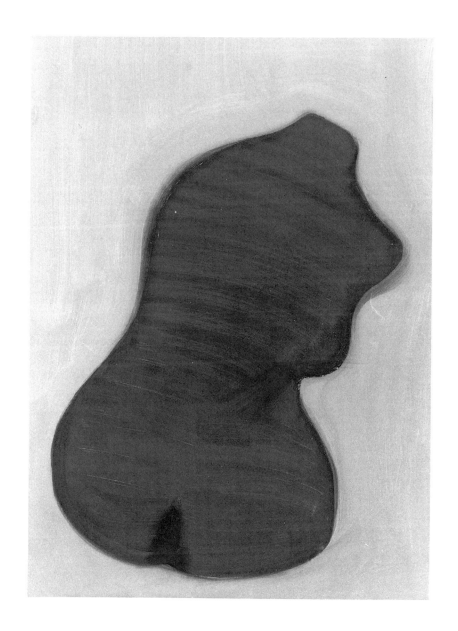

PAT PARKER

"Don't let the fascist speak."
"We want to hear what they have to say."
"Keep them out of the classroom."
"Everyone is entitled to freedom of speech."

I am a child of America
a step child
     raised in the back room
yet taught
     taught how to act
in the front room.
my mind jumps
the voices of students
screaming
insults   threats
"Let the Nazis speak"
"Let the Nazis speak"
Everyone is entitled
     to speak
I sit a greasy-legged
     Black child
in a Black school
in the Black part of town
look to a Black teacher
the bill of rights
     guarantees
us all the right
     my mind

remembers   chants
article I   article I
& my innards churn
they remember
the Black teacher
in the Black school
in the Black part
of the very white town
who stopped us
when we attacked
the puppet principal
of the white Board
of mis-Education
cast-off books
illustrated with
cartoons and
words of wisdom
written by white
children in the
other part of town
missing pages
caricatures
of hanging niggers—
the bill of rights
was written to
     protect
       us

my mind remembers
& my innards churn
conjure images
    police
break up
illegal demonstrations
illegal assemblies
    conjure image
of a Black Panther
"if tricky Dick
tries to stop us

we'll stop him."
    conjure images
of that same Black man
going to jail
for threatening
the life of
    THE PRESIDENT

every citizen
is entitled to
freedom of speech
my mind remembers
& my innards churn
conjure images
of jews in camps—
of homosexuals in camps—
of socialists in camps—
"Let the Nazis speak"
"Let the Nazis speak"
    faces in a college
        classroom
"You're being a fascist too."
"We want to hear what
they have to say"

    faces in
a college classroom
young white faces
    speak let them speak
speak let them speak
Blacks jews some whites
seize the bull horn
"We don't want to hear
your socialist rhetoric"
    socialist rhetoric
    survival
        rhetoric
the supreme court
says it is illegal

to scream fire
in a crowded theatre

to scream fire
in a crowded theatre
cause people to panic
to run to hurt each other
my mind remembers
& now i know
what my innards
      say
illegal to cause
      people
to panic
to run
to hurt
there is
no contradiction
what the Nazis say
will cause
      people
      to hurt
      ME.

For the white person who wants to know how to be my friend

The first thing you do is to forget that i'm Black
Second, you must never forget that i'm Black

You should be able to dig Aretha,
but don't play her every time i come over.
And if you decide to play Beethoven—don't tell me
his life story. They made us take music appreciation too.

Eat soul food if you like it, but don't expect me
to locate your restaurants
or cook it for you.

And if some Black person insults you,
mugs you, rapes your sister, rapes you,
rips your house is just being an ass—
please, do not apologize to me
for wanting to do them bodily harm.
It makes me wonder if you're foolish.

And even if you really believe Blacks are better lovers than
whites—don't tell me. I start thinking of charging stud fees.

In other words—if you really want to be my friend—*don't*
make a labor of it. I'm lazy. Remember.

OLIVIA GUDE, MARCUS AKINLANA,
AND BEATRIZ SANTIAGO MUÑOZ

Innovators and Elders: Painting in the Streets

Olivia Gude, Marcus Akinlana, and Beatriz Santiago Muñoz are artists who often work in the form of community murals. They are members of Chicago Public Art Group, an artists' collective that was founded twenty-eight years ago by William Walker, and John Pitman Weber. Walker and Weber were key figures in the reinvention of murals as a contemporary urban street art form. In this conversation through a long evening of power outages and ice cream, after a long hot day of painting, Gude, Akinlana, and Santiago explore what it means to be mentored into a continuous tradition of collaborative, community-based art. What are the responsibilities, the contradictions, and the possibilities?

Olivia: I see young artists today struggling with questions of audience, authenticity, and balance between individual vision and collective and community vision. These artists are often cut off from their antecedents. Even if they are familiar with the artistic products of earlier political art movements, they are often cut off from the living tradition, from having direct access to the artists. I think this limits understanding of the interaction of social action and aesthetic discussion through which the work was generated.

The three of us, along with others in the later generations of Chicago Public Art Group artists, share that we
are all inheritors of a political, public art tradition. As
members of the Chicago Public Art Group, we've had
access to firsthand knowledge of choices, practices, and
troubles of earlier generations of muralists. For me, it's
been a second graduate education, rooted in practice
and history.

Bea: None of us were part of the original mural movement
and we've come into the movement at different times. I
designed and painted my first outdoor mural in 1992.
Marcus, I believe your first big project was the Roseland
Pullman mural in 1988. Olivia, when did you get started?

Olivia: I painted my first outdoor mural in 1986, but I'd been
doing collaborative murals indoors since the late seventies. Also, during the early eighties I worked with a partner, Jon Pounds, doing non-permission street pieces.

Bea: Along with understanding and building on the community murals tradition, I think we've been actively engaged
in interrogating the tradition as a means to keeping it a
living movement, capable of dealing with the cultural
complexities of today. How does our work fit into the
politics of today? How do we, as artists, reinvent ourselves, reinvent the tradition?
   My relationship to the mural tradition in the Americas—the Mexican Mural Movement and the contemporary street murals—was based on its association with
progressive, grassroots politics. I've been doing some
research on how people have thought about the role of
murals in society, and right next to a Diego Rivera article about the revolutionary power of murals was an
article by the fascist muralist, Mario Sironi, talking about
the wonderful fascist power of mural painting.

Olivia: So we have to face that the wonderful political power of
mural painting to influence people in their daily lives is
not necessarily progressive.

Bea: Yes, the form does not inherently have a politics. It's a very powerful public tool. We are part of a broad tradition of using forms that have a large audience.

Olivia: That's certainly a large part of what attracted me to murals. Another broad theme I've felt connected to is the desire to decommodify the art object. Early in my artistic career, I felt frustrated and alienated by making work that would not be seen by many people. I also had this sudden awareness—if I keep making work, what am I going to do with it? Where am I going to store it if I don't sell it? And how am I going to sell work that's got the kind of politics I want to explore and develop? Why would museums or galleries who are intimately tied into structures of power be willing to show such work?

Doing street art broke the barrier of isolation from a larger public and freed me from some of the constraints of private ownership of work. It was so freeing to do a major piece, take a slide, and be able to walk away. I could think about people and politics, instead of maintaining and placing objects.

Joining CPAG introduced me to a whole other level of process and content. The work was not only about expressing oneself on the street; it was rooted in a conscious choice to see the audience and artist relationship as reciprocal. The word "community" is probably overused and underexamined in the artworld these days, but the muralists have spent three decades asking the questions, "What does it mean to be an artist to the multiple communities to which I belong?" and perhaps, most importantly, "How does collective artmaking contribute to the making and shaping of the community?"

I think some of the best muralists have a kind of love/hate relationship with the form. They are constantly questioning the efficacy and the politics of the murals in interaction with the communities.

Bea: A lot of murals I saw in Puerto Rico were very simplistic. For example, one had an African man, a Taino (the indigenous native people of the Caribbean until the coming of Columbus, when they were virtually wiped out by disease and persecution), and a Spaniard. All were dressed in the garb of the colonial period and were holding hands happily—perhaps the worst example of a false multiculturalism I've ever seen. That's what murals were to me until I had access to art books and saw the possibility of other kinds of mural work.

Marcus: I definitely did not begin with that love/hate relationship, but I was getting exposed to a different type of murals. I was in D.C., looking at books with pictures of murals done here in Chicago and in L.A. from the late sixties and into the seventies. So those murals were different than what Bea is describing. Those sound politically backwards—propaganda for a Babylon system.

Especially when I was younger, I wanted to make art work that would heighten people's political consciousness, particularly in my community, the African-American community. I wanted to heighten their self-awareness as human beings, their self-worth and understanding of their culture and heritage. I asked myself, "How can I do that?" and because I am a painter the best way to do that was through murals.

Murals are big and overwhelming; they overwhelm your senses. Just by their very size they make a lasting impression on you. A studio painting could even be a better quality painting than a mural, but for the most part it will never make the impression that a mural will make on the general public. And a mural will be seen by thousands of people, and, of course, advertisers are using this exact same medium for their purposes. Later I realized that Jeff Donaldson and AfriCobra put forward in the 1970s that African-American artists should make big things to impress the minds of the people. That was its appeal to me.

Olivia: It's wonderful when children paint murals, but it's frustrating that people in the artworld don't differentiate between children's murals and murals that are generated in a complex community process with professional community artists. I think the lack of critical attention has hurt the ability of the mural movement to grow and develop aesthetically.

Marcus: Well, you know we've had numerous conversations about that, about pushing the mural aesthetic onwards as a creative art form, like any other art form. To me, murals shouldn't be a political propaganda machine. It's an art form. Art is concerned with making a piece of quality craft and with being creative, and being creative means you're not doing the same thing for twenty-five years. That's one thing I'd like to see as far as the overall movement—a heightened awareness of people taking their time to become masters. If your art form is working with the community—painting, sculpting, whatever your art calls for—take the time to master your craft so that we can have a movement that's based on excellence.

Now, murals began as a grassroots movement so it didn't necessarily spring particularly from artists. Not everybody who began the mural movement was an artist. It's still a popular movement, but it has grown from its base.

Olivia: When you say, "Push the aesthetic," do you have certain categories that you've thought about that you would like to see developed?

Marcus: I've noticed that quite a few things that artists do in their studio work, they don't bring into their murals. We need to risk, to bring these images out into the public. It's good to have social conscience in your art, but at the same time you should be trying to master your craft. This is nothing new—AfriCobra said this years ago. Number Two of their eight principles was, "Good art, excellence."

Olivia: I'm interested in exploring the social and aesthetic meanings that come out of collaboration and difference within murals. Coming from a painting background, I came to mural making with a painting sensibility. I was very conscious of how the individual mark of the painter was a primary generator of meaning within the work. In 1987, on the Mifflin Cooperative Mural, I worked with a partner, Jon Pounds, and with sixty-five volunteers. Rather than trying to get people to paint the same, we tried to let different parts be in different styles. We wanted the evidence of different hands, different strokes, to be part of the meaning of the piece.

As I've continued in murals, I've gotten away from that. Marcus, I think that you and I got really good at painting together so that people couldn't tell our styles apart within a mural. But, when we work together again, I hope we can emphasize individuality and difference. You've been doing some beautiful things with value and flesh tones on faces and I've been pushing even further the use of separate individual strokes of high chroma color. I'd like to see these two styles coexist and interact on a mural.

Marcus: Yes, that was done by Mitchell Caton and Calvin Jones in the early eighties. If you know their separate styles, it's kind of amazing to see how they just put the two styles together and the murals flow. It is so unified that it looks as though one artist utilized intensive patterning and also his ability to paint volumetrically and realistically. In reality, it is the style of two different artists fused together into an aesthetic whole. That's a whole other way of collaborating. You don't meet in the middle: you just bring both people's strengths to the table. It would be interesting to expand that even more.

Olivia: In Chicago, through CPAG, the emphasis of the mural movement has been on collaborations. This is in contrast to how the tradition has sometimes developed in other cities. We have emphasized the collaboration of the professional artist within the community, but also the equal collaborations of professional artists with each other. Our system has not been one of masters and apprentices. We tend to design projects which allow for the aesthetic input and energy of more than one professional artist. How do you all see the significance of this work?

Marcus: Outside this culture, working collaboratively wouldn't be such a different way of doing things. I saw a TV show on Bali in which five guys were sitting there working on one painting. The painting was only five feet by four feet or so. They were in a studio overlooking the beautiful terraces of Bali and they were all sitting quietly, painting, working on one image. A few feet away, there was a guy working on a painting by himself. Now they were all taking their time painting; there was no obvious rush. They interviewed these artists and the five said, "Well, you know, he's the odd man out. He refuses to work over here with us. He wants to work by himself." From that cultural view, that kind of individualism was odd. They have ways of coming together on some levels that are impossible or unheard of here. Here it is an everybody-out-for-themselves, individualistic society.

I think the fact that we've been able to do that kind of collaboration under this society is phenomenal. People are surprised when they find we have two or three artists working on a project. How do you do that? The assumption they have is that the artist is supposed to have a monstrous ego. It's a role model for the community when they see two or three artists be able to subjugate their egos and their own selfish intentions, and work together to make something lasting for the community.

Bea: It's amazing how people just refuse to believe that this is possible. In the project I am working on now, people keep looking for the person in charge. Who is the "real" artist? To work collaboratively on a project, you have to learn to give up a little bit of yourself in order to open yourself up to new possibilities.

Olivia: Collaboration is a powerful image. It's perhaps especially important in a city like Chicago, which is one of

the most racially divided cities in the world. It's important for a neighborhood to see multiracial teams of
artists working together, having differences, getting mad
at each other, dealing with it and going on with their
mutual work. The mural-making process is a metaphor
for a functional society.

Marcus: Cultural differences and political disagreements are
enough to start a bloody war. Here we have artists of
different cultures coming together to work in the area
of culture, an area that is usually a bone of contention
between peoples. In 1988, when we were doing the
Roseland Pullman mural with 102 people, we had
Latinos, Blacks, and Whites actually working together
on a mural on an underpass that divided and connected the two neighborhoods. That summer in the
news media everyday they kept pumping the issue about
Chicago being racially polarized and we had over a
hundred people working together on a project in peace
and harmony.

Olivia: I think that since the late eighties, many muralists have
done a good job of examining and extending the legacy
of collaboration and community involvement. The
muralists have understood for many years that meaning is created by an interaction between the artist and
the audience. The conventional artworld under the
influence of "continental" theory is now understanding that the work is a co-creation of the receiver and
the sender and has consequently become increasingly
interested in community-based work.

A great deal of contemporary theory examines the
hidden complexities of making representations. How
conscious are we of strategies of representation in our
mural work?

One of the issues muralists face is being called upon
to represent "the people." Often this means representing a multiracial neighborhood or nation. These representations of collective difference can be dismissed as
being like Bennetton ads. I'm sure you've both heard

The Great Migration by Marcus Akinlana. Acrylic paint mural on brick. Cosponsored by the Elliot Donnelly Youth Center and Chicago Public Art Group. (c) Akinlana, 1995. Photo credit: Jennifer Swenson.

me argue that there wouldn't be Bennetton-type ads if there hadn't been a contemporary mural movement. Despite the dangers of abuse and misrepresentation, of false images of a happy multiracial society, I think we must sometimes risk making those utopian images. I believe as artists we have a responsibility not only to critique, but to create proactive future visions.

Bea: Examining community muralmaking closely brings up a lot of questions. When you make a mural, you are doing more than representing the community, the representation itself is what marks what the community is, what is included in the collective. What you represent is where the parameters are drawn; what you leave out is outside the definition. That's one of the strange powers of such a large work—a power I sometimes don't particularly want.

Collectives and communities are organic, fluid things. A particular geographic section of the city might be a community, but within it there are communities that are not geographic at all, that extend beyond geography, like gay and lesbian communities or some political communities. These communities may not be welcomed at the community center, because it is sponsored by people who are excluding them. It's problematic that we rely so heavily on geography. If our job is reduced to talking about community in racial terms and other collective identities are left out, this devalues them in some way.

Olivia: When I did the mural, *Where We Come From. . . Where We're Going*, I was trying to look at that question, trying to think about what it means to constitute ourselves as a community. Just because people live in geographic proximity are they functioning as a community? One of the things that became clear to me in doing that mural and interviewing people and talking to them, was that people can actually exist in the same urban space and not communicate. What makes a community is discourse and sometimes discourse is not happening. Since then I've been increasingly interested in what the possibilities are of using a mural to draw more people into the discourse or even to call attention specifically to who is not in the conversation.

Marcus: I think about it from an entirely different angle. I don't see it as being problematic, because if you work with the community the way many of us have, it is virtually impossible to come up with an image that is not reflective of the lifeblood of that people. Because you are dealing with their input from the foundation you lay on that project and one way or another, you connect. It may be a more profound engagement with the people than only dealing with their verbal input.

Of course, you can't please all the people all the time, but once you have that open-door policy to the community and belong as a member of the community,

Where We Come From . . . Where We're Going by Olivia Gude. An oral
history mural in acrylic paint on concrete. Sponsored by Chicago Public Art
Group. (c) Gude, 1992. Photo credit: Chicago Public Art Group.

I haven't experienced any problems with creating images that speak to people. Now they may not like everything, but it creates something that speaks to them,
that they can understand. It is something that has something valuable to say for that community, because it is
a product of the collective will, power, and vision of the
community.

Bea: The organizations that we often work with are schools
and community centers. This is not an unmediated,
unbiased representation of the community around
you; the images are funneled through a bureaucracy
that has specific needs and is oriented toward a particular liberal politics that are not necessarily truly
progressive. They are not trying to push the enve-
lope of inclusion.

Again I think of the example of the gay and lesbian community. They are not represented in the community centers as gays and lesbians. We are not going to connect with them there. Their history will not be documented through the "normal" channels. We need to work with more organizations that are not geographically based and determined.

Olivia: That's an interesting problem for the medium, because murals are by their very nature territorial. One of the things that is wonderful about murals is that they claim public space. I think one can argue that in some ways murals are one of the few things that are continuing to reinvent public space at a time when there is an increasing privatization of public space and public lands. Billboard space is sold; the space along roadways is sold. So it's interesting to think what it means to represent non-geographical community in a medium so heavily geared toward physically reclaiming territory of the public consciousness.

Beatriz, I know you've been putting a lot of time into rethinking the mural tradition. On your project this summer, you set out to push into new conceptual territory in murals. How's it coming?

Bea: Well, I found that it is harder to do it than to talk about it. Tim Portlock and I are working with ten teenagers on a large outdoor mural project. A lot of our discussion and design is focused on exploring the meaning of being a collective. We're exploring the commonalities and differences amongst the kids and between the artists and the kids. Rather than bringing those differences to a common denominator, we could allow those differences to all live on the wall. The idea is that if we disagree with someone, instead of trying to find consensus somewhere in the middle, we put both ideas on the wall and let them interact. I feel like right now, we're painting a particularly ugly mural.

Olivia: Really?

Bea: I don't think people will walk up to it and say "ugly." Tim and I are trying to achieve some of the things we've been talking about recently, like having fragmented space. Yet instinctively you go "whoosh" with the brush and harmonize the space because that's the thing that makes sense and that your eye is used to seeing on the wall. We really wanted to create fragmented space as part of the meaning of the piece and we're doing it. We have to tolerate the mural looking ugly for awhile until it comes together.

Marcus: Are you talking about the mural being permanently ugly or just until the wall is finished?

Bea: Probably some of both! Formally we are trying to keep things from flowing together. We're trying to maintain visual discontinuity. We've also tried to stay away from images we are used to seeing in murals, even if they are images we like. We asked the students to draw from their experiences. Some drew fictional stories. We didn't show them any murals as we got started because Tim and I know we had seen many murals and been influenced by them. We were putting our hope for newness to come from ideas of kids who hadn't seen many murals. We wanted to know what drawing styles they are attracted to as opposed to the one's we are used to dealing with. We looked at a lot of comic books.

Olivia: Has that showed up in the design of the mural?

Bea: Yes, many figures in the mural have exaggerated features and bodies—the teens were attracted to that. It gave them a way they could bring images up in a sharp and graphic manner without being threatened by realism. But this strategy of not looking at previous murals didn't always work. The students wanted to see a lot of murals to see what the possibilities were—without that it was difficult to get a sense of scale.

Olivia: From what I've seen of the project it looks fresh and interesting and it does seem to throw a challenge to all of us to rethink our strategies. I especially like that you include questions about the role of public art within the mural. It generates its own debate about aesthetic criteria.

Bea: My ideal mural project now is to find a wall and then to experiment aesthetically with the who and how of representing the surrounding collective.

Olivia: How would you organize something like that? Would you drag people in and say "Hey, we need your story here in this mural?"

Bea: I think you'd have to. People who have never seen their themes or politics represented in murals wouldn't necessarily think to approach such a project. On the 53rd Street mural, it was very hard to get some sort of representation of the gay and lesbian communities. The artists couldn't agree on how to handle this. Yet Hyde Park has one of the largest queer communities in all of Chicago. It would have seemed so unfair and untruthful to omit their presence in the mural.

Marcus: What were the arguments that you had amongst the three artists?

Bea: There was concern and lack of comfort, a fear that a large image on the wall would be too confrontational, more than some people would want to deal with.

Olivia: In a practical sense, how would you depict a person being gay? Do you write "this person is gay!" on his or her shirt? Back in 1987 when Pounds and I did the Mifflin Mural, which shows many different people coming together to the feast, the design group decided that they wanted to have one of the people be a gay man. We ran into the problem of stereotyping—how do we represent without falling back on stereotypes?

Bea: Well that suggests that the way you deal with representing gayness is not in terms of realism because then you have to deal with what a gay man looks like. In the

Fishing in Hogarth's Head Bay (The City Hooked a Louie into the Suburbs) (detail) by Beatriz Santiago Muñoz and Tim Portlock. An acrylic paint mural on concrete. Co-sponsored by Prologue High School and Chicago Public Art Group. (c) Santiago Muñoz, 1995. Photocredit: Chicago Public Art Group.

mural we're working on now, there is a huge rib cage where we are painting diagrams of the things you are not supposed to see in the dominant culture and one of the diagrams is of two men kissing. In the part where there are a lot of different wheels and machinery that turn inside a head, there are two wheels and there is a cop chasing the wheel that has this spray-paint guy on it. If we were doing a mural with realistic figures, it would be very hard to get away with painting a cop chasing a guy with a spray-paint can.

Olivia: Yes, in the Mifflin Mural in 1987, we did a cop beating up a stalk of broccoli. I know that sounds really odd, but people at the Coop wanted to remember the violence of the police against the anti-war Coop community, but they didn't want it to dominate or overwhelm the other images. How do you make authentic representations without dragging down peoples' spirits as they encounter these images on a daily basis?

Bea: There are two different issues. One is how do you deal with something which is part of the history of the community, that is painful for the community, that points out contradictions, and that represents problems, trouble, things like violence of one part of the community against the other? The other is how to depict something that is, but should not be, shocking. The fact that someone would find it offensive is offensive in itself. These are two different things.

Olivia: What is allowed to be represented? There is a repression of negativity, but also a repression of difference.

Bea: Right, and those are not the same thing. I don't feel that something that should not be shocking should have to be dealt with as if it is shocking. The assumption should be that it is not shocking.

Olivia: I know what you mean, but I have to say honestly that I think it may require special strategies, new kinds of thought, to get people to deal with things they find controversial in an open way. I do believe that the strategy of shock is often an empty strategy in terms of actually creating change in people.

Bea: I disagree with that. There are some things that shouldn't be considered shocking. That's offensive in itself.

Olivia: I'm not saying that the fact that some things are considered shocking isn't offensive. I'm saying that shocking isn't necessarily politically efficacious.

Bea: It's the difference between talking diplomatically with someone and getting really angry and saying this conversation doesn't even need to happen.

Olivia: When you explain it that way, I do have some agreement. I struggle with this in my life—what is the bal-

ance between passionately expressing oneself, witnessing for one's beliefs and experiences and thinking, and
expressing strategically. How do we as artists negotiate
the territory of sharp differences? How do we reach
people's hearts and minds?

I think that the Names Project, the quilt, which po-
sitioned itself as an American community art form, is
amazing in this regard. It is about the many people
who have been affected by AIDS, and often it is clear
that various panels are tributes to gay men from loving
and beloved partners. I don't know anybody who sees
that project who doesn't come away from it with a ter-
rific sense of loss and of being touched at people's
expressions of loss and love.

Bea: Well, maybe shocking isn't necessarily politically efficacious, but if instead of painting insulting period
pieces of Africans, Tainos, and Spaniards lovingly
holding hands, the muralists of Puerto Rico had been
plastering the walls with images of *independentistas*
being dragged off to jail, or perhaps a period piece of
the suppressions of revolt, or hey, maybe a famous
writer and activist like Luisa Capetillo kissing her girlfriend, things might have been different. Yes, many
people would've been shocked. And some, maybe the
independentistas and the lesbians, who felt oppressed
by the world that found them shocking and unsuit-
able for public viewing, might not have been shocked
at all. Then they might have looked around to see
who was left standing and who was passed out on the
ground from the shock. This might have been quite
informative.

Now, I think that loss and grief are emotions that
can coalesce people who might not normally come together, but not all situations can be expressed through
loss and grief. Maybe the Names quilt is an event that
is easy for people to empathize with because the people
are already dead. They're not people living with HIV;
they're not threatening, they're not demanding.

I think there are many ways of representing "difficult" subjects in a mural. There are many different kinds of strategies that we can use. Some of them appeal through a common sense of loss, others through shock or humor, or at other times just by being clever and biting. Sometimes I think that a lot of the really challenging ideas have a better chance of existing in public space if they are temporary pieces, which, as you were saying, was how you got into making public art in the first place.

Olivia: I do think that people are more willing to take risks in a piece which is not permanent. When I did the banners dealing with racism on the southwest side, I deliberately created a temporary project because I thought it would make people more willing to get into deeper issues.

Marcus: Right, you're doing without the technical problems of working out a big artistic project. That wouldn't fit for this project.

Olivia: People might be willing to talk about things that are more conflicted, edgy, and difficult if they know it's not going to be permanently there on the wall. Something that gets seen and understood and then can fade away. Who wants to be depicted on a wall as a racist who didn't want Martin Luther King in Marquette Park? But people were willing to discuss such things for inclusion in a form that was public, but not permanent. On the other hand, I am not willing to give up the possibilities for permanent public art for people.

Marcus: I definitely am not.

Olivia: I don't want to deconstruct ourselves into not having any monuments.

Bea: I'm not so sure I like monuments.

Olivia: I'm interested in the possibility of creating heteroglossic monuments. Monuments that are multivoiced as opposed to monological. Is it necessarily true that things which are permanent are fascistic? Do they necessarily have that authoritarian, single, averaging tone? Or is it possible to create a permanent multivocal dialogical form? It represents not everything averaged into one, but a snapshot of a moment in the community. You see the monument not as inevitable and immutable, but as the creation of the current discourse.

That brings up a fantasy for a mural I've been having. It's based on the things you've been talking about, Bea. We'd do a mural and leave spaces in the design. The project would be planned for a two or three-year period. In the second year you or somebody else would come back and lead another team. We would talk to people, get their insights and criticisms and then design and add new parts to the mural. The mural would be constructed as a response to itself over time.

Bea:　　Marcus, I know you take the responsibility of being a muralist seriously. What have you been thinking about these issues lately? How do you conceive of this responsibility of stretching the consciousness of the community?

Marcus:　　I'm coming from a whole other time and space. To me, an artist is like a priest. This is for me, I'm not saying this for all artists. Coming from an African cultural standpoint, the artist is a spiritual person, like a medicine man. So if you are going to be a spiritual force, there is a big responsibility that comes with that and you've got to live with it. You can't just live it in the studio. You can't just live this type of work and be a messy, immoral person in your personal life.

One thing I've learned is that one reality doesn't cut it for the whole of humanity. So this is why I'm putting forth that I'm coming from my ancestral tradition. It's a big world and lots of things are going on. I'm not concerned with anything else; I have my sole purpose and focus. If you are in that priestly state or trying to be, things become less of an issue because you learn to take yourself out of it and just be a tool and a vessel.

Then you don't have to do as much thinking and just be about doing what is necessary.

You asked about strategies, Olivia. In this movement there is already one strategy built into what we do. And that strategy is that we consult—consult the community. By doing this, you already get in tune with what the needs are. You can share visions with people. You're not screaming the message you believe to be right at somebody. Not everybody is going to agree, but at least you consulted. You have a working knowledge of the community. If you consult, you'll get better. Your working knowledge will grow. The vision may not come from you; it may come from somebody else and then you being the artist can actually make it, complete the vision, bring it to a place where it can be shared by others. I think you have to be reflective of the community, but also directive; you have to have some kind of vision, some type of crusade.

Olivia: A moral, political, or spiritual vision?

Marcus: I hope the artist has all three, that would be the best, but if you've only got one, that's cool too.

Olivia: A minute ago you were talking about your relationship to ancestral tradition. That has been a strength and some would say a pitfall of the mural movement. How do we deal with connecting to our ancestors, our heritage? How do we deal with representing diverse cultural heritages in a mural?

In the mosaic we did at Lowell School, Bea and I made an image of a parable of creatures talking to each other. It pictures a rooster, a snake, and an antelope with speech balloons based on the ancient Mayan symbol to show the magic of language. I like the mosaic. In the climate of extreme racial divisiveness in the city of Chicago, I like presenting this parable of cross-cultural communication at an elementary school. Bea, looking back at this piece, you have expressed reservations. Reading the mosaic as the rooster representing the Puerto Rican children, the antelope the African-American children and the snake the children of Mexican heritage seems to you to be too reductivist and simplistic.

Bea: Mostly, I feel that a lot of the symbols used for various cultures in public art have lost a lot of their meaning. A particular set of symbols is seen as a general marker of "Mexicanness"—so we recognize them on public walls, but they seem vacuous. We need to ask ourselves if the symbols that we use necessarily convey the specificity of the communities we are trying to represent. For example, in the mural *Meta 4 Icicle Journey,* you and I painted the story of Quetzalcoatl. I'm not sure that this has contemporary relevance. Because it is a part of the ancient culture of Mexico does not guarantee that it represents the culture as it is now.

Marcus: This gets back to innovation and creativity. We all come to this work with our own cultural criteria, our own agenda, our own crusade, the things we have a burning desire to see manifest. Whatever those are, the one thing we don't want to do is to do the same thing over and over and over, whether it is a theme, a style, a content, the way it's done, how it's worked, et cetera.

Bea, I think you are saying that the theme has been dealt with. There is a time and a place for exactly that image, exactly the message that the image contains, but we know that image has been done and similar things have been done quite a bit. So what you are saying, correct me if I'm wrong, is that there are other things that can be dealt with and you want to take this deeper. Innovation on all levels. I basically agree with what you are saying though I don't know about this particular piece.

Olivia: A contemporary culture of hybridity and the fusion of various cultural images is exciting to me. I'm interested in the work that's been done in the field of archetypal psychology. I'm not particularly interested in whether these things represent timeless archetypes or root metaphors of language. I am interested in their use as vehicles for exploration of contemporary issues.

Quetzalcoatl's story is the story of what a man does when he is in despair, when nothing seems to have worked out as planned. When he leaves his city and people ask him, "Where are you going?" he answers only, "I am going to learn." I think that is a rich story. I like bringing that philosophical complexity into murals. I'm especially interested in doing that in terms of metaphor and story.

Bea: Well, to argue with that I'd have to go into our familiar argument of why I don't like mythology. Mythologies survived because they support the ideas which are the foundation of ruling-class power relationships, ruling class ideologies. Mythologies make cultural choices appear as natural and inevitable.

Olivia: This is an area of disagreement. I believe that people continue to tell stories, not only because these stories are forced on them, but because they have profound meaning for their lives.

Marcus: How do you get the idea that mythologies support ruling-class ideology?

Bea: Look at the stories that survive. Take any "girl story." Rapunzel, Cinderella, etc. There are no fairy tales that deal with women living independently.

Marcus: It depends on what culture you are talking about. Bea, that's a broad, broad statement to make. You've got about four or five thousand different cultures in the world and people deal with things in different ways.

Bea: Well, that's true. Here I'm talking about the stories we are used to hearing. For me, it's the stories I grew up hearing in Puerto Rico and the U.S. The story of Quetzalcoatl is the story of a king, a ruler. The story of Psyche is the story of a woman who is kidnapped and who falls in love with her kidnapper. Those are stories that we used in the mural that people reacted favorably to. Do these stories have a positive influence on people's lives?

Olivia: But I would also say that the story of Psyche is progressive. She's a woman who leads an idyllic life, floating along; she hasn't examined things closely, she hasn't even looked at her own husband. Being cast out of her castle, she embarks on a female quest. In order to come to some sort of happiness or fulfillment, she has to grow, she has to go out into the world with her child alone and complete difficult tasks. That's why I like the story— it presents a progressive image of a woman struggling with her own psychic growth. She's psyche. She's soul.

Bea: Let's leave it that we see the story and the issue differently.

Marcus: It may seem strange that I'm not saying that much tonight, but these days being in the movement, being in what I would call the liberation struggle, I find more and more I'm just living it everyday and doing the work. I have less to say, and I think that is reflected in my approach to doing murals and other art.

I find you can just be still and listen and you will be told by a higher spiritual force what to do at a given point in time. You will know how to fit into the plan. You will know what is needed. It's an energy which is driving a lot of people's artwork.

Some people are in tune with this, and they don't even know that they are in tune; they don't even believe in this. It's hocus pocus to them. But you look at their work and what is manifesting through it, and you see the higher power is there. They are in tune with it without even knowing; that's a blessing.

Bea: I agree with a lot of what you say, but I guess I am one of those people on the hocus pocus side of the spectrum. I keep coming back to Mario Sironi writing about murals being the perfect form for fascist art. In his mind he was striving toward the greater good of mankind, but that desire does not necessarily guarantee good.

Olivia: It seems clear that choosing to be muralists keeps us
              from being artists who have the out of saying, "Ulti-
              mately what I do doesn't really matter because who
              really sees it?" or "Only an elite few see this—essen-
              tially I'm without power or *responsibility.*"

Marcus: Bea, it sounds like you have a good healthy respect for
              what murals are about, because it is a powerful me-
              dium and it does carry responsibility.   In America
              (and in other non-reality based societies), people fool
              themselves into thinking that images or cultural pro-
              ductions are not important. "That's just entertainment.
              It's just my art. You can't tell me what to do." I'm not
              talking about censorship, but the consciousness that
              everything is interrelated and you are going to have an
              effect on people's minds, and we are going to affect
              society when it sometimes seems to us like, "Hey, I'm
              doing this and it doesn't even matter. I'm not making
              a dent." We need to keep the faith. To understand that
              art seen does have an effect. We don't even know the
              extent of the effect, but for positive or negative, it has
              an effect.

JOANNA KADI

Moving from Cultural Appropriation toward Ethical Cultural Connections*

My grandmother trudged from the hills of rural Lebanon to the shores of the Mediterranean carrying clothes and a derbeke.** She and the drum survived several weeks in the steerage compartment of a large boat. No small feat. And now she's dead, and the derbeke sits on a shelf far away from me. But I ended up with my *sittee*'s determination, which I've needed to navigate through the stormy waters of drumming.

After experiencing so much anti-Arab hatred growing up, I cut myself off from my culture as soon as I could. I tried hard to assimilate, with the attendant craziness and confusion, but thankfully my journey into political awareness and action brought me back to my racial/cultural heritage and in particular its music. Hearing familiar rhythms, I found myself thinking about—and wanting—a brass derbeke with a chrome finish and intricate engraving. Just like the one my grandmother brought from Lebanon.

So my lover and I embarked on a grand search to ferret out my derbeke. In January 1991, a year after the search began, Jan

---

*Many thanks to Jan Binder for her help with this article.

**A derbeke (pronounced der-beck-ee) is a traditional Arabic hand drum. I've seen several different spellings, but this is the one I prefer. The drum is also known as a dumbek (pronounced doom-beck)—there are varied spellings for that word as well.

and I marched in Washington, D.C., to protest the slaughter of Arabs in the vicious outbreak of U.S. imperialism known as the Gulf War. During that weekend, alternating between grief and numbness, we chanced upon a store specializing in musical instruments from around the world. I found my derbeke.

The end of my journey? No. Just the beginning. Now I needed a teacher and a community that would offer technical assistance and political respect. After much searching, I found a wonderful teacher, Mick Labriola, as well as drumming friends/ acquaintances I connect with politically and musically. Because of this, and because of deep determination to forge ahead in spite of obstacles, drumming has proved an incredibly positive experience. I've reconnected with my roots. Experiencing how much beauty and importance Arabs have given the world has helped me feel pride as opposed to shame about being Arab.

But there is/has also been anger and grief as I continually see derbekes in white people's homes, played by white musicians, banged on at drumming circles. Many players don't even know the name of the instrument, or where it comes from. They don't play it properly, and they don't know traditional Arabic rhythms. But most of this seems to raise little concern, as more and more white people jump on the drumming bandwagon. Why drumming? Why so popular? Because it's a powerful activity? Because it's a wonderfully communal instrument? Because it allows people to learn about other cultures through music? Most days I think these explanations provide a more positive interpretation than the situation warrants, especially when I notice the apolitical spirituality of the New Age movement embracing the concept of "getting in touch with inner rhythms" via the drums of people of color; white people dredding their hair and buying African drums; people "playing" an instrument without knowing its name.

It seems to me those white people use derbekes, perceiving them as generic, no-name drums unencumbered by hard political/historical/cultural realities, never asking themselves the questions that would uncover these realities, such as: Whose music is this? What have imperialism and racism done to the people who created this music? Is it right for me to play this instrument? What kind of beliefs do I carry about Arabs? Ignoring these questions and ignoring Arab musical traditions translates into cultural appropriation—white people taking possession of Arabic culture by commandeering an important instrument and the music it produces. The derbeke and its playing style is an important piece of Arab culture, with thousands of years of history attached. To disregard that and play however one chooses whitewashes the drum, and, by implication, Arab culture. When stripped of its historical legacy, the drum is placed outside Arab culture, suggesting Arab culture and history aren't worth taking seriously; even though Arabs have created something valuable and life-enhancing in our music, that doesn't matter. White people can and will choose to perceive the drum as ahistorical and culturally empty—a plaything that can be given whatever meaning the player chooses.

To perceive a derbeke as a plaything is to carry the privileged attitude that has wrought devastation all over our planet: "Everything is here for me to play with and use." Whether peoples, lands, cultures, it's there for the grabbing. This take-take-take attitude pushed European colonizers through whole peoples and lands on the Asian, African, and American continents. Although brown, black, and yellow people filled those continents, white people perceived them as empty.

This kind of colonization continues, and new forms have evolved. The colonialist attitude has affixed itself to our music, clothing, religions, languages, philosophies, and art. I overheard a white shopper in a music store examining a derbeke: "Cool drum. I'll take a couple." He perceived the derbeke as an empty vessel waiting to have meaning infused into it, as opposed to an important cultural symbol/reality embodying centuries of meaning.

When I come across this sort of attitude, one of cultural appropriation, which says the derbeke is an empty vessel, I begin doubting myself and my community, doubting our very existence. I fight constantly against internalizing the message—if the derbeke means nothing, if it comes from nowhere, I don't exist. I've struggled with this for years, but recently my identity has been strengthened, thanks in part to my derbekes. They help me realize I come from somewhere, my community exists, and we've created wonderful cultural expressions over the centuries.

And so, I find it impossible to examine increased derbeke sales or the increased numbers of white "shamans," for that matter, without discussing multiculturalism. While I am not opposed to a multiculturalism that considers seriously imbalances of power, histories of colonization, and the possibilities for alliances among people of different backgrounds, multiculturalism too often feeds and reinforces imperialist attitudes that grow from attitudes of entitlement and privilege that form part of structural racism. Examples of this abound. Young white schoolchildren are taught to take whatever they want from other culture and use it. White adult consumers snatch our various arts, wanting the stuff but not caring if its creators are systematically destroyed.

As dominant white society casually buys and sells our symbols/realities, the cultural meaning of the symbols is watered down and their integrity diminished. For the most part, the white people whose homes are adorned with African masks, Asian paintings, and Native ceremonial objects haven't done the work necessary to become allies to people of color. They know little or nothing about current global struggles of people of color, as we define and articulate them. They don't engage in acts of solidarity around specific issues such as Native self-determination or Palestinian liberation. They don't read books by radical authors of color. Given the brutal racism endemic to our society, it makes sense that much of what passes for multiculturalism is actually covert and overt cultural appropriation, actually a form of cultural genocide.

Further, these white people haven't analyzed a monster related to racism, that is, classism and the global capitalist system. All of us need to be clear about how and where and why the capitalist system fits into the picture. We need to ask critical questions. Is "multiculturalism" the latest capitalist fad? Who's in control? Who's benefiting? And who's making money, now that it's popular to hang Native dream webs on bedroom walls? Could it be people of color? Hardly. As more and more people of color are forced to live on the streets, white entrepreneurs are getting rich selling our art, music, and spirituality. Watching them profit as they exploit and appropriate our cultures, when for years we experienced hostility and scorn trying to preserve them in a racist society, is truly galling. I grew up with white people belittling and "joking" about my family's choice of music and dancing; now I can watch those same people rush to sign up for "real" bellydancing lessons. Taught by a white woman, of course.

The particular combination of racism and classism that has popularized bellydancing taught by white people has several implications for Arab-American culture. Arab dancers who can't make a living teaching may eventually be forced to give up their serious studies of traditional dance altogether; this is one factor that eventually leads to cultural genocide. If a certain type of bellydancing becomes popular, and another strain never catches on with white teachers, the latter could slowly disappear. Again, this factors into cultural genocide. For every cultural form happily adopted by the dominant culture's racist and classist system, another falls by the wayside. Some expressions discarded by the dominant society will continue to thrive among marginalized communities; some will be lost forever.

Further, many people of color can't afford to buy the now-available music, paintings, instruments, and books from our cultures. We can't afford travel to our countries of origin. Observing white, middle-class people engaging in these activities adds yet another layer of anguish and complexity to these issues. Recently I talked over the phone with a white, middle-class man who has travelled extensively in various Arab countries, attended Arabic language schools, and now speaks Arabic fluently. Upon discovering I am Arab-American, he began speaking Arabic to me.

As is all too usual, I got so choked up with rage I couldn't think clearly. I said curtly: "I don't speak Arabic," and hung up. Next time, I have a response all planned out: "Gee, if only my grandparents hadn't experienced so much racism and been so isolated! Then they wouldn't have tried to assimilate. Then they would have taught us to speak Arabic. Which would be so helpful these days, now that multiculturalism is in. For those who can afford it, which of course precludes most people of color. Oh well, I hope you're having a splendid time with it all."

The discussion of cultural appropriation between white people and people of color is critically important, but I want to push further. If we keep the focus on relationships between colored and white, we come up with an overly simplistic analysis that ignores the fact that many people of color are just as inattentive to these issues and thus act inappropriately toward each other. It implies the only groups worth discussing are *the* white people and *the* people of color, two broad categories that are sometimes helpful but also present problems in terms of under-standing the complexities of race. These simplistic categories feed into the myth that people of color constitute a monolithic group unscathed by differences of skin color, immigrant status, gender, ability, sexuality, language, class, and religion. Further, reduction-ist categories support the lie that we can only be discussed in relation to white people, that our only important relationships exist with white people.

A simplistic analysis of cultural appropriation minimalizes and trivializes what we as people of color from different communities do to each other, glossing over the fact that we can and do commit acts of cultural appropriation, and thus hurt each other badly. I've had the painful experience of watching other people of color using derbekes as no-name drums. Our racial identity doesn't rule out unjust acts toward each other. If I were drawn to an African mask in a store and bought it without knowing where it came from, what it represents, and who made it, would that be accept-able? Of course not. I'd be committing an act of cultural appro-priation as surely as any white person who did the same thing.

Our existence as people of color doesn't mean we know much—if anything—about other communities of color. It doesn't mean we've done the hard work of freeing ourselves from stereo-types and lies about other racial/ethnic groups. I've heard, time and again, the same kind of anti-Arab racism out of the mouths of people of color as I've heard from white people. Unless people of color do the same anti-racist work we want white people to do, we can't become true allies and friends.

However, I don't equate the actions of people of color with those of white people. There's a difference between a white person and a person of color playing derbekes incorrectly. The white person's actions feed into structural racism; they're part and parcel of the systemic oppression of white people over people of color. The person of color's actions stem, I think, from a mix of struc-tural racism and horizontal violence in which the dominant white power structure keeps us carefully divided from each other, du-plicating their mistreatment, and ignorant about the many ways our lives connect.

In addition, many men of color bring a problematic and divisive note to discussions of drumming and culture by insisting women can't drum because it's not "traditional." I have two responses to this. There's historical documentation from many cultures, including Arabic ones, of women drumming in earlier times. Second, even in relation to preserving our cultures, I find the label "traditional" almost irrelevant. If women didn't drum in the past, why would we want to carry on with that aspect of our culture? Are the men who propose this anxious to continue every traditional cultural practice, from the most inane to the most misogynist?* Plenty of manifestations of sexism and misogyny in Arab cultures need to be kissed goodbye.

Returning to the question of careful connections among cultures, as a person of color, I want to do more than react to oppression by white people. As a subject and moral agent with power in the world, it's important to state what I want and what I consider acceptable. I want to share cultural traditions in a context of multiculturalism that has at its root respect, thoughtfulness, a political analysis, and openness. But, while I support the idea of sharing across cultures, I also believe some things should never be shared.

For starters, sacred instruments, rhythms, and rituals. Several years ago I attended a music festival where two white women planned to perform with a sacred instrument from a community of Australian indigenous people. Although an Australian aboriginal woman was present and voiced objections, it didn't matter to the musicians. At the last minute, outcries from a larger group prevented the show. I don't know if these two musicians used the instrument other times, but given the depth of their resistance to restriction of their "artistic freedom," I wouldn't be surprised if they did. Of course, I question whether those women should have been performing at all, since their show consisted of playing instruments from various communities of color. I'm tired of seeing white people get the praise, money, and publicity from public performance.

But, back to making and preserving connections among communities. How to make such links? And what to call them?

---

*Another problem with this attitude is that it feeds into the dangerous lie/myth that cultures are static and unchanging entities.

Words carry critical weight in liberation struggles. Naming ourselves and our desires is vital. The term "ethical cultural connection" embodies my ideas. It focuses clearly on culture, on the life-force of a community. "Connection" speaks a freely chosen bonding experience between people or groups. The adjective "ethical" clarifies the type of connection—one based on respect, justice, and integrity.

Ethical cultural connections are comprised of respect for the community involved; a desire to learn and take action; an openness to being challenged and criticized; a willingness to think critically about personal behavior; a commitment to actively fighting racism. These cornerstones remain the same whether I'm getting to know one Native person or whether I'm buying a carving from a Native museum. They apply to people of color and white people.

I've come to the conclusion I'm not opposed to non-Arabs playing derbekes if it's done with respect, knowledge, and seriousness, and if these attitudes manifest themselves in concrete action. I want drummers to learn the derbeke's culture and history, and the proper way to play. And to take this knowledge a step further by actively countering the imperialism, racism, and genocide Arabs experience today. It's not enough to celebrate cultural difference by learning language, music, or history, when people's whole worlds are at risk.

Of course, this raises a critical question. How do I know if someone's doing these things? By watching? Maybe the person plays the derbeke correctly, maybe he knows Arab rhythms. But that doesn't tell me how much he knows and cares about my people. I can only know for sure if I talk to the drummer. That is the only way any of us will know. Typing out guidelines or policing cultural events won't do it. We need to talk—across cultures and classes. My analysis doesn't help in isolation. It helps as we communicate across all racial groups—Asian (including Arabs), Latino, Native, African, and white.

And talking to one person won't cut it. I'm sure any white person interested in assuaging her conscience could find enough white-identified Arabs to assure her whatever she does with the derbeke is okay. There are many such people in all communities—people who for whatever reasons have become so alienated from our roots and our communities that they casually approve of the worst kinds of cultural appropriation. At the music festival I mentioned earlier, participants discussed cultural appropriation several times, and it appeared the women of color shared a clear and unified response. That is, until a well-known woman of color, a superb drummer, announced from the stage that anyone who wanted a drum from whatever culture should buy it and play it. So much for solidarity.

I don't want white people seeking out white-identified people of color to give them the stamp of approval. I want white people to talk to many people, including political activists. I want discussion around power and privilege, about who benefits from cultural appropriation and in what ways, about who will decide how cultural connections happen and what makes them ethical. I want discussion about actions and the meanings they carry.

I believe politicized people of color and our white allies must start framing discussions with helpful guidelines that make sense to us. Discussions must be cross-cultural and focused on tough questions about racism, classism, imperialist sorts of multiculturalism, power, and privilege. And I suggest we include the ways in which personal experience can help frame critical thinking on cultural appropriation.

Looking at the five derbekes that now grace this home, I'm struck by the connection between my drumming and my political thinking. The deeper I go with one, the deeper I go with the other. The political analysis I push myself to do translates into more meaningful drumming. Playing the derbeke helps me deal with the pain I experience around vivid examples of cultural appropriation. I offer this personal example not as a "feel-good," quick, on-the-surface remedy for oppression and cultural genocide, but rather as a somber statement of possibility. We can plumb the depths of the worst in our society while participating in meaningful cultural activities that ground us and keep hope alive.

CARLOS J. SERRANO

Latino Chess

Dominoes are embedded in our blood
    on the day we Latinos are born.
My friend, Michael, upon sitting in and watching a game,
      had never held dominoes in his life
      but once his fingers touched *las fichás*
      well . . . he's addicted for life.

We call it Latino chess because it involves skill,
      precision, luck, and the ability to count to seven;
and also, we prefer to deal with dots,
      instead of kings and queens;
plus, it doesn't look fashionable to have
      un Palo Viejo next to a chess board.

It's the sounds of the game that make it so attractive
The crack of the bones slammed against an old wooden table,
      the click-clack of the *fichás* being shuffled
Willie Colon y Tito Rojas blaring through the radio of *la bodega*
      while four men sit on milk crates in mid-July
      bonchinchando at just about everything.
Like: The Cleveland Indians will win this year's World Series
  because they
      have the most Latinos in the Major Leagues,
Or, how much Pataki and Giuliani are *Mamaos*,
Or, if Nicole Simpson was Latina, it would be O.J. that would
  be cut up.

The philosophies of life come from Domino tables everywhere
It is said that Don Abizo Campos wrote his plans
     for his revolution against the U.S. on a Domino score card.
Aristotle came up with his *Poetics* after being left
     on *chiba,* but scoring *un Chuchaso y una Capicu* in the
        next game.
And Freud thought the domino 1-5 was a phallic symbol.

Whether it's *los jibarros* up in *las montañas de Puerto Rico,*
     or it's the factory workers who live in *él barrió*
On Friday, *los hombres,* with calluses and blisters on their hands
     and the week's paycheck in their pockets,
will have their escape, without escaping
     the concrete jungle
with dominoes gripped in their fingers.

Visit with Doc to Find My Identity

SESSION 1: VASO DE LECHE

Doctor, I don't know what I should do. You know, the stuff about exploring yourself and finding your identity. You see, I don't quite know who I am. I have serious doubts that I'm a Puerto Rican. It all started when I was a kid. "*Vaso de Leche*," that's what my family called me at home. It means glass of milk. I bet, Doctor, you didn't know I was Puerto Rican by the way I look or speak. It's pretty embarrassing being the lightest skinned in the family . . . well, more like the lightest skinned in the entire Hispanic community. It's uncomfortable, Doc. I feel like an outcast. Whenever one of my parents bring their Hispanic friends over to the house, they always ask, "Who's the white kid?" Sometimes my friends are startled when they find out I'm Puerto Rican. "Hey, you're Puerto Rican? I thought you were Italian!" "Sorry," I say to them (*With a deep Mexican accent*), "Would you prefer me to speak like this?!"

Even the white couple down a few houses from us has a son, my age, who has a tan ten times darker than mine. So, I asked my parents, "Can it be possible that I was switched at birth?" A police investigation is now under way.

I don't know what I can do. If I tan I just get red. Maybe my parents' genes got mixed up along the line. This is crazy, Doc. I don't wanna prove to everyone that I'm a Puerto Rican. Do I have to go around with a card or something as proof?

"Hi. You don't know I'm Puerto Rican. That's o.k., many people don't. That's why I carry the *"I'M DEFINITELY PUERTO RICAN"* identification card. This card helps me out of embarrassing situations in the financial aid office when you're not getting the government grant for college you deserve, or in *el barrio* when you're confronted by the Latin Kings Gang who think you are a 'Gringo.'"

Why, Doctor, why me? This thing is even affecting my dreams. I had this dream where I was defending myself against charges of impersonating a Puerto Rican.

Bailiff:	You promise to tell the truth, the whole truth, and nothing but the truth, so help you God?
Me:	I do.
Lawyer:	O.K. Mister, is it true that you are a Puerto Rican?
Me:	Yes. I am a Puerto Rican.
Lawyer:	Come, come. You expect the court to believe such a thing?
Me:	But it's the truth. I'm a Puerto Rican.
Judge:	Remember, you are under oath. Perjury is against the law.
Me:	I am Puerto Rican, your honor. I'm not lying.
Judge:	That's it! I've had it with you! I'm charging you with contempt! As a matter of fact, I'll give you my verdict now: Guilty! You'll be sentenced to thirty years to life without parole.
Me:	Just because you don't think I'm a Puerto Rican?
Judge:	We're strict around these parts!
Me:	Please . . . let me throw myself at the mercy of the court . . . listen . . . I'll say something in Spanish! Uhmmmmmm . . . Uhmmmmm . . . *Menudo!* How's that?!
Judge:	Bailiff. Take him away! And put a straight jacket on that man. . . . He's psycho!

You see what I mean, Doc. I don't know what I should do. I guess for the rest of my life I'll always be "*Vaso de Leche.*"

SESSION 2: THE SPANISH INQUISITION

Doc, the big reason for my identity problem lies with my family. Instead of encouraging me in overcoming my problem, they tortured me. You see, I came home one day in my freshman year of high school with a 55 in Spanish on my report card.

Don't get me wrong, I had a 95 and over in my other classes, but when you come from a traditional Puerto Rican family like I do, a failing mark in Spanish is the ultimate sin . . . next to marrying someone outside the Spanish community.

The first person I show my report card to is my mother. I don't know how, Doc, but I think mother instinctively knew when it was report card day. 'Cause I never mentioned it to her, and when I came home that day, she was waiting for me at the front door with her hand extended out towards me. *"Dame el reporte."* I was hoping that all those 98s, 99s and 100s would bury the 55 and she might overlook it. *"Que es esto!"* Oh-oh! *"Un cincuenta y cinco en Español! No me enseñes esto! Aye Dios!"* Boy, you'd think I had married a Dominican. My sister comes running in to see what my mother is crying about. *"Que paso, Mami! Que paso!"* Thrusting the report card into my sister's hand, my mother begins to weep. "You came home with this! A 55 in Spanish," my sister yells.

"But look! I got a 97 in Science and . . . "

"A 55 in Spanish! How can you do this to Mami?"

"But . . . but . . . but . . . "

"But nothing!"

Wait a minute. Why was my sister yelling at me? What business was this of hers?

"Idiota! Idiota! Idiota!" my mother yells. Now that's a lot better. Then my brother walks in. My sister says to him,

"Look. He got a 55 in Spanish."

"Yeah. Shit man, you're in trouble."

"Nunca, nunca, nunca," says my mother pointing from my brother to me, *"El nunca trajo en esta casa un cincuenta y cinco en Español. El siempre tenia un noventa y cinco en Español!"*

"But Mami, he had a 95 average in the rest of his classes."

"No importa."

Doc, this was my Spanish Inquisition. I heard the door slam. Then, out of the dark shadow, I swear to God I heard thunder and saw lightening, my father appeared.

"Que pasa aqui?"

"Tu hijo trajo en esta casa un cincuenta y cinco en Español!"

"UN CINCUENTA Y CINCO!"

My father's eyes started to bulge out of their sockets. And with one motion of his hand he loosened his belt buckle and pulled out his belt like he was Conan the Destroyer. And all throughout my father's conniption, my mother is kneeling by her saints with rosary beads asking the lord for forgiveness, *"Por que, el, por que el, por que el. . . . "*

"But look, I got a 99 in English . . . " I said, but they weren't listening to me. My sister was helping my father look through the Yellow Pages for a good military school. Finally, I said, "Look, it's only mid-semester. If I do fairly well in the second half, I could get a 70!"

"Un setenta, un setenta, un setenta!" My mother continues to weep.

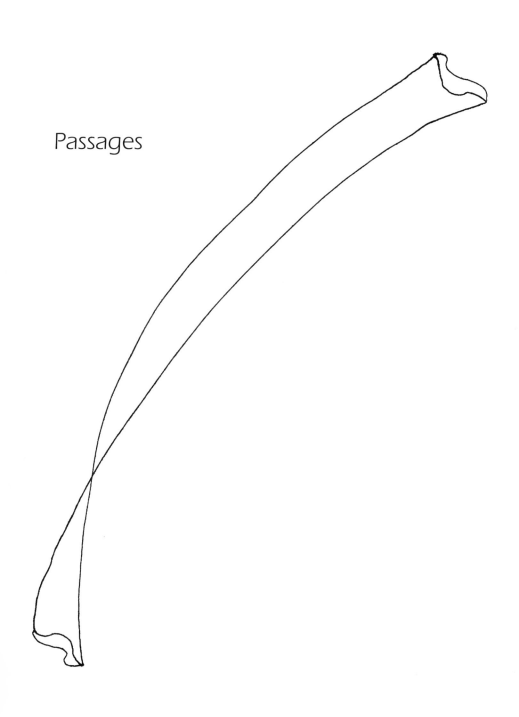

Passages

Drawing on Myself

This is a script for a solo performance with one person playing all the roles, changing "character" through vocalization and physicalization. There is a "Narrative I" that narrates and comments upon the different scenes. This "I" unifies the performance, standing in a special spotlight as she speaks to the audience. Also, all "props" (Barbie doll, soccer ball, etc.) are mimed except for artistic material such as paper and crayons, and Priscilla's mascara and rouge. The various settings (the Bergström home, the interior of a car etc.) are also mimed.

SCENE 1

An easel is placed upstage, turned away from the audience. A sheet of paper is placed under it. Bump up on Priscilla looking at herself in a little mirror, powdering her face. She discovers the audience.

Priscilla: Well, I can see this is going to be a challenging evening, with lots of work. But (*closes her powder case*) that is what I am here for. For example, look at that woman over there in the corner. (*To the spectator*) Yes, you. (*To the rest of the audience*) She has a pair of nice-looking slacks, her sweater is not too cheap-looking but the combination is, as you can all see, (*pause*) awful. (*Turns away in disgust*) I was only five years old when my mother taught me the most important lesson of my life. She took me aside and said, "Priscilla, my beautiful child, life is a box of chocolates, with us women all individually wrapped in it, and when a man opens that package I want you to be wearing the best wrapping." I have been following my mother's advice ever since and I have been very successful. Tonight, I will teach you about wrapping in order to create a desirable image. Therefore, I will take the most pathetic looking one of you all and make a demonstration. (*To an imaginary person by the door*) Here is a little newcomer. Hello (*aims at her victim with intense, judging eyes, approaching slowly*), would you like to be my (*pause*) assistant? What is your name? Bridgette? Spell that. B-r-i-t-t? That is a queer little name. Come on, Bridgette, this is going to be so much fun.

Adult Britt: No, I don't want to.

Priscilla: Yes you do, this is going to be so much fun. (*The "two" pulling, dragging and resisting, Britt with her left hand and Priscilla with her right hand*) (*At the easel*) Draw a little picture of yourself. Take any crayon you want. Make a picture as I talk to you, inspire you. (*Priscilla is turned toward the audience as Britt draws behind the easel*) Draw the pleasure of watching yourself being looked at. Draw the wonderful feeling of being gazed at, becoming a woman in the eyes of someone else. (*pause*) I think our little Bridgette is done. Let us see what she has drawn. (*Priscilla turns toward the easel, her face changes into a grimace*) Really . . . (*Priscilla walks downstage*) . . . I can see that I am not being appreciated here. I came here to help *you*, and Lord knows you need it, but under no circumstances do I tolerate being insulted. (*Exits downstage right*)

Adult Britt: (*To Priscilla*) Priscilla, you forgot your easel. (*Walks back to the easel to take a look, shies away from it. Turns toward the audience*) This is not a very pretty picture.

But I wouldn't have drawn it if she hadn't asked me to. You saw how she dragged me up on stage. Do you want to see it? I'll show it to you in a bit, I just have to change it a little first . . . (*Touches the picture with her fingers, gets all smudgy, walks downstage toward the audience who still does not get to see the picture*) I just did the impossible — I made that picture even worse. (*Looks at her hands*) . . . It is a good thing Mrs. Olofsson can't see me now. Mrs. Olofsson was my Kindergarten teacher in Göteborg, Sweden, where I grew up. She was always on my case, nagging, especially about cleaning my hands. She would say:

SCENE 2

Mrs. Olofsson: Britt Alice Coles, show me your hands.

Britt (about five years old): (*Shakes her head, hides her hands, and backs up*) No!

Mrs. Olofsson: Show them to me now!

Britt: (*Slowly brings out her hands from behind her back, raises them slowly, then suddenly turns around and runs away, twisting and turning, shaking her body in triumph*) My hands are supposed to be all smudgy because I am an artist, and artists always have color all over them, because they are always drawing. I am going to draw a picture of myself right now. (*Runs to easel and takes out the paper under the easel. Throws the paper on the floor and starts drawing with a bright orange color as she talks*) I am drawing a big head, big eyes, and a big mouth, 'cause I have all these things to say . . . skipping feet, and smudgy, really smudgy hands. Now I am going to write my name, B-r-i-t-t. (*Gets up from the floor with a drawing of a big head and a little body*) I am going to put it on the wall so everyone can look at it and tell me what a great artist I am. *(Tapes the drawing on top of the first drawing, onto the easel and then turns the easel around)* Look, this is me. *(Poses proudly)*

Narrative I: *(Pointing to the orange drawing on the easel)* That is a face in a phase where I still believed in the myth that we are all born as clean slates with a crayon in our hand, ready to draw any picture we want and make it come true. Only to one day discover that some pictures are more "true" than others . . .

SCENE 3

Mrs.
Olofsson: *(Downstage left)* Children, today I would like you to draw a picture of an animal that you saw when you were on summer vacation with your parents. *(Bends down to look at the children's drawings)* Richard, that is a nice little dog that you are drawing. Let us all spell that: D-O-G. Good. What did you draw, Lena? A cat. That's nice. C-A-T. Very good. And what did you do Britt? A what? A kudu? *(Change of tone)* Don't spell that.

Young Britt
(5 years old): K-U-D-U. *(Repeats the word triumphantly)*

Mrs.
Olofsson: Shhhhh! Since you are so intent on talking today, why don't you come here, in front of the other children and tell us about this *(pause)* animal.

Britt: A kudu is sort of like a deer with twisted horns that I saw when I was in Swaziland, where my daddy works—

Mrs.
Olofsson: *(Interrupts)* And where is this, Swaziland, Britt . . . *(leaning over)* . . .

Britt: It is in the southern part of Africa. *(Suddenly, Britt stands on her toes as if she is pulled by her right ear)* Ouch! Let me go, that hurts.

Mrs.
Olofsson: *(Holding onto Britt's ear)* I told you not to be lying like that. *(Drags Britt downstage right)* You were trying to make your self special, weren't you? Don't you know what Mrs. Olofsson thinks about little girls who lie?

Britt: *(protesting)* Let me go. I am not lying. *(Starts to cry)*

Mrs.
Olofsson: *(To the other children "sitting" next to the audience)* Look at Britt. She is crying because she is ashamed of having lied to Mrs. Olofsson, trying to make herself special. *(To Britt)* Let this be a lesson to you. *(Stops)* You will sit here in this corner, all by yourself, until you learn to be a good girl and tell the truth!

Narrative I: *(Cleaning her hands with a wet rag downstage right)* I *was* telling the truth. But I guess it was a good thing that the kudu drawing was the only picture I drew that day. Had I told Mrs. Olofsson not only that I went to visit

my father in the southern part of Africa in the sum-
mers, where he was working at the time, but that he
himself grew up on a second continent, that I was
born on a third, and that my mother decided to raise
me on a fourth, where she was born . . . had I told Mrs.
Olofsson all this I would still be sitting in that corner.
But my mother got me out of that corner that afternoon and she would do it again and again and again . . .

SCENE 4

Britt
(About eight
years old):   Mom, this Barbie doesn't look like me . . . *(Gives Barbie
to Mom, reaching up, then stands and waits for her Barbie,
grasping at her mother)*

Narrative I: *(downstage right)* My mother cut off Barbie's long hair,
curled what was left on top and dyed it dark brown.

Britt: Thanks mom. Look, it is a Barbie-Britt. I am going
to go and play with Lena. Bye. *(Skips away)*

Britt: *(Upstage right. Starts talking to another child)* Hello, what
is your name? Did you just move into the valley? I'm
Britt. I live in that apartment over there with my
mom and our dog. I am off to play with my friend
Lena who lives up on that hill. *(Points)* She lives in
a big house with *both* her parents. She isn't really my
friend but she lets me play with all her Barbie stuff,
but only if I play *her* stupid Barbie games. "This is
what my mom does," she says. Then we sit and comb
Barbie's hair, go shopping, cook food, and wait for
Ken to come home. *(Sighs)* But now I have my own
Barbie-Britt. *(Shows the child her Barbie)* Look! So now
we're going to play *my* Barbie game. You want to
play with us? *(In a condescending voice)* You can't,
because you're too small. *(Skips away, going around
the stage. Stops to reach up for a door bell. Waits for someone to open the door. Turns around.)* Hi Mr. Bergström,

I have come to play with Lena. *(Enters after cleaning her feet on the doormat)* Hi Mrs. Bergström, look at my Barbie-Britt. *(responds in a subdued voice)* No, she doesn't look weird, she looks just like me. *(Smiles as*

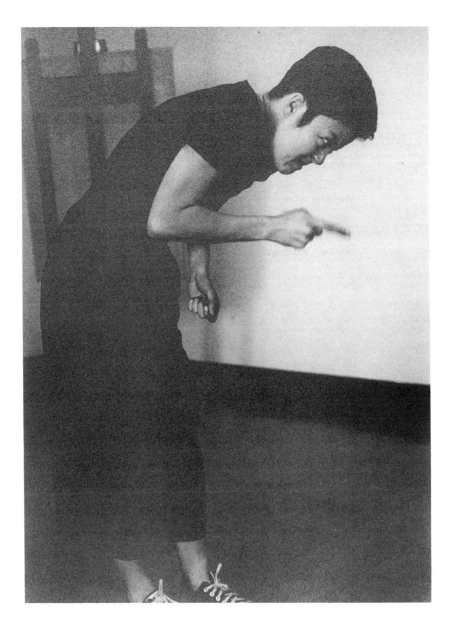

*she skips away to Lena's room, then realizes what it is that
Mrs. Bergström just implied. Britt makes a grimace, then
greets Lena sitting on the floor)* Hi Lena. *(Pause) (Stomps
her feet on the floor)* No! Today we are going to play *my*
Barbie game. *(Britt puts Barbie's hands up into the air.
She bends down to walk her Barbie on the floor. In this
scene the performer acts a stiff silent Barbie with hands up
in the air, and the lines are spoken by young Britt talking
to the Barbie)* No more spending money on shopping,
Barbie. *(Barbie swaggers, looks troubled)* You have di-
vorced your husband *(Barbie turns to the audience with
a worried look)* and as a single mom you are going to
have to leave your daughter at the day care center
because . . . *(Barbie refuses to walk)* What is the matter
with you Barbie? *(Britt struggles with resisting Barbie)*
Walk, *(in a very happy voice)* because you are off to
work! *Barbie screams silently in protest, then starts running. Britt chases the runaway Barbie)* Come back,
Barbie, you will be late for work! Come back Barbie.

SCENE 5

Britt: *(Britt stops chasing after Barbie)* Well I don't care about
                 Barbies anyway . . . They're stupid. *(Walks around aim-
                 lessly)* Ouch! *(Mimes getting hit by a ball, picks it up.
                 Britt to some other kids)* No, you can't have it back.
                 (Pause) Okay, but only if I get to play too, because
                 (realization) I am going to be the best soccer player
                 in the world.

Narrative I: *(Upstage right)* I practiced and I practiced. On the
                 weekends, my uncle Börje took me to all the soccer
                 games in town. One day I was good enough to make
                 the team, as the only girl on it. *(Kicks ball)*

Britt
(about eleven
years old):   *(to another player)* Good game, Richard.

Richard: *(Center)* Good game Britt. Okay, you all, let's talk tactics. Tomorrow we are going to play the Vallhamra school. It is going to be a tough game. *(Draws the field and the various positions in the sand with his right foot)* Stefan, you will be the goalie tomorrow. What? Oh, *(turns around to establish Lena)* hi Lena.

Lena: Hi Richard, Kristina and I were wondering, if we could play too, tomorrow?

Richard: *(Turned away from Lena)* No, girls can't play. *(Continues to draw in the sand with foot)* Britt you will be playing forward—

Lena: *(Interrupts)* But Britt is playing!

Richard: *(In a freeze position, irritated over having been interrupted and "caught")* Yeah, but Britt is . . . *(Turns to Lena)* Britt is different! *(To the playmates)* See you guys tomorrow. *(Exits upstage right)*

SCENE 6

Narrative I: *(Upstage right in a happy voice)* I was different . . . but then came a day when different got to be *(change of tone as if pronouncing something disgusting)* different . . .

Britt: *(Center. Walks around with a soccer ball under her arm. Sees Richard)* Hi, Richard, why aren't you dressed? Don't we have a game?

Richard: No, we cancelled it because we are going to have a party and we invited all these hot chicks. But if we decided to start playing again we might give you a call. Bye. *(Exits upstage right)*

(Britt stops, puts ball down, then sits on it)

Narrative I: *(Upstage right. Looks down at the imaginary, younger Britt)* There I was, without a team, a spectator watching the others play. I wasn't invited to the parties since

I wasn't considered to be one of the desirable chicks. But I wasn't one of the guys again which left me trying out for a new team, playing a girl. I started to observe what the other girls my age thought that meant, what music to listen to, what to talk about, how to dress, all the codes one had to learn for being accepted into girlhood in a coastal city on the West coast of Sweden in the late 1970s. Our school's music classes proved to be one of the hardest challenges. Whenever Mr. Toft, our music teacher, would play a song on the piano, Lena and the other girls would urge him to play each song in a higher and higher pitch, competing which one of them could sing the highest note.

SCENE 7

Mr. Toft: Today, we are going to sing "Gläns över sjö och strand." *(Swedish song)* Lena, why don't you start singing.

Lena: *(In a lovely high soprano voice)* "Gläns över sjö och strand . . ." *(Lena stops, turns around to challenge Britt)* Britt . . .

**Britt
(About
thirteen
years old):**   *(In her deep voice)* " . . . natten är fjärran, du som i Österland . . . " *(Her voice cracks as she tries to hit notes)*

Mr. Toft: Now everybody together!

Lena: " . . . tändes av herran . . . "

Britt: " . . . barnen och herdarna" *(Voice cracks again. Britt holds her hand to her throat, and starts miming to save her voice. As she looks around she realizes that nobody is noticing that she isn't singing. She takes her hand away from her throat and really gets into the miming)*

Narrative I: *(Downstage left)* Nobody noticed that I wasn't singing. Mr. Toft was too far away to hear me and the other

students were too concentrated on their own singing, the only thing that distracted them was if I sang
out of tune. I developed a very "feminine" voice by
being silent. Then one day finals came along.

Toft: Today, I would like to try something different. I want
you to sing one by one. Let's start with you Britt, I
haven't really heard your voice since you are always
standing in the back. *(Plays distinctly on his piano,
moving his right hand a bit more, hits one of the keys a
couple of times and signals with his head to Britt to start
singing. Britt starts to sing but soon her voice cracks, then
no sound comes out of her mouth)*

Toft: Britt, let us try one more time.

Britt: "Gläns över sjö . . . " *(Her voice cracks again and she
instinctively starts miming, only to stop as she realizes that
this time she can't get away with miming)*

Toft: *(Irritated)* Enough! *(Turns toward the other students and
changes his tone of voice as he looks at his favorite pupil)*
Lena . . . *(Britt walks away)*

Narrative I: *(Downstage right)* After all those years of miming I
had convinced myself that I could not sing. Even
when I wanted to, with the whole class looking at
me, the mental block made it impossible for me to
sing out. I failed the music class and I failed in my
attempt to be one of the girls. But the next semester
my mother and I moved in with her boyfriend on
the other side of the city. For me it was a much
needed beginning: my new classmates knew nothing
of my singing failure, nor of my soccer past. I was
also growing my hair really long. This time everything would be okay.

SCENE 8

*(Britt walks on her new school yard looking at the new brick build-
ings and her new classmates standing around the school yard)*

Ulrika: *(Observing Britt as she talks to the other girls.)* Do you
see that new girl? What is that she has on her head?
Oh, it's her hair. It looks like a bird's nest or something. *(Laughs, then stops as if she remembers something)*
Did you hear her in English class, talking away? She
says that her father is American. *(In a menacing voice)*
I bet she thinks that makes her *special.* Let's show
her what we do to people who think they are *(pause)*
special . . .

Britt: *(Walks over)* Hi, I am Britt.

Ulrika: We know, we could spot that hair from a mile away.

Britt: Yeah? *(Takes it as a compliment)* I guess that is what
happens when you have long hair.

Ulrika: With that hair and those *(pause)* clothes you would
be great in a show we are doing.

Britt: Really? What do you want me to do? I can do anything.

Ulrika: Oh, just be yourself. You would be the *(pause)*
troll . . . *(Strolls away laughing. Then to the other girls)*
Did you see her face?

SCENE 9

Britt: *(Walks center)* Hi mom. *(Pause)* It was okay *(Pause)* No
I didn't get to know anyone today. *(Pause)* No mom,
it is not going to get better. Mom, they won't leave
me alone.

Harasser 1: Hair! *(Britt gets slapped a first time from the left. The first
to the third slap makes Britt fall toward the ground little
by little and by the fourth blow she collapses onto the ground)*

Harasser 2: Geek! *(A second slap from the right)*

Harasser 3: Ugly! *(A third slap from the left again)*

Harasser 4: Freak! *(A fourth slap from the right again. Britt collapses)*

Britt: *(On the floor almost crying)* Mom, it doesn't matter where we go. It's me. It was always me. The rules keep changing and I can't keep up.

Mother: *(Talks in Swedish)* Britt, håll ut. Bry dig inte om de där ungarna. Jag älskar dig. Var stolt. Sköt om dig och mig. Du är det bästa jag har!

Narrative I: *(Upstage right)* My mother was right . . . And when I did meet others, I realized how much I needed other people, other *(pause, realization)* women. Women I didn't have to compete with, but instead, women that came together to inspire one another. When I moved to Stockholm it seemed only logical that I should look up all the women's centers to start a new network of friends. The first name I ran into was a center called "All Women's House."

SCENE 10

Catherine: *(Talks in a sing-song voice that she keeps all throughout the scene, even when she is irritated)* My name is Catherine. I want to say how happy, happy, happy I am to have you here with us, Britt. I want you to know this is a space for all women, of all generations, and I hope that we will be able to exchange experiences across the generational lines. Next to me sits . . .

Susan: My name is Susan and I just want to say how important Catherine has been to me—

Catherine: *(Interrupts)* Thank you Susan. Next to Susan sits . . . Annie!

Annie: *(Wakes up)* Huh? What?

Catherine: Ann, I want you to . . . Never mind. Britt, why don't you introduce yourself to us. If there is anything you would like to talk about please feel free to do so. You might want to talk about some problems you have with your boyfriend.

Britt
(In her early
twenties):   My name is Britt and I am curious to know what sort
of positive and supportive energies can be generated
in a group like this. But I also feel that we must
critically examine any prejudice or discrimination
we might have toward each other and other women.
In this context, as a woman who is in a relationship
with another women, I just want to remind you,
Catherine, to make this important inclusion, "if you
have problems with your male *or female lovers*," but I
am sure that is what you meant.

Catherine: *(Clearly uncomfortable but keeps her gentle sing-song voice)*
Britt, first of all I am really ha-*(stops halfway)* no, I
don't think that is the word I want to use. *(Pause)* I
am honored, I think that you wanted to share this
personal and dark chapter of your life with us. I
understand that you people must have a lot of inhi-
bitions and depressions that you need to talk about,
but I am sure that there is some crisis-line you can
look up in the yellow pages. This is not one of *those*
conscious-raising groups, if you know what I mean . . .

Susan: Exactly, Britt, this is not one of those groups—

Britt: *(Interrupts)* I thought you said this was a space for all
women—

Catherine: *(Interrupts)* There is no need for a conflict here, just
because you happen to mention the *(pause)* L-word.

Susan: The L-word? You mean liberal?

Catherine: No, Susan, that is what we are.

Susan: Oh, we're lesbians? Exactly, we are—*(interrupted by
Catherine who puts her hand over Susan's mouth)*

Catherine: *(Holds a hand out. Smiles to Susan as she takes it away)*
Susan, no! Britt, I knew this would happen with
people like you, you have made us all a bit confused
here. Well, now that we have thoroughly discussed

the L-word, let us go to the next step on my agenda, I mean *our* agenda. I think that we ought to discuss the M-word. I know this might be hard for you, Britt, since this is your first time with us but feel free to say anything, don't feel shy. Today I would like us to discuss how we experience our *(pause)* menstruation. *(Looking at Britt)* Britt, I can see that you are already feeling inhibited just by me saying the word. With what exactly did you have a problem and needed us to help?

Britt: Actually, I was thinking of another M-word.

Catherine: You mean you know another happy, happy M-word?

Britt: Yes, I do. I feel that women need to talk about desire. Women need to talk more about their own bodies. Therefore, let us discuss masturbation.

Catherine: Certainly not.

Britt: Why not? We all do it.

Catherine: No, we don't. There are certain things that a proper woman does not talk about, and if you were in the least concerned with trying to pass as one you would know this.

Britt: You're right. Let us not talk about it. *(Pause)* Let's do it. *(Drops her slacks)* Let us all—*(Turns to Catherine and Susan only to discover that they have run away)* Catherine? Susan? *(Runs a couple of steps with her pants down by her feet.)* Come back. Catherine, you said you would give me a ride home.

SCENE 11

(Britt pulls her pants up. Looks at her watch. Sighs as she realizes that there are no buses around at this hour. Puts her thumb up to hitchhike. She follows the cars passing her with her gaze. The fourth time a "car" stops in front of her.)

Britt: Sir, are you going downtown? Great *(Steps into car by sitting down on the bottom part of the easel)*

Driver: *(Right foot on gas, left hand on wheel)* Did you just miss the last bus?

Britt: *(Changes position, to simply sitting)* No, a friend was supposed to give me a ride but she bailed on me.

Driver: I thought you women were supposed to stick together.

Britt: Well, this time I guess I said the wrong thing, again.

Driver: Like what?

Britt: I don't know . . .

Driver: Let me guess, you were too adventurous for them?

Britt: Sort of, how did you know?

Driver: For one thing, you don't see that many women out hitchhiking by themselves. It takes a certain women to—

Britt: *(Interrupts)* To miss the bus? Listen, I'm not very adventurous. I just need to get from point A to point B.

Driver: Seems like you've been around.

Britt: I have done some travelling if that is what you mean.

Driver: Yeah, I hear you and I think I know what you have been looking for. *(Raises his right hand and moves it to the right toward the "passenger seat")*

Britt: *(Left hand grabs her left leg. She pushes the left hand off her leg with her right hand. In an angry voice)* Don't you dare do that again! *(Looks out at passing cars. Hand on thigh again. She pushes it off again)* Didn't you hear me? I said leave me alone or I'll . . . *(Pause. Britt is thinking of her next move. Takes out lighter from her right hand pocket and lights it in the driver's face to observe him more closely as a counterattack)*

Driver: *(Irritated)* Put that light out! I can't drive with that.

Britt: Where did you get that birthmark by your eyebrow? It is very small.

Driver: *(Irritated and a bit nervous as he is losing control over the situation)* I said, get that light away from my face.

Britt: *(Her voice gets calmer as the driver gets more nervous)* Actually, it looks like a scratch, did you get in a fight with someone? Is that how you got the scar in your chin or is it that something you were born with?

Driver: *(Hits the brakes)* Listen, I have to pick up a friend. There will be no room for you. Get out.

SCENE 12

Narrative I: First, I was okay. I felt relieved. *(Pause)* Then . . . *(Gets more and more agitated as she realizes how violated she has been)* I wanted to rip away the skin on my thigh where his disgusting hand had been. *(Pause as she tries to hold back the tears)* Looking at myself through his eyes made me feel . . . I felt so dirty . . . *(Runs toward easel)* I felt like—*(Tears up the drawing made by the young Britt. Beneath it is a grotesque drawing of a woman with a minuscule head, big breast, and a big triangle, symbolizing the sexual organ of a woman, all drawn with a dark blue crayon. This is the picture drawn in the beginning of the performance)* This is what I felt like *(Points to the drawing on the easel)* and it wasn't the first time. He and so many other people had made me shrink when I thought I was growing . . . *(Britt looks at the picture)*

Priscilla: *(Enters)* Bridgette, I have been sitting in that corner over there listening to your story. If you only knew more things about wrapping, you would be so much better off in life.

Adult Britt: I don't think that's the problem, Priscilla.

Priscilla: *(Sighs)* Bridgette, didn't your mother teach you anything?

Britt: *(Stiffens, turns around slowly)* Excuse me, what did you just say?

Priscilla: I said, didn't your mother teach you anything?

Britt: Priscilla, let me take that mascara and show you exactly what my mother taught me.

(Priscilla takes the mascara out of her pocket and hands it to Britt who takes the brush out, after filling it with mascara by pushing it up and down first. She then puts the brush up her nose.)

Britt: Priscilla . . . Priscilla . . . Don't you like it? Priscilla, where are you going? Priscilla I did this for you! *(Takes a couple of steps towards Priscilla)* Wait, Priscilla. *(Stands still as she watches Priscilla run away. Takes the mascara brush out of her nose. Rubs her nose with her hand and gets streaks of mascara on her hand. Looks at her hand)* I am all smudgy again. *(Pause. Realization. Turns around and looks at the pieces around her)* But an artist is supposed to be that way and I am going to draw my picture right now. *(Walks up to the easel with the grotesque picture)* But I can't draw myself as others look at me. *(Britt pushes the easel away. Then she picks up the crayons and walks back to the spot where the easel used to be. Starts drawing on herself as she says the following lines)* This is a picture of a kudu. *(Draws on her left leg)* This is a picture of the best soccer player in the world. *(Draws on her stomach)* This is a picture of my desire. *(Draws on chest)* This is a picture of my voice. *(Draws on her throat)* But I am not only drawing the past and the present, I am also drawing as I imagine my future. And as I am drawing, I am not only getting older but I am also transforming. Transforming, evolving, and growing as I draw upon myself. *(Drawing frantically on her arms and face)*

The end

MARCIA DOUGLAS

The Ascania Docks in Southampton, circa 1955

All that's left now is a black and white photo from an old
   Daily Mirror.
One thousand West Indian immigrants on board the *Ascania*—
mostly men in felt hats.
Flooding the decks, they lean over the rails,
their shoulders pressed together.
On the far left is someone's Uncle Morris.
He has left behind half an acre of yellow yam
and a girl with a pretty black mole on her upper lip.
The dream in his eyes shines like the lighted window far away,
where by candle light,
the girl washes her hair in a plastic basin.
Wearing new shoes and a relative's old wedding suit,
the young man behind him searches the dock for the queen.
Certainly, she will come to greet him,
her gloved hand waving like the white wing of a dove.
Short men. Tall men. Husky men. Frail men.
Men with five pounds in their pocket
and a carboard suitcase with a broken latch.

Come to the Mother Country.
The Mother Country needs you.
The cry crossed the Atlantic,

ringing from Trinidad and Tobago
and along the curve of the Leewards,
past Anguilla and on to the Cockpit Country of Jamaica.
Brave men. They packed their bags,
their ancestors' fear of ships almost strained from their blood,
the Atlantic spread before them like a banquet table.

Now on the upper deck, the fifth person from the right—
a man smiles and rubs his chin.
Union Jacks are stuffed in the bags beneath his eyes.
Later, he will take a train to Victoria Station.
In the cold and the rain, there will be no one to meet him.
He will work in an asbestos plant,
rent a flat with a mattress
and a clothes line strung from one corner to the other.
He will dream of children playing on warm rocks by the
    Martha Brae,
their mothers bathing silently in the water.

CHARLES PETERSON

A Long Way from Home

Early migrations were dwarfed by the surge of Black people
northward after 1900, and especially after 1910. According to
various contemporaneous estimates, between 1890 and 1910
around 200,000 Black Southerners fled to the north; and
between 1910 and 1920 another 300,000 to 1,000,000 followed. The Department of Labor reported than in eighteen
months of 1916–17 the migration was variously estimated at
200,000 to 700,000. (Florette Henri, *Black Migration*, 51)

silk blue skies wash into darker cramped tones. the dust of
the road and the fields rises and rises blurring the past. a past
better left behind, children's teary curious eyes asking questions
of hunger and filth. questions that can't be answered without my
own questions rising up like the dust that clouds my footsteps.
there's word that up north there's work. so much work that
word spreads down as far as the snowy cotton field, we were
standing in the middle of. my fourth plantation in two years.
wandering from field to field doing the only thing i ever learned,
pickin'. a new wife with two children of her own and one more
which is mine, don't help my journey along any faster. my wife
picked in the rows along in the next acre and she takes in wash.
snow white cotton and snow white shirts soaking up our sweat
and stretching out like years in front of us.
there's trucks that leave carryin' north any that wants to
bend their backs to steel. my cousin that went before me writes

back sayin' its twice the pay, enough to get your own place, feed your kids and no crackers to look over your back or tell you where to go or how fast to get there or to eat the shit that they're feedin' you off their boots.

leonard couldn't stay down home, he'd got caught up in some trouble outside of sardis. over the past 15–20 years he, his brothers and they daddy had been working a good stretch a land for a mr. harris. chip'n a piece here and a piece there, they managed to take over the place from mr. harris. working damn can't see to can't see, they almost killed themselves over it but finally it was theirs. seventy of the greenest acres i've ever seen. enough to break up for your family and fertile enough to turn over. enough to get yourself a little something in this world. but a little something for a colored in this world spells too damn much for whites. after a month a trying to get my uncle to sell out to 'em, a small committee of "concerned" citizens wanted to negotiated in a more direct way. from what leonard tells me, bout half past three in the morning a final offer was made. lit oil cans crashed through their windows and rounds of buckshot peppered their porch. leonard was the youngest, 15 at the time. his daddy managed to push him out the back door with a burn to the arm and a bit more space instead of hair on his scalp as a memory. my uncle leonard was the baby and had lost his two older brothers (one of whom was my daddy) to the southern hazard of thinking you was a person when you was told you ain't nothing but a dog.

this truck i'm ridin' to gary, indiana (or detroit or chicago or cleveland) feels like a drop in the river that's headed for the lake, a great flowin' stream of tired hopin' bodies, tired of hopin' for what they cain't get. every day more and more leavin' home, lookin' to go to some place where home can mean more than the same o' same o' of just hangin' on. colored's just streamin' with boxes and bags and some with nothin' whatever, just a bunch of bad memories and hurt hearts that they got like they was gifts on christmas day. leonard told me that i could stay with him until i get myself right. my wife's waitin' on me and i'm thinkin' about her and the children when i see them grey winds begin to swirl. the markings in the sky got their own little flavor and scent. char and coal and other smells i don't quite recognize. it ain't like home, the clouds ain't puffy and the land looks beat on. but it's a job i'm here for not to appreciate my surroundins. maybe in a few months i could scrape some money together to send for rose lee and the children, maybe i could see the baby girl again before she starts walkin' . . .

> Between me and the other world there is even an unasked question: unasked by some through feelins of delicacy; by others through the difficulty of rightly framing it. All . . . flutter round it. They approach me in a half hesitant sort of way, eye me curiously or compassionately. . . . To the real question, How does it feel to be a problem? I answer seldom a word. (W.E.B. Du Bois, *The Souls of Black Folk*, 43–44)

flakes—dry, charred—float on icy blast winds. somber sweeps on the currents of flame that kick me in the face like a angry mule—ornery mean-hearted and proud—demanding and makin' no exception for livin' weaknesses.

full blast of flame and smoke reminds me to keep shovelin' coal, keep earnin' fifty cents an hour, keep runnin' so's i can stand still. standin' at the mouth of an open blast furnace in the heart of five miles of a thick metal hope on the lip of lake michigan, in the middle of a wakin' dream, the weight of wood and iron in my hand and the scrape of metal against coal anchor me to this gravel. my nights have been gettin' longer and sleepin's on a need to have basis. my eldest boy sits up all night sweatin' and coughin', with a chill that seems to be worse than anything the wind off the lake could give. rose lee stays up late to see to 'em and wakes up early to see to the rest of us. i suspect the boy's got t-b from the way it was driftin' through the streets. rows and rows of two room hazy shacks, squattin' on sheets of ice and leanin' on one another, tired children looking for some rest. houses so close you can catch the blues from the next man's moans. all with coughin, shiverin' kids and saggin' red-eyed parents. somethin's sweepin' in the air, somethin' that's tirin' us out and layin' us down.

two weeks ago a man from the school comes down to see why emmet ain't been makin' it. come with him was a sweaty-faced doctor, that, between lookin' down his nose and scrunchin' up his face, assumed too damn much and told us more than we asked to hear. he was so surprised at how neat the house was and how clean the children were and made so many suggestions about what we should do to pull ourselves up that he forgot to tell what was wrong with emmet. he only scratched on his piece of paper and said his fee would be comin' out my check. company houses, company stores and to top it off a company doctor.

the boy's cough and the scared silence of the other children are the long night to the days of steel mill screams and worker shouts. twelve hour days dizzy with bendin', scrapin', and chokin' back an anger that feels good enough to be the truth. all shift long i'm gawked at and ignored all at the same time. for the most part if you colored in this town, you're a piece of the nothing that sits on the east side of broadway. a long winding gray forgettin' that's only something cause it's between white folks and the beach. but in the mill, one colored in a shop with a bunch a whites seems to become a presence to be reckoned with, at least that's what they think. i see what they see and they don't know it. to them one colored'll mean two, then three, then four, then a pay cut, then a lay off then no chance for them to eat less dirt in their lives. i also see what they don't see and don't know i see. a scared and hungry look in their eyes. a look that sees me takin' their jobs, their chance and their lives. the same look i seen in the eyes of a thousand poor white farmers back home. they buy their food from the same grocer as me, no one's said hello. they pay rent to the same landlord as me, no one's offered me their hands. union man walks by me like i was best friends with the boss. there's not a dime in my pocket or no spoon in my mouth, all i got is my family, my friends, and my past. but everywhere i go i'm treated like the fox in the henhouse.

rose lee sees it a little, but most times her kinda help is always wanted. somebody to cook or hold a baby or wash a shirt. somebody to be the body that somebody else didn't want to be. she tells me the women she works for treat her like she always 'sposed to be there, like a door or a rug or a step, "why, what else would you do if you weren't here with me?" the night's cold stains frost lines on the window and rose lee sleeps heavily. because of emmet's illness she at home most times takin' in wash. i hear her move as i sit up with emmet, he sleeps and i talk to him to tell what little i know of livin' this life. a story here and talk there things that i remember my mother tellin' me, her hair twisted up in two long braids her eyes clear and her voice low to not wake the others. i'm seven again and shiverin' despite the night's heat. high john the conqueror and brer rabbit keep my eyes on her and her eyes in the dim lamp light, i can smell her warmth and weariness with flashes of sweetness from the honey she put in my tea.

in the next room my daddy moves in the dark and rose lee turns and i think back to when i seen her that first time out front of a grocer's in sledge, mississippi. her and emmet with blanche ridin' her hip. a stranger in town, she was bein' eyed by the kind of folk that think bein' alone is a flower to have its petals pulled off. questions and questions, rose was a woman alone with clear eyes and a low voice. low but firm in her answers and stiff in her replies. it was back and forth with the crowd and the crowd didn't seem none too satisfied with the show. blanche starts to whimper a little and emmet's thumb just wasn't enough to steady his little knees. that's when i think it's maybe time rose lee met her new cousin, her cousin that would introduce her to sister jones who was always lookin' out for them that was new and didn't know their way around. with my head down and eyes low i didn't see rose's clear eyes that had gone watery or her tremblin' jaw until we had left the circle and i heard her dry tight thank you. i remember thinkin' we do what we can.

five or six months of tippin' in to say hello and play with the baby and show her round and two or three months of quiet talkin' and sly smiles and sunday dinners and puttin' the babies to bed led to emmet and blanche gettin a new daddy, rose lee a husband and me a reason to start thinkin' about more than the next payday . . .

> *Requiem*
> Home to the cooling hearth
> nestled in the bosom
> of the deathly vibrant
> pockmarked body
> of industrial illusion
> Sold on a glittering dream
> ever were you a wasteland
> amid mortuaries
> Ungrateful your child
> cold comfort is the steel
> you gave birth to

shocking splashes of light crystal spires spin dazzle and fall on the edges of the sky sun bathed clouds unveil their hearts before the earth promising more to see as the sun's rays smack tearin' at my eyes caught starin' too long at the sun . . .

caught up in a seagull's path struttin' across the sky the sun hits me smack dab in mid wish. comparin' those seagulls to the ducks back home, they move the same. it's a different bird, a different time and a different place but the way they move . . . a lazy stroke takin' its own time, no rushin' no hurry—just a freedom i cain't even taste on my off days. the time now moves so slow that more and more i'm losing track and miscounting the things that mean somethin'. i've crossed the middle of the field, lookin' at my young manhood from a tent that's pitched a little bit closer to the river. rose lee tells me it's just the years of work and worry, the years of tryin' to build on foundations made of sand. the kids, that are too old to be called kids anymore, say it's time for me and rose to rest. but it's more than that.

my youngest boy, walter, moves and i see my moves, how they were. my eyes blur and the light which covers more and more of what i'm seein' dances, drops of, sweat bounce off a strong back that once again don't pay no 'tention to time or weariness or wear and tear. eyes that cry dry tears for days ahead that i cain't see. in the light i'm twenty two again with only a few things to do but so much time to do 'em. comin' out of that glow into the gray mist after sundown and me and that boy glowin' beneath the sun are on opposite ends of the same tether, with a few more things to do and even less time to get them done.

my friends and me spend more time than we used to sittin' around not wantin' to move. it's not just that it's an effort but it's the idea of chasin' after something, always wantin' always empty and tryin' to fill some space that was always either your stomach or a pocket or a heart. but damn on all that now. i've been running all this time and i'm tired of it. anything that i got comin' had better present itself to me. but i know what it is that's comin' and on those days where the light of things i'd thought i'd forgotten is warm and soft, i think "my, my but it's takin' its time gettin' here." but more often than not those days where there's a mean chill blowin' across a summer's day, i don't feel like goin' down so easy.

i see walter and his moves, his dreams, and fears, lookin' at him i see forty years waitin' to happen and feel forty years come too soon. he's my youngest and looks so much like me that i feel like we're breathin' the same breaths. eighteen and he's lookin' for a chance to get a little something for himself in this world. just finished high school and signed up to go into the airforce. he's got a few weeks left of biding his time to get his life started. he's excited and he's scared. all his life whenever the boy's been scared or nervous or unsure he's been talkin'. so we talk. and with walter you talk and talk.

my time at the mill is growin' short and i got friends who punch the clock and pull favors for me, so's my short time to retirement ain't so much trouble. with my longer days, me and walter spend more time together. his eyes are so bright when he talks about the things he can do and the places he can go in the airforce. i hear in his voice a chance. he's not my first to go, three of my older ones been off to the service. fought in wars, seen places and all, thank god, come back to us. they're young men now and do what they can for the family. naw, walter's life ain't the first time i've seen that look. i've seen it years past as i've looked into mirrors and into the mirrored eyes of my friends, their children and my own. sons lookin' to be fathers and providers, daughters hopin' to be mothers and providers. all hopin' to avoid the sadness and questions in their parents eyes. naw, it's not the first time i seen that look. and that's what gets my heart pumpin' and my eyes tearin' from the taste in my mouth.

this life's bein' lived over and over. the haint's runnin' long for me and my strength grown sho't. that boy in the field forty years ago rooted like a tree. rooted in this life to soil that won't turn over or take new seeds or yield to changin' seasons. my walter's got to sign his life away and run clean across the world, fight wars risk his life and carry the heartache of that, just to try his hand at the same game me and his momma been playin' for more than his life. the same losing game his grandparents played. when my grandmama died she closed her eyes in some sweet peace. she'd been born a slave, lived to see her children get some schoolin' and get some pay for their sweat and pain. so with some sweet peace she died, her life had changed somethin' and made her children's lives different from hers. my time gone short and the dry golden thoughts of passing times is where i'm spending more of my moments, unable to fix it. unable to fix the lie that a northern steel mill is different from a southern plantation. the lie that say hardwork is all negroes need. the lie that say it takes time and all the wrongs will be righted. i've made the moves and i've worked the jobs and i've passed the time. no, there won't be no sweet peace as these eyes close, no gentle rest and no lie big enough to tell me that anything's changed. . . .

MYRA LOVE

Reality's Friends

Oh no, I thought, when trying to write a few words about my relationship to academics and the reason I've chosen to write a novel with a distinctly surreal tone, a novel that has, on occasion been called "demented" (by readers who liked it), instead of doing the scholarship I have been trained to do. I don't want to offer explanations and justifications of what is, ultimately, a personal choice, particularly since some people may, upon hearing what I have to say, forget my insistence on the subjectivity of my comments and commitments and feel attacked or invalidated. This is certainly not my intention, but stranger things have happened.

Over the past ten years, since I finished my dissertation and became a more or less full-fledged member of academia, I have, despite my best efforts and my determination from the very beginning to avoid the pitfalls of ivory-towerhood, noticed in myself a direct relationship between the degree of my commitment to academics and the extent to which I experience what I can only call a loss of reality or better yet an increasingly broken or distorted relationship to reality.

What I mean by this is not all that hard to explain. I knew when I saw colleagues experiencing more anxiety over issues pertaining to their own academic careers and standing, the financial solvency of the universities and colleges that employed them, and the relative status and security of their academic department than over violence against women, all-pervasive racist and homophobic attitudes and behavior, homelessness, and poverty that the state of mind into which I would have to enter to be fully integrated into academe deserved to be characterized as unreal because it presupposed my separateness from multiple human sufferings, a separateness which I know to be unreal.

Well, you may say, someone who admits (confesses?) that she is writing a surreal and possibly demented novel has a lot of nerve talking about reality, doesn't she? Be that as it may. In any case, the notion of a broken relationship to reality isn't a phrase that stems from me. The German author Christa Wolf, about whom I recently published a scholarly book, used it in conversation with me in 1983 and it stayed in my mind. Wolf is the same author, who, in a speech that quickly became famous, especially among feminist academic scholars, insisted on the extreme ambivalence of the positions of women, even of privileged women, with what she called the "citadel of reason," the phallocentric or masculinist structures that determine what counts and what doesn't count as valid thought that deserves to be taken seriously. She said:

> *Paradoxically—yes: her entrance into the citadel [of reason] subjects her to its laws!—paradoxically she had to assist in the misunderstanding. To become free, she yielded to new entanglements. To find herself, new forms of self-denial were demanded of her.[1]*

For whatever reasons—my success in graduate school; my naively optimistic belief that if people only understood the restrictive ways in which knowledge is constituted and institutionalized in our society, and in the academic world in particular, they would be willing, if not eager to extend the boundaries of knowledge, especially our knowledge of ourselves, and stop producing books and articles "in Martian, by Martians, and for Martians"; and, perhaps most important, my inability to distinguish between what I was really searching for, call it wisdom or insight, if you will, and what passes for and is institutionalized as the highest achievement of the human mind and spirit, intellectual knowledge and scholarship—for all of these reasons I believed that I could live with the paradox of which Wolf had spoken, and even use it to my advantage and to the advantage of everyone committed to the expansion of what we call mind, intellect, reason, scholarship, to include what has been traditionally excluded and rendered invisible and invalid.

I am sure that there are some people who manage to do what I could not. At least I hope there are and wish them all success. With time, however, I realized that the practices expected of me if I were to succeed,

*that is, to have a career, and those that would enable me to be effective
as a teacher and a scholar in calling into question the limits imposed
upon the rational and the real were mutually exclusive. For all the
advances that feminist and lesbian and multicultural studies have supposedly made, I have not noticed a willingness on the part of anyone
truly established in reason's citadel to abandon what Audre Lorde called
"the master's tools," which, as she, quite rightly, understood "will never
dismantle the master's house."*[2]

*Perhaps I overgeneralize, but I can only report on my own experience.
I chose quite deliberately, I think, to do what I could as a teacher, helping
people rearrange the furniture in their minds, as a friend of mine put it.
At this I was quite successful, and I hold that success to be the crowning
achievement of my academic labors. I have done scholarly work and have
received recognition for it, but I could not help but notice that, whatever
the ostensible radicalism of its topic, its acceptability depended on its con-
formity to academic norms, i.e., its remaining within a discourse designed
to display its own sophistication at the expense of communication.*

*Of course, other scholars in academe knew what I was writing about.
Some of them appreciated my work too. At least I thought they did. However, I found that acceptance of what I had done often took the form of what
I could only experience as a strange reinterpretation of whatever I had
written to suit the intellectual frameworks of others, frameworks that often
diverged quite radically from my own. Now, although I have little use for
the concept of intellectual property, still, finding articles I'd written cited as
support for Freudian arguments was quite disconcerting. Although I have
no control and have never desired control over what other people make of
what I do, it would be nice to hear my own voice played back once in a
while, even if in a key that I myself would never use.*

*If one hears or reads one's own words but cannot come to terms with
the contexts in which they are cited, one easily loses one's sense of one's
own voice, and that is what disturbed me most of all. The loss of my own
voice in my academic writing troubled me deeply because I interpreted it
as a mark of my complicity, however unintentional, with structures and
ways of thinking that I had never wished to embrace. How else could I
interpret it? This was then inevitably accompanied by the loss of my sense
of humor in all matters intellectual. My writing of a somewhat surreal,
possibly demented, novel about a woman named Wisdom, her squirrel
Jesus, and their assorted friends, acquaintances, and antagonists is an
attempt to recoup these losses, maybe also to write in a manner that no*

academic scholar in her or his "right mind" would care or dare to appropriate. It is also one hell of a lot of fun.

The passages that follow consist of brief excerpts from the early chapters of Reality's Friends. *Those chapters introduce Wisdom and Jesus and set the scene for the rest of the novel.*

from: Chapter 1

BEGINNINGS

Wisdom

You never thought I would actually sit down and write this, did you, Nin? I probably wouldn't have gotten started today if it hadn't been for the TV. Yeah, that's right, the TV is responsible for this, believe it or not. Even though I would probably tell you that I don't like to watch TV if you asked me, sometimes I turn it on just because I don't feel like doing much of anything but have already slept as much as I feel comfortable sleeping. You know how you feel when you sleep too much, don't you? Kind of blurry with a headache? Well, today was kind of like that, so I turned on the TV and heard them announce a show coming up featuring women who fell in love with and married convicted murderers. Then someone said that the sexiest thing in this society is murder, so I turned off the TV and came in here to ask you a question: when does the next spaceship leave?

Now don't look at me as if I were crazy. *I'm* not the one who thinks that murder is sexy. I just want out of here. I know that you sometimes tell people you pilot spaceships when they ask you about your career. And yeah, I know you're only kidding, but I figure that if you can say that convincingly enough, you probably know something about it, and since you could only learn it from someone who really does pilot spaceships, I am asking you as a personal favor to fill me in on the flight schedules. . . .

Oh yeah, before I forget. My name is Wisdom. Now don't laugh. I like that name, picked it myself. Don't call me Teeth or any other smartass thing either! I think Wisdom is a great name. Hell of a lot better than Money, isn't it?

CJ

Hi there! I see that Wisdom has been introducing herself to you. She's really something, isn't she? She decided to move in here about a month ago. At first I wasn't sure that I wanted her around since the place is a little crowded with me and Abby and Lua. And then there's that squirrel she keeps as a pet. A rabbit is one thing, but a squirrel is more destructive and sure makes a hell of a lot more mess. Not to mention noise. She calls the squirrel Jesus, even though it's a female. Jesus really annoys Lua no end. Lua really doesn't want any other animal sleeping on her rug or eating out of her dishes. Not that Jesus ever really sleeps. She sure does eat though. She got into the peanut butter jar somehow earlier today. Almost a whole pound of the stuff gone in nothing flat! Oh well, at least Jesus doesn't like spider plants or pansies for between meal snacks. That's Lua's specialty.

Anyhow, we have Wisdom and Jesus living with us here for the time being. At least I hope it's for the time being. Wisdom says she's only going to stay until she can figure out where she wants to move next. Of course there is always a chance that she may never figure that out. Actually I'm not too worried though. We're only going to stay here until next summer and then be moving on ourselves. Once I have to start teaching again in a few weeks, I figure Wisdom will keep Lua company if she's still hanging around. She and Lua can watch TV together.

❦

Wisdom

. . . What's that? You want to know why I named her Jesus? Well, I didn't; she picked her name herself, just like I did mine. About three weeks after I stopped having to feed her with an eyedropper, I was sitting out back watching the cars slow down and park near the creek out there. Baby Squirrel, as I called her then, was sitting on my right shoulder, chewing on my hair, and we were pretty contented and relaxed. Then this guy got out of one of the biggest of all the cars, marched up to us, pointed at us with his right forefinger, waved his bible, and thundered: "Now tell me, sinner, have you found Jesus?" Well, I was pretty taken aback for a minute but realized pretty quickly that it was, as an old pal of mine would say, a message. All I'd found recently had been this baby squirrel, who wasn't any too happy about the guy barking at us and waving his finger. She began to chatter at him and took a flying leap (a very short flying leap since he was breathing in my face) from my shoulder onto the left-hand page of his open bible. She grabbed the page, ripped a swatch right down the length of it, crumbled it up, and kicked it right at his face. Then she scrambled to the edge of the page and leaped right back onto my shoulder. The guy tumbled backwards, as if he'd seen a ghost, mumbled Jesus Christ under his breath, and took off back to his big old ugly car. When I picked the piece of bible page off the ground, the only word on it that was still legible was "Jesus." So I figured that was another sign and started calling the baby squirrel Jesus. She doesn't seem to mind too much. Never laughs when I call her by her name. It kind of makes some other people uptight though, but I tell them not to blame me. Blame the squirrel; she tore the name right out of the book herself. Let me tell you, Jesus is one very smart squirrel.

from: Chapter 3

WORDS OF WISDOM

. . . You know (this is a *non sequitur*, but I'm gonna say it anyhow), I'm real tired of people taking their identity from sex. I mean, I'm especially tired of lesbians doing it, though I understand how a society that judges you by who you have sex with could make you want to define yourself by constantly having, thinking about, talking about, or otherwise obsessing about sex. How do I define myself? Well, I try not to mostly, but when I am forced to, I pick something really goofy, like my shoe size or the circumference of my head. Hell, I'm not against having an identity. No way, but all this crap about defining yourself seems a little questionable to me. Hell, if you know who you are, you don't have to go around defining yourself, and if you don't, then no amount of defining is gonna do you a damned bit of good.

Yeah, I know I talk a lot of negativity about sex. It's not that I'm against it, it's just that love seems more important and gets less attention. I don't mean romance either, I mean love.

Like I was sayin', love gets a lot less attention than sex. That's because we live in a materialist culture, and I don't just mean a culture that values only money and possessions, but one that turns everything into things and discounts whatever can't be turned into a thing as unreal. I guess that's why we obsess about bodies so much, our own and everyone else's. To me, it's like standing in a beautiful meadow under a huge clear blue sky and only seeing the dust particles that come to rest on your shoes. Know what I mean?

Anyway, things can get weighed and measured and evaluated. This culture is totally hooked on evaluation. It's as if everyone has to know what's bigger, faster, better to know what's real. It's like you can't enjoy what's around you unless you compare it to what everyone else has around them.

๑๖๑

I picked up one of CJ's books that was in German, and it had some lines underlined in red with a big exclamation point next to them. When I asked her what they meant, she told me that they said something about people getting mad at poets for expressing dissatisfaction at the reduced life they were all living, but not noticing or trying not to notice that they are living. I kind of like that about reduced life, and it sure surprised me that someone else was thinking stuff like that besides me. Makes me feel kind of glad though, and a hell of a lot less lonely.

A reduced life comes from not doing what you really want to do, and that's exactly what most people are like, yours truly included. I mean, to do what you really want to do, you gotta know what that is. As for me, when I think about what I want to do at any given time, it's different from what I want to do at any other time. And you can't earn a living from any of it. I mean, who'd pay me to take walks or eat hamburgers or talk to people on street corners between here and the Burger King?

But you know, the idea of earning a living is sure a strange one. It's like you don't have a right to live unless you earn it.

Sometimes I think that I'll never come up with what I really want
to do until the pressure about earning a living and the whole
idea that you have to *do* something that earns you money to
justify your existence is gone from my mind. I mean, how can I
know what to do when I'm not really free to consider all the
possibilities? And how can I consider all the possibilities when so
many are automatically excluded when you can't get paid for
them?

I keep trying to talk to CJ about this stuff, but I think it
makes her a little nervous. Guess she's afraid I might stay on
here forever if I can't figure out what I want to do to earn money.

JESUS SPEAKS

i, jesus, am the squirrel who teaches the world the truth of
the matter. it does not matter what matter; all that matters is that
what matters. this does wisdom have yet to learn. cj as well. and
possibly a lot of other two-leggeds, if they are mentally and spiri-
tually capable of learning, which i occasionally have reason to
doubt. so if it confuses you, you're not the only one. but think
about it and everything that could be understood if only words
did not intervene and allow one to refer to it without specifying
its essence, nature, and edibility. and remember that the sages
always speak in parables when they speak at all, which is not all
that often, since their mouths are often full of food, and they are
too well-bred, not to mention fastidious, to speak whilst eating.

i was born into the most tragic of all possible circumstances:
a large family with many mouths to feed living in an environment teeming with canines and other predators. orphaned at an
early age when a german shepherd ate my mother and siblings,
i was left to the tender mercies of a two-legged, who was fortunately less vicious and insensitive than many, though her sensibility was far less refined than that of even the most ill-bred squirrel.
in saying this, dear reader, i do not mean to attack your species,
but am merely recording the truth about it in order to enable
you to reflect and accept your responsibility to other species,
among whom there may be (no, not may be, but assuredly and
indubitably are) not only other enlightened entities like myself,

but also many fine and distinguished, though less evolved speci-
mens still deserving of your admiration and respect.

unfortunately, wisdom, the name by which the two-legged
who appropriated me refers to herself, had no fixed address
when she retrieved me from the garbage can into which i had
fled after witnessing the savaging of my nearest and dearest. so
i was forced to survive for weeks on end perched precariously on
her head, a position whose awkwardness was matched only by
discomfort due to the extreme shortness of her headwhiskers.
even after she moved into her chosen residence, a small cabin
not far from the captive animal domicile at which she worked, i
was obliged to remain balanced on her head because she insisted
on my accompanying her to her place of employment every single
day. she claimed that this was for my own safety, but how could
she even speak of safety while forcing me to hazard my existence
by exposing myself to the inquisitiveness and intrusiveness of
enormous creatures of limited intelligence of the bovine and
equine varieties? it is true that when she did leave me alone in
the cabin for a few short days after we moved in, i tore the place
to absolute shreds and got myself trapped in the bottom of a
deep and capacious cooking implement, but that is hardly grounds
for keeping me imprisoned on her person day after endless day.
i think she did it and tends to do it still because she is totally
indecisive and insecure, and thus incapable of making rational
decisions without my assistance. . . .

it's not that i underestimate my importance to wisdom or
the strength of her attachment to me. and i certainly don't understand the extreme partiality of abby and cj to rabbits, who are,
after all, merely lagomorphs, deviants from the rodent species.
but it certainly is wonderful to wake up every morning and be
able to wander around the place, eat a nut or a bit of peanut
butter, chatter with abby or lua, who, though not fluent speakers
of squirrel, seem to be remarkably able to make out most of what
i say, and chew up whatever papers or magazines cj leaves around
that lua doesn't get to first. it's a safe and easy life, and i like it
a lot. i know that cj worries about her tendency to create what
abby has referred to as nauseating security wherever she goes,
but when you've lived the kind of life i have, you really appreciate security and comfort, let me tell you. i just hope wisdom

doesn't do anything stupid the way she usually does and get us kicked out of here.

naturally i don't want to end up the way lua is: a domesticated creature, afraid of her own shadow. i am, after all a squirrel, and as such a member of a higher order of life than the domestic lapine. lua is afraid of cats, afraid of other rabbits, afraid of birds, even afraid of squirrels.

i can't say that i miss a life of freedom in the great outdoors, having never experienced such within recent memory. besides, i do have contact with other squirrels when wisdom, dependent though she usually may be, allows me a few moments alone to enjoy peace and quiet and the dignity of my own exceptionally sage thoughts. then my fellow animals who surround this building in which we spend the greater part of our days approach the window and inform me of all that a squirrel of status and dignity needs to know: the state of the nut harvest, the relative proximity of cats and dogs, and other essential bits of information about the condition of the world, which is, i must admit, lamentable.

lately, some members of my species, which does, i must admit, tend to indulge in unseemly gossip and backbiting, have been making rude comments about me concerning both my relationship to wisdom and my residence within this domicile. i hope it will not prove necessary for me to sally forth and offer a defense of my lifestyle with my teeth and claws, though sometimes that is the only way to transmit an emphatic message about the unacceptability of certain behaviors. intolerance is so petty and so unbecoming a superior species. really quite unworthy. it exists so much less frequently among us than among humans that we sometimes fail to be on guard against it and to recognize it when it occurs. i would prefer not having to deal with such nonsense, especially since wisdom gets absolutely frantic whenever i go forth on my own to engage with my peers. it may, alas, prove necessary, however, that i beat some sense into those recalcitrant squirrely heads, and i am certainly equal to the task if it is required of me.

lua, on the other hand, could not defend herself against a butterfly. stamp and run, stamp and run, that is all she had the courage to do when abby showed the bad taste of allowing a cat into the apartment. can you imagine allowing a cat into your very residence? i was so disgusted that i nearly peed on abby's foot. i did manage to bite cj quite hard, since she did nothing to prevent that obnoxious occurrence, but she was too busy on the floor trying to pacify lua even to notice my outrage.

i will never understand those two-leggeds.

from: Chapter 3

STAY TUNED

Wisdom

You know, no matter what else happens, you can always count on TV to give you a sense of what's really going on in the popular mind of the great American John Q. Public. Today, while CJ was out, I turned on the TV and accidentally tuned into a show where a British male to female transsexual was being interviewed. A really famous transsexual who's been on lots and lots of talk shows and does a really good imitation of a femmy straight woman. I thought, wow, this is so amazing. The transsexual talked about having three x and one y chromosome and then told about having had a rich boyfriend, who, prior to the actual surgery but after the patient had breast implants, had wanted to marry him just as he was. He claimed that they had this wonderful and loving relationship in which the transsexual-to-be had felt that his suitor truly loved him the way he was and didn't want him to have the surgery, which he had anyway though he had to leave the relationship to do so. Also, his suitor had given him all sorts of presents and stuff. This really impressed the talk show lady, who seemed really envious of that kind of relationship. Weird, I mean, is that weird or is that weird? I guess I wonder if that's the ideal of many women involved with men. You know, the ones who claim to be "normal"? Like I say, TV really gives you a lot of insight into the popular mind.

Right now, I'm not feeling too popular though. I mean, when your very own squirrel puts you down, you can't feel too great about yourself. I didn't even know that Jesus could type. Must be Lua's influence. But at least I know she isn't hanging out with me for security or jewelry or anything like that. She sounded like she thought I might be hanging out with her for security.

Kind of hard to believe how differently we see our relationship: she thinks she's taking care of me and I think I'm taking care of her. I guess people are like that too with each other, and they don't even have the excuse of species-based differences. But then on the other hand, you'd think a squirrel would have more sense.

Anyway, that TV show got me to thinking about men and women, which I don't do very often because it kind of turns my stomach. Basically, I think the species should mix, but sexes should live separately. Lua is sitting right here, meditating, and she won't say whether she agrees or not, but I have noticed that her behavior suggests she does agree: she doesn't take real well to men coming in here.

Now you may wonder why I feel the way I do. I mean, I know lots of lesbians who don't. Fact is, that I'm just going on the basis of what I see and what I hear. I mean, there is this really unhealthy symbiosis between men and women, and I think that it's polluting the environment. Don't ask me for scientific proof, but I'll bet you that most of the damage done to the planet is done by breeders, both men and women. I know you're going to say that's because there are more of them. It's true there are; they multiply like flies, but even proportionate to the distribution of sexual orientations within the population, they do a hell of a lot more damage. That's because they don't know how to communicate with each other or with other species in positive ways.

And you know what's worse? The fact that most of us have heterosexual parents makes us dangerous because we inherit and pass on their infection. Unless we put time and energy into getting free of it. Most lesbians and gay men I know are really deviant heterosexuals. Then there are a few of us who are really a different sexual orientation. That doesn't just mean that we have sex along different lines, but that we really feel and do something different.

Now most so-called gay people won't admit that they know what I mean, even if they do. They're so busy trying to be normally gay, and that means deviantly heterosexual. Those of us who do know usually have a hard time figuring out why we feel so different and so differently and what to do about that. If we're really lucky, we find each other, but you know what? We never or almost never become lovers. We're too busy using each other to help us cope with our relationships to all the deviantly hetero types to whom we're attracted because they are closer to the norm.

from: Chapter 6

BRAIN CHILDREN

Wisdom

. . . You know, I wish people could learn to be wise. Then my name wouldn't sound so funny and out of place. It would be natural to name your kid or yourself after something valued like that. Only we don't value it the way we value status and money.

Anyway, I was watching TV the other day, and I saw four talk shows that directly or indirectly had to do with rape and violence against women. I could only stand to watch one of them where the woman hosting had some tough questions to ask about the way the legal system deals with rape victims. Otherwise the shows were the same old shitty blame the victim stuff. You know what amuses me about it all? All these men talking about how much more sensitive the legal system has gotten to women who are victimized. Ha? The only reason there's anything like increased sensitivity is because women have been making a stink. And it's about time. I just wish there were more to do, but I can't figure out what. That's part of what frustrates me.

Another part is that CJ and Abby can't seem to make up their minds about what they're going to do next year. I know that they're going to move, but the question is to where. And do I want to travel with them? Jesus is for it, I'm sure, but I don't really know how I feel. They have weird priorities. I mean, CJ doesn't even seem to care if they live around lesbians or not, even though just about all her friends are lesbians. (Yeah, all three of them! She's not exactly outgoing, if you know what I mean.) And Abby is so used to working with lesbians, that she hardly gives it a thought. Neither has given a thought to what it would mean to live in a place totally devoid of any but the most closeted folks. I can hardly believe how oblivious they are sometimes.

⊙⊺⊚

You know, I just wish I didn't see and hear so many things that upset me. Sure Nin thinks my comments on TV are pretty amusing, but I wish I didn't have to make them. Wouldn't it be nice if there were nothing to complain about, nothing to mock, because everything made sense?

CJ made one of her classes write essays on their idea of utopia. Utopia for me would be having nothing to complain about. I'd be so happy, you'd hardly believe it.

When I told that to CJ, she laughed so hard she cried. When she calmed down, she told me that I'd always find something to complain about because I'm just like that by temperament. Claimed that if I ever found myself in a world with nothing to make fun of, I'd just shrivel up and die. I don't know. I think I might like it. A world with nothing to complain about. Yeah, I think I would like it a lot.

Anyway, I was just watching TV, and the news is going on about national AIDS day. It's incredible. Ever since they figured out that it's not just a gay disease, they're panicking. So much for the news. I think I'm gonna go play with Jesus. She's kind of restless.

NOTES

1. Christa Wolf, "Shall I Garnish a Metaphor with an Almond Blossom?: Büchner Prize Acceptance Speech," trans. Henry J. Schmidt, *New German Critique 23* (Spring/Summer 1981): 8.

2. Audre Lorde, "The Master's Tools Will Never Dismantle the Master's House," *Sister Outsider* (Freedom, Cal.: Crossing Press, 1984), 112.

SUSANNE DE LOTBINIÈRE-HARWOOD

ACTING THE (RE)WRITER: a feminist translator's practice of space

Five years ago, I came out of performance retirement. My last show, a multi-media bilingual solo piece, part of a parallel gallery series, had been a searing experience. For specific personal reasons, I'd been unable to focus my energy that last night in 1984, and got a strong taste of the "F" word in front of an audience full of family, friends, artists, non-friends. Failure. So I "retired from the stage" as they say. Haunted by the question: *Must* the show go on? Should I, could I, have just stopped the music to say: Sorry, I can't do this. Everybody knew it anyway. But I plowed on for twenty miserable minutes. They kindly applauded and quickly left.

Needing to lick my wounds, I dug into my writing, published creative texts and literary translations in Québec, Canada, and the United States, started to write my book. I was missing performance, though. It activates so many selves in me.

Doing performance offsets writing's solitude and physical harshness. The writer gets to produce a text and perform its sounds and silences to a live audience. Through performance the translator can further her auther-translator[1] experience of collaboration, for she will require the participation of other women working in various artistic mediums. The would-be visual artist explores new creative dimensions through experimenting with audio and visual mediums, with matter. The lover of style enjoys the sensual gratification of costume, makeup, accessories. The body-worker is challenged to stretch into deeper levels of awareness to find the gestures and movements expressive of her intention. The spiritual seeker is drawn to performance's ritual aspects, such as the manipulation of objects invested with meaning, the opportunity of psychic self-transformation, and the real-time unfolding in real-space shared with a live audience creating a sense of community.

So the performer within is huge. She is the agent of my desire to put the "show" into the ". . . and tell" of writing. Of creative writing as well as of diary writing, for performance provides a direct outlet for self-disclosure. Also, of writing as a feminist translator. In the act of translating, the translator is acting for the writer being translated. Rewriting her in a second language. But the translator has things to say too, and the feminist practice of translation as co-creation, instead of mere reproduction, has given her voice as a writer. The performer, then, is a means of acting the (re)writer.

ৰ৽৽

In 1989 came an invitation from the University of Western Ontario (London) to speak as a literary translator on a writers' panel at a colloquium addressing "*Les discours féminins dans la littérature postmoderne au Québec.*" I was delighted but couldn't imagine myself discoursing in the feminine while seated behind a microphone. The time had finally come to translocate my performative desire from the art space into academia. The show must go on. . . .

ৰ৽৽

In that five-year interval I'd attended many performances by women artists, always fascinated to see what their bodies were knowing and how their bodies were speaking. And many lectures too, where I became increasingly distressed listening to feminists speaking about writing the body, *l'écriture du corps*, thinking through the body, *la pensée corps*, etc., while their seated bodies were neatly folded away behind a table or standing out of sight behind a lectern. Signifier and signified seemed in such contradiction.

My malaise peaked during the 1988 Montréal International Feminist Book Fair where I listened to women sitting on stages, solo, in pairs or all in a row, bodies collapsed out of sight, the edge of the table cutting into their diaphragm, the muscle membrane vital for breathing. Breath, the vehicle of sound.

The Fair's venue, *l'Université de Montréal*, has huge windowless lecture halls where much energy was spent straining against the distance separating "them" there on stage and "us" here in the audience. Famous women writers from around the world were reduced to talking heads by these cavernous, hierarchically-constructed spaces, their voices swallowed by the sound system which seemed to be retransmitting the architecture's static masculinist ideology instead of the speakers' dynamic feminist meanings.

Afterwards, I often couldn't remember what they'd said. Because our senses were not directly engaged, little energy circulated and communication was incomplete. I was left feeling disembodied and frustrated.

I decoded my frustration as an effect of syntax. As feminists we were subverting patriarchal language's hold on our voices, yet our flesh, blood and bones were still held captive by architecture's syntax. We were challenging straight thinking though our writing, yet were framed in and by conventional order when presenting work at academic/feminist events. It appeared to me that the codes of the lecture space needed problematizing too. My questions: What are our bodies doing while we're speaking about the body? Why not attend to the physical body as well as the theoretical one? Could we not translate the desire and politics driving the innovative form and content of these texts into a corresponding physical practice of space? Could we not break the lecture setting's prescribed spatial arrangement for speakers' and listeners' pleasure?

☙❧

I decided to perform excerpts from my book-in-progress, *Re-belle et infidèle: la traduction comme pratique de réécriture au féminin/ The Body Bilingual: translation as a rewriting in the feminine*, at the

London colloquium.[2] To embody the traditionally silent and invisible figure of the translator, whom feminism has empowered to speak in her own voice. Also to out myself as a partner in a full-fledged relationship with "my" authers, for feminist writers and translators have rejected the longstanding "master-slave" paradigm of writing versus translation, and replaced it with the love relationship paradigm, making her and me co-authers of the translated text.

I'd translated work by several writers participating in the panel, so this first lecture-performance would be a highly charged event for me. Not only would I be coming out of retirement from the stage but also, despite the autonomy conferred to the translator by her acknowledged co-auther status, I was aware of not wanting to disappoint them when acting the (re)writer.

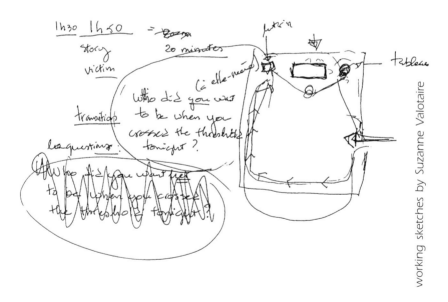

working sketches by Suzanne Valotaire

Live performance art sprang from visual arts scenes in Europe in the early twentieth century, and "became accepted as a medium of artistic expression in its own right in the 1970s," writes New York performance art historian RoseLee Goldberg. "At that time, conceptual art—which insisted on an art of ideas over product, and on an art that could not be bought and sold—was in its heyday and performance was often a demonstration, or an execution, of those ideas."[3] Not surprisingly, as this coincided with the rising Women's Movement, performance became and remains an important vehicle for feminist artists to give their ideas body.

Performance art mostly remains outside of academia, unrecognized as a formal art discipline because it is interdisciplinary and interdisciplinarity has not yet been conceptually defined, thereby implying that it cannot be taught.[4]

Meanwhile, in academia, feminists are constantly "giving 'papers'" as the saying goes, when in fact it's female bodies they/ we are giving while lecturing. Their voices, presence of mind and spirit, energy and knowledge. So why not use the deviance of performance art to crack the rigid code of academic public lecturing? Being institutionally unattached at the time, I was free to enter that uncharted space.

Early on, I ask my London hosts for a description of the lecture hall. There will be a long rectangular table, a lectern to its left, microphones on both sides, several chairs onstage, a rolldown slide screen behind, no windows, a door to the left of the stage raised from the floor by several stairs on both sides. Will all the panelists be sitting on stage while each one speaks? Will our legs under the table be visible to the audience looking up at us? Is seating fixed or arrangeable? Organizers are understandably puzzled by my questions.

(I'm not sure I know what I'm doing either . . .)

Home alone, I simulate the lecture set-up with table, chairs, and the printed-out pages of my text. And realize that in order to subvert the text-based lecture format through body-based performance art, I must first free my eyes, hands and body from lecturing's page-dependency. This means learning much of my written text by heart. Then the performer will be free to establish eye contact with audience members, to speak with her hands, to walk her talk.

To perform my intended subversion on stage, I'll have to start by foregrounding lecturing's habitually invisible support, the actual pages of the "paper" being given. For example, by letting a page fall to the floor to mark a passage, or crumpling one up into a ball and throwing it on the floor when I've finished reading it. Only once the "paper" has been made visible can I then make it disappear and proceed to work "off the page," as photographer Nina Levitt put it.

I hire performance artist and friend Suzanne Valotaire as coach. Rehearsing in my kitchen, in hers, in a rented studio, we work to let surface the body language underlying the signs already written, to choreograph movements that will move my performing body through space the way print moves readers from one paragraph to the next. Recalling the translator's body, constantly in motion between the source text, the target-language text-in-progress and the readers she aims to entertain with her work.

> *Her search for equivalence of meaning keeps her travelling through the standard intertext (dictionaries, reference books) and the feminist one, activating her memory, plumbing the auther's imaginaire and her own, making her body one of the most moving/performing bodies in language-centered work of any kind.*[5]

Intention = emotion + reason. *What do you mean by that movement?* asks my coach. *If you're not clear, they won't be.* I want to sit at the lecture table with my back to the audience to read a passage concerning the past. I know it's risky. It can backfire if my intention isn't focused, if I don't speak loudly enough, if something in my performing body makes the audience feel shut out. *Here, let me do it and you be the audience.* Watching her, emotion + reason make a powerful click. I love it. We keep it.

It's a rough passage, translating a written essay through the body. My voice keeps colliding with the linear hardness of print. My real physical body feels so absent from even my own theoretical writing (so informed by French male postmodernism) that I don't know how to connect head to body. I find myself falling into literalness, i.e., mimicking a word with a redundant gesture.

Etymologically, "theory" means *to see*, and "discourse" originally meant *oral delivery*, verbal interchange of ideas. My intention with this hybrid form is to create visual images and to open discursive spaces using my body as well as my words and my voice.

That's good but take your time! We're in rehearsal and I'm removing my little Balinese hat to indicate an inner voice shift before moving on to the next paragraph. Valotaire is telling me to slow down and grant the gesture its fullness. True, I'm rushing through. Time's emotional reality unfolds much more slowly for the performer than for the audience. What seems like an eternity to her is a mere moment to them. Breathe! I realize that I'm afraid of leaving a few seconds' silence in between words to remove my hat because I dread "dead air." *The audience will breathe with you* . . . Unlike a performance art audience, this audience will not be expecting the performative content of my lecture, so if I don't give them time to absorb the double decontextualization, I will literally make no sense.

What to wear? In performance art the performer intentionally draws attention to herself as speaking subject whose sexual body is the spectacle. Everything about her body matters because everything about her body makes meaning. Colours, shoes and jewelry as much as movement and shaved or unshaved armpits. Female academics who lecture know they are scrutinized for appearance, body language, etc. differently than are their male colleagues, and most resort to disembodiment as a way of registering in male public official spaces. Most but not all . . .

I remember how Jane Gallop thrilled me when she lectured at Concordia University wearing a side-slit skirt made of men's ties, which she described as "a phallic displacement" as she crossed her legs, exposing a thigh. Sexy and savvy, she was. And a feminist and a scholar.

(So, I thought: the show *can* go on . . .)

At some point during rehearsal I remove the scarf I'm wearing and drape it over a chair to delineate an imaginary space I want to invest with meaning by inscribing it with a trace of my presence before moving on to the next one. The scarf is big and bold enough to make a clear statement when seen from the audience. The image works conceptually, yet has the sensuality of wafting perfume.

(Plus, wearing my favorite scarf on stage will make me feel more secure—so I figure, go for it.)

How I'm using my hat and scarf, and later on a reversible jacket, reminds me of the dressing and un- and cross-dressing recurrent in feminist artists' performances, again revealing where I've come from. These gender-specific articles of clothing sexualize my performing body, which, thus languaged, enacts a subversion of the desexualizing female academic dress code, the same way my translating body performs its subversion of sexist grammatical codes (gender-marked French, gender-neutral English) through the practice of translation as a rewriting in the feminine.

I'm questioning the codes and conventions of the panel format, too. As a panelist I'm ambivalent about sitting side by side with other speakers. I enjoy the physical closeness of women gathered together on a panel, and the statement it makes. However, sound travels forward, so when I'm sitting next to her speaking, I can't hear what she's saying. I try to imagine a situation where panelists could see one another and grasp all the non-linguistic expressive content of language as she is spoken.

My coach Suzanne and I devise ways I can be and can be seen to be a participant in this panel as well as a performer physically problematizing the format. Throughout the process she makes working sketches that help guide us. I decide to sit in the front row to listen to the other panelists. And to begin my performance from there. And to progressively become the figure of the translator as I perform my/her way through the space between the front row and the stage, that rarely crossed physical boundary space enforcing power relations between audience and speakers, then up the three stairs onto the stage—stopping at each one to speak something—finally reaching the panel table.

But to me that boundary space resembles the passage that is the translation process, a crossing from auther to readers operated by the translator. It can be empowered as a site of meaning when made visible by naming. Feminist discourse on translation exists because translators have things to say about their practice. That boundary space can be reclaimed from dominant syntax when crossed into by a transgressive speaking body.

As my written words become absorbed into my mouth and body during rehearsal, my text—"paper" becomes a script covered with stage directions to guide my body through performance space and time: Move to panel table—Look at panelists (make

eye contact with each)—Touch table (to assert participation in panel)—Sit—Breathe.[6]

See the discourse?

I love what you're doing with that chair but if you want to do that, do it bigger! Valotaire is reminding me how unaccustomed women are to taking up space. As my intention is to signify "my" auther's presence, I pick up the chair again and really handle it as if someone precious were sitting on it. "Signing in a bigger space," as I once heard American ASL interpreter Sherry Hicks express it.

Reworking the spatial code raises questions of ethics concerning the presence of my co-panelists, whom I don't want to take by surprise or offend by what could be construed as mere grandstanding. I'm relieved to find them receptive and curious when I explain my intentions beforehand.

೦೪⊙

Finally, London, November 1989 rolls around. In the bathroom applying lipstick minutes before going on, I vow never to do this again, it's too hard, especially far away from home.

Although I felt awkward (still!) about taking up so much space in front of all these writers (a new take on "the translator as traitor"?), and struggled for legitimacy in this very large hall lined with very large portraits of the university's past deans (something the organizers could not know to tell me nor I to ask), the show went well. The mostly female audience of writers, professors, literary critics, and students reacted strongly. Audible stirrings when I spoke with my back turned confirmed that the move was a good one. Questions put to me later gave me the impression they had understood what I was doing. Except for the boots. . . .

I'd insisted on removing my cowgirl boots during the performance. I wasn't sure why, I just wanted to. Well, my coach was right. Audience members picked up on it. Quite a few asked: What did that mean?

ॐ

Several papers delivered on the remaining days of the colloquium alluded to my presentation, which was exciting. But the most revealing comment of all came from a professor who said to me: "I teach here, so I could never do that, but I enjoyed it." Though I'm aware of its pedagogical potential, and am not suggesting that every feminist professor and lecturer "do that," she perfectly voiced my point.

ॐ

My developing practice had no name at that time. A year later, some Concordia University students invited me to speak on "Sexuality and Language: the '*problemès de genre*' when translating." As video artist Chris Martin, who was then living in Montréal, had once asked to come and play with me some time, I proposed that we act out parts of the piece *à deux*. The day we went to rehearse, Chris excitedly brought me an article entitled "Has the Body Lost Its Mind?" by American feminist art critic Joanna Frueh, in which she is photographed topless and uses the crossover term "performative lecturing" to describe her own practice of space.[7] I've used it ever since.

So far I've done about ten performative lectures. In English, in French (my first language), in both, depending on the event or topic. When it's translation, for example, I can posit a somewhat bilingual audience. Each one site-specific, a feature of much performance art. Difficult when presenting out of town. Even with a floor plan, I'm working in the dark. I have to remember to ask what kind of lighting is available. If seating is arrangeable, how many chairs will be set up? And how?

To subvert the authority and unicity of the lecturing voice, I sometimes ask another panelist to read out a specific sentence of mine or a quote from another writer. Our voices compose a live intertext resonant of dialogue and community. Or the passage can be from something I've translated, in which case she stands in for the auther by reading the original text while I read my translation and the audience stands in for the readers. Our momentary "we" recreates translation's collaborative, feminine plural process.

The Concordia venue has three blackboards, an upright piano and large rectangular tables informally arranged in a square around which students will sit. Chris and I map three interactions. She will follow me around the room as I write on the blackboards, questioning the feminist language strategies I'm explaining: "Your gender-marking and deconstructing are fine for writing—but what about when we're talking . . ." She will sit atop the piano flashing her gold tooth and ankle strap biker boots to quote a Kathy Acker review that starts: "The mouth is and continues to be the most threatening opening of the feminine body . . ." (Luisa Valenzuela, "Dirty Words"), her sexually aggressive body posture and statement performing my radical stance as a feminist translator while my lecturing body continues speaking. And we will physically mirror-image a sentence in French and in English to enact the body bilingual. "Make sure your lipstick isn't too dark," Chris recommends as we leave the venue after rehearsing. "Let's wear the same one," I suggest. Nobody notices, but our meaning gets across to the amused—and bemused—audience.

Ah! the wild syntax of spaces. In a studio arts classroom, I'm faced with a wall-sized mirror and a paint-soiled sink. The mirror's doubling effect becomes an opportunity to once again turn my back to the audience to perform a flashback autobiographical passage, but this time I can see them and they can see me front and back. Our eyes meet in the mirror, framing "us" in a kind of *tableau vivant*. The effect is startling, especially because we are so close.

I can't resist the dirty sink, which is all the way across the room. So I dare to have my art profs-and-students audience pick up their chairs and move them over there as I shift the scene to "my kitchen" by running the faucet for a few seconds. I'm talking about how, when the creative process hits a snag, I procrastinate by, for example, doing dishes to counteract the anxiety. Hoping that the hot water will inspire. There is the laughter of recognition.

During the question period afterwards, I realize that for me classrooms are a great setting for performative lecturing. Perhaps the best. Though situated inside academia, they elude the formality of official lecture halls. And while students come expecting a lecture as usual, they are delighted to get something more. Also, a fairly long question period is usually possible in classrooms and, because performative lecturing is an experimental form, this time of exchange is really important for performer and audience alike. And when the audience is students, the feminist pedagogue in me merges with the acting (re)writer, and we are all very happy.

⊙⦿⦾

Last year, invited solo to a Halifax University art gallery to speak as a translator on the theme of "Cross-cultural Issues in the Arts," I took the risk of sandwiching a French performance piece between two English lecture sections. Why not act the body bilingual's cross-cultural issues instead of just talking about them? I knew that if I didn't show my roots, I'd pass for an Anglophone.

I rehired my coach Suzanne V., another body bilingual, so she was well aware of the challenge and danger involved. I wanted to perform *Manu Opera*, an erotic essay I'd written in the lesbian translator's double voice-of-love addressing both her auther and her real-life *amante*. I'd read the text in French and in English at the 1992 Fifth International Feminist Book Fair in Amsterdam, and later published it. Now I wanted to translate the original French version into a body piece. Its (re)writerly doubleness seemed appropriate for the Halifax theme.

Again Valotaire was relentless about intention. *Are you doing this just to provoke? Who are you to this audience when you're speaking*

French? We strategized at length, carefully balanced the piece so as not to alienate my mostly English-speaking audience. Painstakingly worked out the two extremely important hinge moments when I'd be switching languages and personae. Counting on the sounds of French, on the performance visuals and movements to carry the meaning until I resumed in English (standing right at the front row):

> *When I decided to perform* Manu Opera *in French here tonight, you were on my mind. It was a matter of necessity, representing difference instead of just talking about it. Yes, I took the risk of losing many of you, of failing to communicate, of losing some laughs, of creating boundaries between our bodies, of merely provoking. . . . But I was also taking the risk of making myself more vulnerable, because French is my mother tongue, it's my roots language. If I was to go all the way, it would have to be this way . . . I've taken the opportunity of tonight's invitation to make the complex reality of this body seen and heard. Thank you for being here to cross the threshold with me.*

I was shaking like a leaf when I finished. Reactions I had sensed during the presentation and questions afterwards confirmed that most had been able to stay with me throughout. My gamble had paid off: it *is* possible to speak this body of possibilities.

☙❧

Reflecting on my five years' practice of performative lecturing has proved difficult. There's been a lot of resistance in my body. This shouldn't come as a surprise. It's a first attempt at producing discourse about it. Any writing I've done related to performative lecturing to date has been the scripts themselves, which are written to be spoken, not to be printed on a page. Writing it all down in intelligible form, in English, for publication, has required applying ordered thinking to exteriorize a process I've mostly carried in my body. It feels strange. Very exposed.

Although many avenues remain unexplored in this article as in my practice—I haven't learned to handle a microphone like a rock singer yet, I haven't produced any visual documentation of my performances yet, I . . . —what started out as a small piece became much more important than I thought it would be. Which means that I didn't know everything my body already knows about it. Which could mean I'm taking the practice more seriously now that it's seen print. I guess I'll live with the paradox. . . .

NOTES

The title of this piece was inspired by Myriam Diaz—Diocaretz's "Translator as Acting Writer," in *Translating Poetic Discourse: Questions on Feminist Strategies in Adrienne Rich,* John Benjamins, Amsterdam/Philadalphia, 1985.

1. Originally but no longer a typo: *auther* is my feminized spelling of author.

2. *Re-belle et Infidèle: la traduction comme pratique de réécriture au féminin*/The Body Bilingual: translation as a rewriting in the feminine (Montréal/Toronto: *Les editions du remue-ménage*/Women's Press, 1991). Both French and English sections contain discussions of "translation as performance."

3. Goldberg, RoseLee, *Performance Art. From Futurism to the Present,* revised and enlarged edition (London: Thames and Hudson, 1988).

4. See Danielle Boutet, "Interdisciplinarity in the Arts," *Harbour 2,* no. 2 (Winter 1993).

5. de Lotbinière-Harwood, *Re-belle et Infidèle,* 160.

6. See "*La Voir Sa Voix,*" a visual presentation of a 1990 script, layout designed by Lani Maestro, hand-scripted by SLH in *Harbour I,* no. 3 (Fall 1991).

7. Joanna Frueh, "Has the Body Lost Its Mind?" *High Performance* (Summer 1989).

What I Have to Do

Mary had done one thing since her father sold her into prostitution. She had ceased to anticipate. That was, so far as she could tell, her lone accomplishment. Everything else that had happened there, behind the sealed windows and above the street she saw every day but had traversed only once, everything else had been done to her. But this *she* had done. Herself.

Unfortunately, it took her several months to achieve this. Once she had looked forward to many things. The day when her mother would look back at her from the mirror, or when P. would find some other reason not to need her. The day when she would be able to go to a market for herself; when she could stare at the sky by herself, whenever she chose, from someplace other than a roof. The day when privacy would mean that the nearest person was more than a closed door away.

With the futile anticipation of a child eyeing a toy far beyond her parents' means, she had looked out of the sealed windows at the narrow shop across the street. Above its door was a white sign, rectangular but for its rounded edges, which bore the words "Neil's Deli" in raised blue letters. Thick black lines in the shape of a steam-producing coffee cup separated the words. On the day when P. terminated the arrangement she would cross that street for the second time and order a cup just like that. Then she would stand in the window and drink it like the other people did when it was raining or during their lunch breaks.

But Mary was able to extinguish her anticipation when she realized what her work signified. It was like helping her parents, hauling the nets with her father and cleaning the fish they didn't sell with her mother: it was her contribution to the wellbeing of the household that sustained her. Without P. and the bodyguards and the other women she would be alone in a foreign country whose language she hadn't studied in five years. And so she turned away from the future and from the sealed windows, and she stopped thinking about Neil's Deli.

P. assigned her clients of all types, big and small, old and young, but none noticed any more of her than they needed. They made her touch them here, moved her limbs there; they offered praise and criticism of her performance, or demanded her running evaluation of theirs. The Americans often objected when she responded in English. *Say it in Chinese* they'd exclaim. And though she spoke Chinese she'd repeat herself in Thai, to see if they'd notice the difference. Since they never did she sometimes thought about insulting them instead of simply repeating herself. But to do so seemed a waste. Novelty was too precious in Mary's routinized world for her to squander it without achieving anything.

Some of her clients really valued the holding, kissing, and caressing that came with their purchase. Others valued these things solely as ways of coaxing semen from their bodies, into, or onto, hers. Whatever the clients valued, whatever they needed, they paid P. for the right to get it.

One night one client seemed bored and lonely and curious, and he asked if they could talk about her work. She agreed, on the condition that they do it in the bed—so her boss wouldn't think that she was slacking or that she'd repulsed him somehow. When he asked how anyone would know she simply repeated herself, so he accepted the terms and joined her beneath the clean white covers she'd just put on the bed. He started to remark on the tiny yellow flowers dotting the sheets at distant, regular intervals, but she interrupted him by pulling him on like a blanket.

When he asked how she'd come to work there, she described how her uncle's debt here in America had eventually forced her father to his knees in the sand of the beach facing the Andaman Sea, begging for his life before a tall man in a dark suit. (She remembered but didn't tell what her father had said: *think of my children, growing up without a father.*) She explained how the tall man's boss walked past her to her father and agreed to give her passage to America even though her father had not suggested it; how when her father had looked at her in alarm the man dangled before him the prospect that she would find work so lucrative that she could pay the debt and send money home. (She didn't tell how her father explained the details and the duty of it to her, in a slender boat on the dull, placid water of the Bangkok canals. She always enjoyed going with him to the markets where she would sell the few bird nests she'd collected; she fingered the rough twigs and looked at the oarsman's remorseless left foot while her father spoke.) She told him how eight months passed before she was smuggled through what she thought was China and California to Manhattan. And how upon her arrival she was brought to the building across the street from Neil's Deli, ostensibly until such time as the cost of her conveyance to America was recovered.

When he asked about the daily mechanics of the brothel she told him that the building they were in was a mostly self-contained community, or an outpost of one. The off-duty women waited downstairs and washed all those sheets and towels and did all the cooking. P. and the guards did everything else. They helped themselves to the women's work and maintained the building's relations to the rest of the community. They shopped, procured reliable doctors to keep the women in shape, brought in manicurists and hairstylists to keep them presentable, and negotiated with authorities to keep their business unnoticed.

She said as much as she could within thirty minutes and without aspiration. He thanked her and on his way out asked her to remind him of her name. P. had told her long ago that her real name, the name which marked her as a member of one of the few Christian families in southern Thailand, was too boring. He had told her then to think of something better and stick to it. She looked at the figure waiting in her doorway.

What can I call you, he said. I mean, if I come here again, how do I ask—

She told him the name she'd given P. and turned to make up the bed.

The next time she lay on him and he talked. She rested her head on his chest and deciphered the vibrations as his speech rumbled through him. He told her that he was half-Korean: his father was probably an American serviceman, and his mother was a prostitute who had contracted to get pregnant and deliver for a baby broker, only to find herself stuck with the baby, him, when he turned out black. He told her that his adoptive parents had finally, reluctantly, told him all that the nuns at the orphanage had told them about his background; that in the six months since the news his girlfriend had declined to move to New York with him and had broken up with him to get engaged to someone else, he still hadn't made any good friends in the city. She didn't know what to say to all that, so she told him his time was almost up.

After that she saw him at least twice a week. They rarely had sex, but they always talked. She helped him practice and improve the halting academic Chinese he'd learned in college—his school hadn't offered Korean—and he helped her build on the English she'd learned before the law let her father take her out of school. He started smuggling in the things P. wouldn't buy for her, like nail files, or the mouthwash strong enough to eliminate the more objectionable tastes (the customers complained about medicine breath, though she didn't know how they noticed through the free beer they received in the waiting area). In return she started tying her hair back the way she knew he liked it, though she didn't much care for it and had to undo it anyway when he left.

One night he asked her what she thought about leaving. She ignored the water stains and peeling plaster on the ceiling arranging themselves into patterns the way clouds and stars do. She took as deep a breath as his weight on her would allow and spoke the truth. She didn't think about it. She didn't know how it could happen and anyway, she didn't know what else she could do. All she knew was this and fishing and birds' nests.

He pushed up from her so that he was no longer talking into the pillow. If I could get you out and you could be with me, would you want that, he asked.

What I do, she asked.

What *would* I do, he corrected. Just be with me, he said.

What I have to do, she asked.

He smiled and said, Don't worry about that: I'll take care of everything. He'd misunderstood the question, but she declined to pursue it.

After that his questioning became singleminded. How many guards are there with you when they take you to the roof? Has anyone ever tried to get away up there? What happened? Then the next time: How many guards are here at any given time? Have they ever taken anyone to the doctor instead of calling their doctors? Did she come back? Then: Do you ever see the police around here? Do you ever see them *patrolling* around here?

Soon after his change she noticed that Neil's Deli had changed. It was gone; a pizza place had appeared beneath the nearly rectangular sign, which was now green, red, and white. Against her will she imagined herself in the place of one of the restaurant's customers, standing at the red horizontal shelf that jutted from the front window, folding a slice the way P. showed them once.

Within two weeks he stopped asking questions. Instead he gave reports. Checking on immigration laws. Seeing about a police investigation. Looking into hiring some people. The one day he just stood by the door. When she reminded him that they had to get in the bed or she'd get in trouble, he said that he was going to offer to buy her from P. He'd thought and thought, but he didn't know what else to do. Tonight he was going to make the offer.

Wait, she said. Not yet.

Why, he asked.

She wouldn't tell him until he got into the bed. He complained that he didn't know how long he could keep the money lined up.

Only take two days, she said. Wait two days, then return and do what I say.

❧

On the night of the first day the customers proceeded as always. They touched her and felt her and moved her like they always did. Until they noticed that she was different. Some of them tried to go on, but even most of these had to stop. Some of them hit her, thinking it was part of the illusion. Then they left and complained to P., who put on his leather gloves and hit her some more. But it didn't matter. She wouldn't confirm their *You like that shit don't you bitch* or indulge their *please just put your arms around me* or participate in their *Suzy Wong* china girl buddha bitch fantasies. She just lay there, spread-eagled, staring at the stained and peeling stars and clouds.

On the second day P. brought one of the doctors to examine her in the sleeping area where she and some of the other off-duty women lay. Afterward they went out into the hall to talk, and she listened.

"Sometimes they just go, you know?"

"Some handle it better than others. Yes. Some last longer than others."

"Yeah, sometimes. . . ."

"What do you do with her now?"

"This one motherfucker used to come by all the time, you know, for her. Black motherfucker. Next time he comes I'll see if he wants to work out something."

"He has never come to see any of the others?"

"No, man. Never. That shit happens sometimes, too. But you know; it's alright. Cause then we can do a little side business, like one of those mail-order bride deals, only no, you know, shipping and handling."

"I see. Yes."

"Sometimes it don't work out. Sometimes they'd rather, you know, rent than own. But I'll give that motherfucker a shot."

☜✧☞

The stairs were slick from rain the night before. He had come to make his offer during the day, when Mary was off duty, so they walked out into a sliver of sunshine that had fallen between the buildings. She had arrived at night two years ago, so as soon as she was out of the door she started turning to see where she'd been all this time. The building was indistinguishable from the neighboring structures stretched innumerably down the block. Three floors of dull urban colorlessness behind an uncertain fire escape, freshly painted black. Blinds were drawn in front of all the windows. They reached the bottom of the stairs and she looked higher. On the roof two women leaned over and waved goodbye, until a guard came and guided them back to hang more things on the clothesline.

Then she saw the sky. The clouds had exhausted themselves the previous night and had yet to reappear. The stars would be in hiding until—

Let's go, Edward said, guiding her down the sidewalk for the second time in her life.

She stopped and asked: A coffee? At the deli? She knew he wouldn't understand. He had been rushing, to get as far away as possible as quickly as possible. But she looked him in the eye and said it anyway. Maybe she could explain it to him the way she'd explained her father's pleading. Maybe he'd see it in her eyes.

He looked puzzled. The deli's gone, he said. It's pizza now, he said. Novelli's Pizza.

She looked at the sign, green, red, and white, and looked down. She had forgotten and had lapsed into the old aspirations, the old anticipations. She wanted to cry, but before the tears came she found herself wanting pizza more.

A slice, she asked.

We'll order some at home, he said. Okay? Whatever you want: pizza, coffee, tea. Whatever.

Okay, she said, submitting to his hasty guidance down the street. Mary still didn't know what she would have to do, or what she could do. All she knew was what this man had given to her. The clouds and the stars, when they bothered to show themselves. Pizza, later; maybe coffee. Mouthwash and nail files. And she knew what giving meant.

JAMES BALDWIN

The Price of the Ticket

My soul looks back and wonders how I got over—indeed:
but I find it unexpectedly difficult to remember, in detail, how I
got started. I will never, for example, forget Saul Levitas, the
editor of *The New Leader*, who gave me my first book review as-
signment sometime in 1946, nor Mary Greene, a wonderful
woman, who was his man Friday: but I do not remember exactly
how I met them.

I *do* remember how my life in Greenwich Village began—
which is, essentially, how my career began—for it began when I
was fifteen.

One day, a DeWitt Clinton H.S. running buddy, Emile
Capouya, played hookey without me and went down to Greenwich Village and made the acquaintance of Beauford Delaney.
The next day, he told me about this wonderful man he had met,
a black—then, Negro, or Colored—painter and said that I must
meet him: and he gave me Beauford Delaney's address.

I had a Dickensian job, after school, in a sweat shop on
Canal Street, and was getting on so badly at home that I dreaded
going home: and, so, sometime later, I went to 181 Greene Street,
where Beauford lived then, and introduced myself.

I was terrified, once I had climbed those stairs and knocked
on that door. A short, round brown man came to the door and
looked at me. He had the most extraordinary eyes I'd ever seen.
When he had completed his instant X-ray of my brain, lungs,

liver, heart, bowels, and spinal column (while I had said, usefully, "Emile sent me") he smiled and said, "Come in," and opened the door.

He opened the door all right.

Lord, I was to hear Beauford sing, later, and for many years, *open the unusual door*. My running buddy had sent me to the right one, and not a moment too soon.

I walked through that door into Beauford's colors—on the easel, on the palette, against the wall—sometimes turned to the wall—and sometimes (in limbo?) covered by white sheets. It was a small studio (but it didn't seem small) with a black pot-bellied stove somewhere near the two windows. *I* remember two windows, but there may have been only one: there *was* a fire escape which Beauford, simply by his presence, had transformed, transmuted into the most exclusive terrace in Manhattan or Bombay.

I walked into music. I had grown up with music, but, now, on Beauford's small black record player, I began to hear what I had never dared or been able to hear. Beauford never gave me any lectures. But, in his studio and because of his presence, I really began to *hear* Ella Fitzgerald, Ma Rainey, Louis Armstrong, Bessie Smith, Ethel Waters, Paul Robeson, Lena Horne, Fats Waller. He could inform me about Duke Ellington and W. C. Handy and Josh White, introduce me to Frankie Newton and tell tall tales about Ethel Waters. And these people were not meant to be looked on by me as celebrities, but as part of Beauford's life and as part of my inheritance.

I may have been with Beauford, for example, the first time I saw Paul Robeson, in concert, and in *Othello*: but I know that he bought tickets for us—really, for me—to see and hear Miss Marian Anderson, at Carnegie Hall.

Because of her color, Miss Anderson was not allowed to sing at The Met, nor, as far as The Daughters of The American Revolution were concerned, anywhere in Washington where white people might risk hearing her. Eleanor Roosevelt was appalled by this species of patriotism and arranged for Marian Anderson to sing on the steps of the Lincoln Memorial. This was a quite marvelous and passionate event in those years, triggered by the indignation of one woman, who had, clearly, it seemed to me, married beneath her.

By this time, I was working for the Army—or the Yankee dollar!—in New Jersey. I hitchhiked, in sub-zero weather, out of what I will always remember as one of the lowest and most obscene circles of Hell, into Manhattan: where both Beauford and Miss Anderson were on hand to inform me that I had no right to permit myself to be defined by so pitiful a people. Not only was I not born to be a slave: I was not born to hope to become the equal of the slave-master. They had, the masters, incontestably, the rope—in time, with enough, they would hang themselves with it. They were not to hang *me*: *I* was to see to that. If Beauford and Miss Anderson were a part of my inheritance, I was a part of their hope.

I still remember Miss Anderson, at the end of that concert, in a kind of smoky yellow gown, her skin copper and tan, roses in the air about her, roses at her feet. Beauford painted it, an enormous painting, he fixed it in time, for me, forever, and he painted it, he said, for me.

Beauford was the first walking, living proof, for me, that a black man could be an artist. In a warmer time, a less blasphemous place, he would have been recognized as my Master and I as his Pupil. He became, for me, an example of courage and integrity, humility and passion. An absolute integrity: I saw him shaken many times and I lived to see him broken but I never saw him bow.

His example operated as an enormous protection: for the Village, then, and not only for a boy like me, was an alabaster maze perched above a boiling sea. To lose oneself in the maze was to fall into the sea. One saw it around one all the time: a famous poet of the twenties and thirties grotesquely, shamelessly, cadging drinks, another relic living in isolation on opium and champagne, someone your own age suddenly strung out or going under a subway train, people you ate with and drank with suddenly going home and blowing their brains out or turning on the gas or leaping out of the window. And, racially, the Village was vicious, partly because of the natives, largely because of the tourists, and absolutely because of the cops.

Very largely, then, because of Beauford and Connie Williams, a beautiful black lady from Trinidad who ran the restaurant in which I was a waiter, and the jazz musicians I loved and who referred to me, with a kind of exasperated affection, as "the kid," I was never entirely at the mercy of an environment at once hostile and seductive. They knew about dope, for example—I didn't: but the pusher and his product were kept far away from me. I needed love so badly that I could as easily have been hit with a needle as persuaded to share a joint of marijuana. And, in fact, Beauford and the others let me smoke with them from time to time. (But there were people they warned me *not* to smoke with.)

The only real danger with marijuana is that it can lead to rough stuff, but this has to do with the person, not the weed. In my own case, it could hardly have become a problem, since I simply could not write if I were "high." Or, rather, I could, sometimes all night long, the greatest pages the world had ever seen, pages I tore up the moment I was able to read them.

Yet, I learned something about myself from these irredeemable horrors: something which I might not have learned had I not been forced to know that I was valued. I repeat that Beauford never gave me any lectures, but he didn't have to—he expected me to accept and respect the value placed upon me. Without this, I might very easily have become the junky which so many among those I knew were becoming then, or the Bellevue or Tombs inmate (instead of the visitor) or the Hudson River corpse which a black man I loved with all my heart was shortly to become.

❦

Shortly: I was to meet Eugene sometime between 1943 and 1944 and "run" or "hang" with him until he hurled himself off the George Washington Bridge, in the winter of 1946. We were never lovers: for what it's worth, I think I wish we had been.

When he was dead, I remembered that he had, once, obliquely, suggested this possibility. He had run down a list of his girl friends: those he liked, those he *really* liked, one or two with whom he might really be in love, and then, he said, "I wonder if I might be in love with you."

I wish I had heard him more clearly: an oblique confession is always a plea. But I was to hurt a great many people by being unable to imagine that anyone could possibly be in love with an ugly boy like me. To be valued is one thing, the recognition of this assessment demanding, essentially, an act of the will. But love is another matter: it is scarcely worth observing what a mockery it makes of the will. Leaving all that alone, however: when he was dead, I realized that I would have done anything whatever to have been able to hold him in this world.

Through him, anyway, my political life, insofar as I can claim, formally to have had one, began. He was a Socialist—a member of the Young People's Socialist League (YPSL) and urged me to join, and I did. I, then, outdistanced him by becoming a Trotskyite—so that I was in the interesting position (at the age of nineteen) of being an anti-Stalinist when American and Russia were allies.

My life on the Left is of absolutely no interest. It did not last long. It was useful in that I learned that it may be impossible to indoctrinate me; also, revolutionaries tend to be sentimental and I hope that I am not. This was to lead to very serious differences between myself and Eugene, and others: but it was during this period that I met the people who were to take me to Saul Levitas, of *The New Leader*, Randall Jarrell, of *The Nation*, Elliott Cohen and Robert Warshow, of *Commentary*, and Philip Rahv, of *Partisan Review*.

These men are all dead, now, and they were all very important to my life. It is not too much to say that they helped to save my life. (As Bill Cole, at Knopf, was later to do when the editor assigned to *Go Tell it On the Mountain* had me on the ropes.) And their role in my life says something arresting concerning the American dilemma, or more precisely, perhaps, the American torment.

I had been to two black newspapers before I met these people and had simply been laughed out of the office: I was a shoeshine boy who had never been to college. I don't blame these people, God knows that I was an unlikely cub reporter: yet, I still remember how deeply I was hurt.

On the other hand, around this time, or a little later, I landed a job as messenger for New York's liberal newspaper, *PM*. It is perhaps worth pointing out that *PM* had a man of about my complexion (dark) in the tower, under whom I worked, a coal black Negro in the cellar, whom nobody ever saw, and a very fair Negro on the city desk, in the window. My career at *PM* was nearly as devastating as my career as a civilian employee of the US Army, except that *PM* never (as far as I know) placed me on a blacklist. If the black newspapers had considered me absolutely beyond redemption, *PM* was determined to save me: I cannot tell which attitude caused me more bitter anguish.

Therefore, though it may have cost Saul Levitas nothing to hurl a book at a black boy to see if he could read it and be articulate concerning what he had read, I took it as a vote of confidence and swore that I would give him my very best shot. And I loved him—the old man, as I sometimes called him (to his face) and I think—I know—that he was proud of me, and that he loved me, too.

It was a very great apprenticeship. Saul required a book review a week, which meant that I had to read and write all the time. He paid me ten or twenty dollars a shot: Mary Greene would sometimes coerce him into giving me a bonus. Then he would stare at her, as though he could not believe that she, his helper, could be capable of such base treachery and look at me more tragically than Julius Caesar looked at Brutus and sigh— and give me another five or ten dollars.

As for the books I reviewed—well, no one, I suppose, will ever read them again. It was after the war, and the Americans were on one of their monotonous conscience "trips": be kind to niggers, for Christ's sake, be kind to Jews! A high, or turning point of some kind was reached when I reviewed Ross Lockridge's sunlit and fabulously successful *Raintree County*. The review was turned in and the author committed suicide before the review was printed. I was very disagreeably shaken by this, and Saul asked me to write a postscript—which I did. That same week I met the late Dwight MacDonald, whom I admired very much because of his magazine, *Politics*, who looked at me with wonder and said that I was "very smart." This pleased me, certainly, but it frightened me more.

But no black editor could or would have been able to give me my head, as Saul did then: partly because he would not have had the power, partly because he could not have afforded—or needed—Saul's politics, and partly because part of the price of the black ticket is involved—fatally—with the dream of becoming white.

This is not possible, partly because white people are not white: part of the price of the white ticket is to delude themselves into believing that they are. The political position of *my old man*, for example, whether or not he knew it, was dictated by his (in his case) very honorable necessity not to break faith with the Old World. One may add, in passing, that the Old World, or Europe, has become nothing less than an American superstition, which accounts, if anything can, for an American vision of Russia so Talmudic and self-serving that it has absolutely nothing to do with any reality occurring under the sun.

✧

But the black American must find a way to keep faith with, and to excavate, a reality much older than Europe. Europe has never been, and cannot be, a useful or valid touchstone for the American experience because America is not, and never can be, white.

✧

My father died before Eugene died. When my father died, Beauford helped me to bury him and I then moved from Harlem to the Village.

This was in 1943. We were fighting the Second World War. *We*: who was this *we*?

For this war was being fought, as far as I could tell, to bring freedom to everyone with the exception of Hagar's children and the "yellow-bellied Japs."

This was not a matter, merely, of my postadolescent discernment. It had been made absolutely clear to me by the eighteen months or so I had been working for the Army, in New Jersey, by the anti-Japanese posters to be found, then, all over New York, and by the internment of the Japanese.

At the same time, one was expected to be "patriotic" and pledge allegiance to a flag which had pledged no allegiance to you: it risked becoming your shroud if you didn't know how to keep your distance and stay in your "place."

And all this was to come back to me much later, when Cassius Clay, a.k.a. Muhammad Ali, refused to serve in Vietnam because he was a Muslim—in other words, for religious reasons—and was stripped of his title, while placards all over New York trumpeted, *Be true to your faith!*

I have never been able to convey the confusion and horror and heartbreak and contempt which every black person I then knew felt. Oh, we dissembled and smiled as we groaned and cursed and did our duty. (And we *did* our duty.) The romance of treason never occurred to us for the brutally simple reason that you can't betray a country you don't have. (Think about it.) Treason draws its energy from the conscious, deliberate betrayal of a trust—as we were not trusted, we could not betray. And we did not wish to be traitors. We wished to be citizens.

We: the black people of this country, then, with particular emphasis on those serving in the Armed Forces. The way blacks were treated in, and by, an American Army spreading freedom around the globe was the reason for the heartbreak and contempt. Daddy's youngest son, by his first marriage, came home, on furlough, to help with the funeral. When these young men came home, in uniform, they started talking: and one sometimes trembled, for their sanity and for one's own. One trembled, too, at another wonder—as one could not fail to wonder—what *nation* they represented. My brother, describing his life in uniform, did not seem to be representing the America his uniform meant to represent. Had anyone? did he know, had he met, anyone who had? Did anyone *live* there? judging from the great gulf fixed between their conduct and their principles, it seemed unlikely. *Was it worth his life?*

For he, certainly, on the other hand, represented something much larger than himself and something in him knew it: otherwise, he would have been broken like a match-stick and lost or have surrendered the power of speech. *A nation within a nation*: this thought wavered in my mind, I think, all those years ago, but I did not know what to make of it, it frightened me.

☙❧

We: my family, the living and the dead, and the children coming along behind us. This was a complex matter, for I was not living with my family in Harlem, after all, but "down-town," in the "white world," in alien and mainly hostile territory. On the other hand, for me, then, Harlem was almost as alien and in a yet more intimidating way and risked being equally hostile, although for very different reasons. This truth cost me something in guilt and confusion, but it was the truth. It had something to do with my being the son of an evangelist and having been a child evangelist, but this is not all there was to it—that is, guilt is not all there was to it.

The fact that this particular child had been born when and where he was born had dictated certain expectations. The child does not really know what these expectations are—does not know how real they are—until he begins to fail, challenge, or defeat them. When it was clear, for example, that the pulpit, where I had made so promising a beginning, would not be my career, it was hoped that I would go on to college. This was never a very realistic hope and—perhaps because I knew this—I don't seem to have felt very strongly about it. In any case, this hope was dashed by the death of my father.

Once I had left the pulpit, I had abandoned or betrayed my role in the community—indeed, my departure from the pulpit and my leaving home were almost simultaneous. (I had abandoned the ministry in order not to betray myself by betraying the ministry.)

Once it became clear that I was not going to go to college, I became a kind of two-headed monstrosity of a problem. Without a college education, I could, clearly, never hope to become a writer: would never acquire the skills which would enable me to conquer what was thought of as an all-white world. This meant that I would become a half-educated handyman, a vociferous, bitter ruin, spouting Shakespeare in the bars on Saturday night and sleeping it off on Sunday.

I could see this, too. I saw it all around me. There are few things more dreadful than dealing with a man who knows that he is going under, in his own eyes, and in the eyes of others. Nothing can help that man. What is left of that man flees from what is left of human attention.

I fled. I didn't want Mama, or the kids, to see me like that.

And if all this seems, now, ridiculous and theatrical apprehension on the part of a nineteen-year-old boy, I can say only that it didn't seem remotely ridiculous then. A black person in this democracy is certain to endure the unspeakable and the unimaginable in nineteen years. It is far from an exaggeration to state that many, and by the deliberate will and action of the Republic, are ruined by that time.

White Americans cannot, in the generality, hear this, anymore than their European ancestors and contemporaries, could, or can. If I say that my best friend, black, Eugene, who took his life at the age of twenty-four, had been, until that moment, a survivor, I will be told that he had "personal" problems. Indeed he did, and one of them was trying to find a job, or a place to live, in New York. If I point out that there is certainly a connection between his death (when I was twenty-two) and my departure for Paris (when *I* was twenty-four) I will be condemned as theatrical.

But I am really saying something very simple. The will of the people, or the State, is revealed by the State's institutions. There was not, then, nor is there, now, a single American institution which is not a racist institution. And racist institutions—the unions, for one example, the church, for another, and the Army—or the military—for yet another, are meant to keep the nigger in his place. Yes: we have lived through avalanches of tokens and concessions but white power remains white. And what it appears to surrender with one hand it obsessively clutches in the other.

I know that this is considered to be heresy. Spare me, for Christ's *and* His Father's sake, any further examples of American white progress. When one examines the use of this word in most particular context, it translates as meaning that those people who have opted for being white congratulate themselves on their generous ability to return to the slave that freedom which they never had any right to endanger, much less take away. For this dubious effort, and still more dubious achievement, they congratulate themselves and expect to be congratulated—: in the coin, furthermore, of black gratitude, gratitude not only that my burden is—(slowly, but it takes time) being made lighter but my joy that white people are improving.

My black burden has not, however, been made lighter in the sixty years since my birth . . . and my joy, therefore, as concerns the immense strides made by white people is, to say the least, restrained.

Leaving aside my friends, the people I love, who cannot, usefully, be described as either black or white, they are, like life itself, thank God, many, many colors, I do not feel, alas, that my country has any reason for self-congratulation.

If I were still in the pulpit which some people (and they may be right) claim I never left, I would counsel my countrymen to the self-confrontation of prayer, the cleansing breaking of the heart which precedes atonement. This is, of course, impossible. Multitudes are capable of many things, but atonement is not one of them.

A multitude is, I suppose, by definition, an anonymous group of people bound or driven together by fears (I wrote "tears") and hopes and needs which no individual member could face or articulate alone.

On the one hand, for example, mass conversions are notoriously transitory: within days, the reformed—"saved"—whore, whoremonger, thief, drunkard, have ventilated their fears and dried their tears and returned to their former ways. Nor do the quite spectacularly repentant "born again" of the present hour give up this world to follow Jesus. No, they take Jesus with them into the marketplace where He is used as proof of their acumen and as their Real Estate Broker, now, and, as it were, forever.

But it does not demand a mass conversion to persuade a mob to lynch a nigger or stone a Jew or mutilate a sexual heretic. It demands no conversion at all: in the very same way that the act demands no courage at all. That not one member of the mob could or would accomplish the deed alone is not merely, I think, due to physical cowardice but to cowardice of another order. To destroy a nigger, a kike, a dyke, or a faggot, by one's own act alone is to have committed a communion and, above all, to have made a public confession more personal, more total, and more devastating than any act of love: whereas the orgasm of the mob is drenched in the blood of the lamb.

A mob is not autonomous: it executes the real will of the people who rule the State. The slaughter in Birmingham, Alabama, for example, was not merely, the action of a mob. The blood is on the hands of the state of Alabama: which sent those mobs into the streets to execute the will of the State. And, though I know that it has now become inconvenient and impolite to speak of the American black (*I hate to say I told you so*, sings the right righteous Reverend Ray Charles, *but, I told you so*), I yet contend that the mobs in the streets of Hitler's Germany were in those streets not only by the will of the German State, but by the will of the western world, including those architects of freedom, the British, and the presumed guardian of Christian and human morality, the Pope. The American Jew, if I may say so—and I say so with love, whether or not you believe me—makes the error of believing that his Holocaust ends in the New World, where mine begins. My diaspora continues, the end is not in sight, and I certainly cannot depend on the morality of this panic-stricken consumer society to bring me out of—: Egypt.

A mob cannot afford to doubt: that the Jews killed Christ or that niggers want to rape their sisters or that anyone who fails to make it in the land of the free and the home of the brave deserves to be wretched. But these ideas do not come from the mob. The idea of black persons as property, for example, does not come from the mob. It is not a spontaneous idea. It does not come from the people, who know better, who thought nothing of intermarriage until they were penalized for it: this idea comes from the architects of the American State. These architects decided that the concept of Property was more important—more real—than the possibilities of the human being.

☙❦❧

In the church I come from—which is not at all the same church to which white Americans belong—we were counselled, from time to time, to do our first works over. Though the church I come from and the church to which most white Americans belong are both Christian churches, their relationship—due to those pragmatic decisions concerning Property made by a Christian State sometime ago—cannot be said to involve, or suggest, the fellowship of Christians. We do not, therefore, share the same hope or speak the same language.

To do your first works over means to reexamine everything. Go back to where you started, or as far back as you can, examine all of it, travel your road again and tell the truth about it. Sing or shout or testify or keep it to yourself: but *know whence you came.*

This is precisely what the generality of white Americans cannot afford to do. They do not know how to do it—: as I must suppose. They came through Ellis Island, where *Giorgio* becomes *Joe*, *Pappavasiliu* becomes *Palmer*, *Evangelos* becomes *Evans*, *Goldsmith* becomes *Smith* or *Gold*, and *Avakian* becomes *King*. So, with a painless change of name, and in the twinkling of an eye, one becomes a white American.

Later, in the midnight hour, the missing identity aches. One can neither assess nor overcome the storm of the middle passage. One is mysteriously shipwrecked forever, in the Great New World.

The slave is in another condition, as are his heirs: *I told Jesus it would be all right / If He changed my name.*

If *He* changed my name.

The Irish middle passage, for but one example, was as foul as my own, and as dishonorable on the part of those responsible for it. But the Irish became white when they got here and began rising in the world, whereas I became black and began sinking. The Irish, therefore and thereafter—again, for but one example— had absolutely no choice but to make certain that I could not menace their safety or status or identity: and, if I came too close, they could, with the consent of the governed, kill me. Which means that we can be friendly with each other anywhere in the world, except Boston.

What a monumental achievement on the part of those heroes who conquered the North American wilderness!

The price the white American paid for his ticket was to become white—: and, in the main, nothing more than that, or, as he was to insist, nothing less. This incredibly limited not to say dimwitted ambition has choked many a human being to death here: and this, I contend, is because the white American has never accepted the real reasons for his journey. I know very well that my ancestors had no desire to come to this place: but neither did the ancestors of the people who became white and who require of my captivity a song. They require of me a song less to celebrate my captivity than to justify their own.

spinning memories

Arachne

Arachne spun by day and by night and with her threads wove sunset and dawn. Her loom was a story-telling loom. If a flying squirrel glided one night into the nest of another, by dawn its gliding was spread wide across the sky. If a snake slithered over a cypress knee and, meeting another, looped and entwined, sunset was streaked with twining and looping. Whatever the tale, the loom was the tattler. Nobody minded, the gossip was harmless. In those days, lust traveled in both directions. There wasn't a color for secrecy. Dawns were pink and mauve, sometimes streaked with grey; sunsets were red-rimmed orange.

But what if the snake were a goddess minding goddess business? Creating a shell, painting an egg, not eager to join with another? And what if some randy god knotted his snakeself around her?

Or, if the god were a quailcock pinning an unwilling quailhen? Or a rapacious boar covering a sow, her piglets scattered, squealing?

These happened, and more. Arachne's loom seethed. Blood-red smeared blue-black with fury and grief, dawn burned the eastern sky. Boats that embarked those mornings didn't come back to their moorings.

One morning Arachne sat next to a late-summer river. Her distaff held sumac and nightshade. A shadow darkened her spindle.

"Are you spinning my father again?" Athena, upright, owl-eyed, unsmiling, fingered a purple thread already warped on the loom. "He wasn't pleased this morning's dawn, you know." She pulled the thread from its knot and rolled it between her fingers.

"And are you pleased with your father's engenderings?" Arachne kept her eyes on her own thread twisted between forefinger and thumb. Silence, except for the *burr-burr-burr* of the spindle. "He swallowed your mother whole, you know. She died slowly, smothered in his esophagus. Is that a pretty sunset? And you, you went from her belly to his head, but you didn't come out on your own. When the wedge split his skull, whose hand do you think guided the beetle?"

Athena turned abruptly. "Stories," she said. "Gossip. Anyone can tell tales." She smacked her sword against a rock. Two oak saplings shaped themselves into a loom. An elderberry became a spindle with fat threads. "We'll have a contest," she said. "The loom first filled will spread its story for sunset. Are you willing?"

"Is there a choice?"

As the relentless sun drove across the afternoon sky, the shuttles coursed: *thwap, churr, thwap, churr.* Nightshade and sumac grew across one loom, silver goathair and willow on the other. Strand after strand, the woof entered the warp. As the sun tipped toward the western horizon, Athena unknotted her loom and flung her cloth into the sky.

"There," she said, "is the true story. Victory to the father."

Arachne watched the triumphant golds and silvers cloak the setting sun. She took her own cloth and floated it on the river. "Go," she whispered. "Sing high around one rock, sing low around another. Let the stories flow in many voices."

Then she folded her loom into branches and multiplied her legs. She spins still. You can see her on an untraveled river path. Her web may shiver with white dawn. Or a struggling fly.

D. H. MELHEM

Plain String

Thanksgiving evening. I have just wiped
a few plates left to drain; I wipe them
clean of spots, they sparkle. And I remember
you, Grandmother, carefully drying
the spoons we had quick-dried
after holiday dinner,
how you studied each spoon for dampness
that might blemish it,
how you sought to impose
on the plain order of your life
perfection, an Aristotelian sense
of ideal form and purpose.

And these causes, your humble act instructed
in other tasks: basting stitches were to be
small and even, before a final sewing,
so that even the things unseen
might leave their aura of excellence.
I remember the string full of knots:
a peculiar chore to untie them.
A work of patience. I learned it.
And then the reward:

cat's cradle—forms
for their own sake.
The white string, the depth of line,
the quick twist into
simplicity, both of us holding it.
That I could share with you something fine,
designing the air into epiphanies!

String, an instrument,
four hands to conduct and orchestrate
with filaments and webs and geometries
together, together not only our hands to their
single tasks, but joined now in dialogue.
You speak, then I speak.
Our language of plain string.

When the sky is rent asunder; when the stars scatter and
the oceans roll together; when the graves are hurled
about; each soul shall know what it has done and what it
has failed to do. —Qur'an, 82:1

Eighty thousand sorties nonstop express over Baghdad
a sound-and-light show takeout boxed into your livingroom
(you can only see the nightskytop on TV;
the bloody bottom of the picture mars the image).
Look at the stars! look, look up at the skies!
O look at all the fire-folk sitting in the air!
Smart bombs and cruise missiles, F-16 fighter jets,
Patriot antimissiles and rocket hardware.
Everyone wants them now.
(Was this a carnage
commercial?)

In the bomb shelter children are sleeping
in the arms of their mothers. Not hungry,
having supp'd full with horrors.
Are targeted. Deliberately hit.
Well, enemies are enemies.
May hide anywhere.

Your red-and-white kaffiyeh was edged with lace
crocheted by your mother in the family's pattern.
You wore a blue bead to ward off evil.
It didn't work.

Iraq is a dry place, mostly, dry as cobblestones,
and hot. "Iraq, with its Soviet-style strategy and
Soviet-made arms, was the kind of opponent the Army has
spent decades preparing to fight." No figures, as yet,
on civilian deaths. Maybe a hundred thousand.
Plus a hundred thousand soldiers.
A thousand of theirs to one of ours.
We're still number one.

Try to make sense of it—
boys who will kill other boys who will kill
children asleep in the arms of their mothers
and their mothers asleep with them.
Arms and armaments twist into smoke.
Even the tanks writhe and scream.

Men and women kneel in the prayerful dust
of ancient cities, in the new museum
of bones and shell fragments.
Daily they kneel five times,
facing Mecca.

Between the Tigris and the Euphrates
Mesopotamia once flourished.
The Tigris and the Euphrates
carried great deposits of silt.
The Tigris and the Euphrates
carry dead bodies to be oiled
in the Persian Gulf.

Cheetah, hyena, wolf, jackal, desert hare,
and small mammals, the jerboa, The vulture,
the raven, the owl, the hawk. In the west
the country is nearly treeless. Places
devoid of vegetation except for
the bush of Christ's thorn.

"Although many think of it as a lifeless place, the desert
is actually a teeming, though fragile, ecosystem. Home to a
variety of spiders, snakes and scorpions as well as larger
creatures like camels, sheep and gazelles, it is literally
held together by microorganisms, which form a thin surface
crust. This crust catches the seeds of sparse shrubs and
prevents surface soil from blowing away. Once it is
disturbed—by the maneuvers of a million soldiers,
say—recovery can take decades. The Libyan desert still
shows tank tracks laid down in World War II."

The Mesopotamian desert is strewn
with the ruins of ancient cities,
their royal tombs and hecatombs. In Sumer,
five dynasties ruled before the Flood.
The first capital was founded at Kish by 4000 B.C.
Sippar lay on the edge of the glacial shore-line.
South of Sippar rose Akkad and its armies of Sargon.
Below Cuthah stood the great temples of Kish.
Fifteen miles westward lie the ruins of Babylon.

When the Euphrates changed course it deserted
its settled embankments. In the south,
lakes became marshland. Now
ancient cities are mounds, waterless, bare.
Kish, Akkad, Babylon, Nippur,
Nineveh, Borsippa, Uruk, Ur.
Levels of excavation
on caravan routes
from Baghdad.

Baghdad, the Abode of Peace, foremost city
of Mesopotamia, preserved the name it has held
for 4,000 years. It was once a fertile land of gardens,
the home of merchants and scholars, renowned for learning,
for silks and tiled buildings, enlightened caliphs,
tales of the Arabian Nights.

In 1258 Hulagu Khan, grandson of Genghiz, sacked the city.
The Mongols destroyed irrigation systems
and converted Mesopotamia into a desert.

"Already a U.N. report concludes that Iraq has been bombed
back to the 'pre-industrial age,' its infrastructure
destroyed, its people beset by famine and disease."

I prayed for the people and I prayed for
food, water, electricity, and I prayed
for the museums, that our history not be obliterated
into a footnote of rubble.

"It was a great sight—all those fireworks,
like Christmas," said a U.S. airman.

The tank was running out of gas and the planes kept coming
and everyone was running and I prayed to Allah that I not be
burned in the tank and we were just like everyone else,
scared and running like the people on the road,
running to Basra.

"It was a turkey shoot," said a U.S. airman.

"After the third day as I say, we knew we had them. I
mean we had closed the back door. The bridges across the
Tigris and Euphrates were out. We had cut highway 8 that
ran up the Tigris and Euphrates valley on this side of the
river. There was no way out for them. I mean, they could
go through Basra. There were a few bridges going across Al
Fao to the Al Fao but there was nothing else and there was
literally about to become the Battle of Cannae, a battle of
annihilation."

Schwartzkopf at Cannae, Scwartzkopf as Hannibal,
the Carthaginian general, who stunned the Romans
by a rapid march to the city.

Caritas. *Though I speak with the tongues of men and of*
angels, and have not charity, I am become as sounding brass,
or a tinkling cymbal. —1 Corinthians 13.1.

And Cato the Elder cried, "*Delenda esi Carthago.*"
Carthage must be destroyed.
Carthage destroyed Tyre and ruled the Mediterranean.
It warred with the Greeks and was defeated at Salamis.
It fought three Punic Wars with the Romans

and was destroyed. *Delenda est Carthago.*

Madam, Saddam Hussein is mad, bad, and
dangerous to know. A Hitler.
(*Have I no friend will rid me of this living fear?*
His soldiers? his generals? his people?
The Kurds? The Shi'ites? Rambo?)
Saddam Hussein must not remain
to retain his domain. He must eat
the Breakfast of Humiliations.
And yet, if his neighbors
come nibbling at his table
they may elect to dine well,
so let his helicopter blades
whip the dissidents
into a mix, a sort of blend,
not too crumbly, one that can
hold together when pressed
in the fist.
This is called
stabilizing
the region.

"Increasingly, it becomes hard to distinguish victim from
victor in the gulf crisis." . . . "What we have now is worse
than what we had when Iraq was in Kuwait."

They want the oil
But they don't want the people.
They want the oil
But they don't want the people.[1]

Everything ventured, chaos gained.
Everything ventured, chaos gained.

Feast on scorpions
on jackals
the petroleum-dipped

tongues of politicians
the excrement of bombers
dropping their loads
on the people.

Sorties of sound and light
Fuel-bombs of flaming blood.

They took everything.
Who did?
Enemies. They shot my father
in front of us.
What did this teach you?
To hate them.
My children will hate them
and their children, also.

The oil burns and will burn.
The eye of the sky
will glare through a tear
in the ozone. (Oh-oh. The ozone.)

My child is a beggar.
My child is a running sore in the street.
She looks for food, for water.
I must find our lost family.
I can hear them laughing
under the rubble of our house.
The planes do not stop.
Why must they kill us all?

"The burning wells emit a daily load of 50,000 tons of
sulfur dioxide—a prime cause of acid rain—and 100,000 tons
of sooty smoke into the atmosphere. . . . Saddam Hussein . . .
had plainly warned that he would do it, however; so the
U.S., by its decision to launch the war anyway rather than
rely on non-combat pressures, bears some responsibility . . .
the Kuwaiti well fires . . . 'the most intense burning

source, probably, in the history of the world.'" Meanwhile,

The Country Is in a Better (or Worse) Economic Mood.
Kurdish Refugee Plight Worsens. The "Star Wars" Program
Will Go On. The Third World Seeks Advanced Arms. Wars Will
Become More Destructive. The Baseball Season Begins.

"From the overcast skies drips a greasy black rain, while
sheets of gooey oil slap against a polluted shore.
Burned-out hulks of twisted metal litter a landscape
pockmarked by bomb craters, land mines and shallow graves
scraped in the sand. . . . No one knows how long it will
take to undo the damage done by the war. Most of the oil in
the gulf will probably be left for nature to dispose of, a
process that could take decades given the sluggish movement
of the water. The job of disarming or exploding the land
mines is also likely to go on for years; 50 years after
World War II, people are still stumbling on mines in Egypt's
western desert."

Pilgrim, behold Death Highway, afterwards. A road that
stumbles into next year, groans into the future. Mother of
Battles, pray for us now and in the hour of our
devastations.

NOTES

1. "They want the oil . . . " "Nigerian/American Relations," Jayne Cortez, *Firespitter*" (New York: Bola Press, 1982). Other notes in sequence. "Look at the stars! . . . " Gerard Manley Hopkins, "The Starlight Night." . . . "Having supp'd full with horrors." Shakespeare, *Macbeth*, V.v.13. The reference here is to an actual occurrence, in which the air force corrected the misconception that the bombing of an air raid shelter was accidental. . . . "Iraq, with its Soviet-style strategy. . . . " *New York Times* editorial, March 30, 1991. . . . "Although many think. . . . " *Time*, March 18, 1991, p. 37. Information on Iraq is culled from various reference works. . . . "Already a U.N. report. . . . " Tom Wicker, *New York Times*, April 3, 1991. . . . "After the third day. . . . " General H. Norman Schwartzkopf, excerpt from TV interview with David Frost, published the following day in the *New York Times*, March 28, 1991 . . . "Mad, bad and dangerous to know." Written of George Gordon, Lord Byron, by Lady Caroline Lamb in her *Journal* (1812). "A Hitler," an opinion notably expressed by President George Bush. . . . "Have I no friend . . . ?" Shakespeare, *Richard II*, V.iv.2. . . . "Increasingly, it becomes hard. . . . " Christine Moss Helms, Middle East scholar, *New York Times*, March 30, 1991, and (to Patrick E. Tyler) in the newspaper the following day. . . . "The burning wells emit. . . . " Tom Wicker, *New York Times*, April 3, 1991, ending with quotation from Joel S. Levine of NASA. . . . "From the overcast skies. . . . " *Time*, pp. 37, 36, March 18, 1991.

ALISON MARCHANT

Wall Paper History

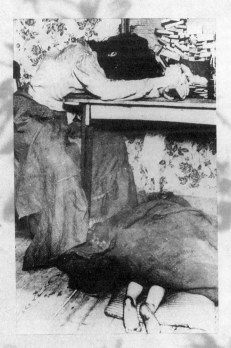

Inside the frame of the photograph,
lining the walls of her room,
the imperial
rose blooms
in the
background

ice Peacock Bridget Lee Sarah Coddard Mary Gutridge
Julia Donovan Alice Smithers Ada Smith Mary Begley M
ah Webb Ellen Bouquet Eliza Martin Lizzie Ince Marga
llen Cary Ellen Thirsty Mary Murphy Lilley Hayes Bri
nnie Waters Tilley Hall Sarah Branton Rachel Leonard
n Annie Prouse   O'Brien Esther Carthy Mag Raffe
nningham Bec   iza Goodwin Annie Elsley Eliza
 Carter Ne   Price Maria Briscoe Louisa
wling Jan   Jones Mary Flood Bella D
Anglin Ca   oodwin Eliza Jane Tate Bri
a Sulliv   s Annie Nicholls Annie Ha
rince Em   Toohy Kate Carthy Jane Eva
bert Est   Connor   Lickford Sar
s Charlo   e Bla   Doyle Ell
se Evans   ie   ngham L
Ann Ready   ie   w Eliz
ust Alice   oll   ily E
Delane Thor   rat   garet
er Alexander   Worch   Annie
heehan Laura Stanton Harriet   Mil
n Fenwick Annie Hardy Marga   orbel
ny Holmes M   Maskell Alic   rpenter
Susan Ri   Mathews Nel   Lane M
Elizab   eth Lawrence   th Perkins
phia   han Clara Clayden Harriet Cook
lfor   Ellen Abrahams Maria Springfo
sher   isa Coford Jane Coford Elizabe
 Cunn   s Sarah Chapman Susan Cane Ali
Marga   n M   t Pa
ily F   elau   ills
izzie W   ash Ma   Eliz
ennings Eli   h Jennir   Half
 Maria Tucker Ellen Cour   e Tu
ayden Lizzie Thorn Mary   nnie
 Kate Ripsher Eliza Hest   tant
 Carr Mrs Chambers Annie   Her
Sermon Alice Lloyd Marth   Har
Sheen Liz Butler Kate St   arne
 Norrie Murphy Nellie Sa   nie
Mog Pier Jane Smith Mary   Sara
zie Cole Mary Marney Emm   Mog
ker Jane Mathews Margaret Plummer Ellen Cronin Kate
Martha Taylor Ellen Roley Mary Shedwick Clara Peacoc
n Annie Elsworth Rose Goss Emily Morr Minnie Canon F
ah Tant Alice Dow Annie Sawle Lucy Dabbs Mary Baker

Wall Paper History is an installation series which toured Britain independently. Focusing upon the Match Women's Strikes of the nineteenth century in relation to the present, the installation utilizes a documentary approach within a contemporary art practice and raises questions about aspects of the socio-political class construction of people's lives. One such aspect was the current redevelopment of the match factory as yuppy flats and the eradication of the match women's radical history.

My family history drifted me back to East London, where I live now. My home, which is situated not far from the old Bryant and May match factory, stirred my interest in stories passed on through my family several years ago. I began researching into the match women's histories in 1985, prompted by three images from the Museum of Labour History, where I was tracing my family tree and matriarchal stories. I came across two images of women seated in corroded interiors lined with rose-covered wall paper. The flipside details identified the women as match makers and home workers.

The archivist pointed me to the strike register, where I rediscovered my great-aunt Elizabeth Marchant's name. Beside her name I read "lives with sisters," the words resounding like a metaphor for encountering and reclaiming a female, working-class, social space. What first struck me about these images was that direct knowledge was elusive, yet the meaning contained in those images was apparent as visual records. My response was to empathize with the women depicted.

The Wall Paper History series marked a turning point as I uncovered class and gender histories anew from my position as a working-class woman through the 1980s and 90s in relation to the experiences of a social-political climate in London's East End that my great-aunt must have encountered in the 1800s.[1] A hundred years on I retrace her steps and the journeys of other working-class women, many unnamed and some, my great-aunt among them, listed in the 1888 strike register.

In the construction of the installations, a past is identified and reclaimed, uncovered through a process of critical research. The personal journey is also political; it is a quest for self-identity spreading out into wider social landscapes. In addition to collecting, describing, classifying, analysing, and presenting data, I approach the historical subject matter as "process" so that the formerly objectified content is replaced by an effort to convey a sense of reality of the struggle, including the experience of making and installing the work in the present time. My presence is as a working-class woman creative practitioner.

At first, when looking into the archive photographs, I focused on the women and the wall paper. I gazed across the famous postcard image of a group of match women and noted something unusual in their faces. By enlarging their portraits, I found their faces contained the presence of phosphorous neurosis. I read history books recounting the match industry to try to map the women's faces. As I read these official histories, I became interested in the spaces between the patronising words of the middle-class writers. I am interested in silence, the untold story. I pieced together clues from the fragments and re-presented the working-class women's history anew, refusing stereotypical notions that we as working-class women are unable to speak for ourselves.[2]

RECLAIMING HER MISPLACED HISTORY: THE WOMAN'S VOICE SHATTERS THE EXISTING STRUCTURE

Annie Brown is twenty years of age. She went to work at the match factory putting lids on match boxes when she was nine years old. She could smell the phosphorous at first, but soon grew used to it. At night she could see her clothes glowing on the chair where she had placed them; her hands and arms were glowing too. After she had worked there for about four years, the complaint began as toothache. She covered her face as her jaw had been removed at the infirmary seven years ago.[3]

The Wall Paper History installations concentrate on the ever-evolving arrangements of collected information, images, and archive material on the Match Women's Strikes, with the aim of re-representing history and "allowing events and people's voices to speak for themselves."[4] Some of the installations incorporated sound and live work—continually changing depending on the space, location, and time span of each exposition. Not only did the re-represented historical text, which accompanied all the installations, provide context and information for the viewer, but the text and images also raised questions about the means available to us for knowing about the past.

Wall Paper History Installation—Version I

The first Wall Paper History installation was shown at Rochdale Art Gallery, England (10 January—5 March, 1988), in an exhibition entitled *The Medium and the Message.* I enlarged to 9 by 11 feet and photo-silk screened archive images of the domestic conditions of home workers onto adjoining pages of traditional English history books (*A Shorter History of England* and *The New Imperialism*) to reflect a juxtaposition of two existing but conflicting cultures and to tell two different stories, one "complete" and detailed, the other fragmented and fading into obscurity. The monumental prints, placed side by side, filled one wall of the installation and appeared as new printed pages suspended on an open but representationally and historically closed book.

> *In 1888, my great aunt lived with my grandmother, both young women existing in domestic poverty. My family said "the match factory thrived on the blood of its workers."*[5]

The Match Women's Strike happened over a hundred years ago and little is known of the women who actually took part. The Strike Register came to light ninety years after the event, and so it is only fairly recently that even the strikers' names have been revealed. This list of names became another representation, another layer in the installation, as the names were projected onto hanging prints, echoing pages of a book on a vast scale.

But like the original photographic images, the installations were like an illustrative memento, a collection of fragments pieced together in the present. To the factory owners, the women's lives seemed almost to be a waste product; their individual lives flitted across the backdrop of match production. The installation tried to reflect this fragmented history in the museum through which viewers passed, their own shadows flitting across the spaces of

light cast upon the walls. Out of this fragmented, transient collection of images, text, installation artist, and viewers, a past was
identified and reclaimed, a visual narrative extended, and a language and history based on metaphor and intuition (and in
opposition to "official" history text) highlighted.[6]

Underscoring the installation's divergence from "official"
text was another work, "England's Glory." An enlarged detail
from the most well-known postcard of Match Women revealed
the visible effects of phosphorous contamination of the women's
hands and jaws. These images were scattered "ironically against
a background of photocopied wall paper printed with huge black
roses."[7] The final element of this piece was a contemporary Bryant
& May match box—"England's Glory"—with the date 1888 re-
printed on its surface. Below the empty match box lay its former
contents in a dead pile on the floor.

I located two twin home worker prints, identical to those in
the gallery, outside. I pasted one on the wall of a demolished
house; the other filled an empty shop window. Both drew attention to domestic labor and voicelessness. With weathering over
six weeks, the work undermined itself as a permanent public art
work. The prints peeled away once more into fragmented pages
mingled with piles of rubble. The print on the abandoned shop
window connected commodity culture with the often-neglected
producers of the commodities that drive and are driven by that
culture—the women workers and the conditions under which
they live(d).

INSIDE THE FRAME OF THE PHOTOGRAPH, LINING THE WALLS OF THE ROOM, THE IMPERIAL ROSE BLOOMS IN THE BACKGROUND

Wall Paper History Installation—Version II

At the Collective Gallery in Edinburgh, Scotland, during the Fringe Festival (1988), "Wall Paper History" was shown as two installations. One of these installations became a live work over seven hours.

I placed the archive photograph, "Exhausted Match Workers—1888," over the entrance of a former living room space. I tinted and toned the photograph to draw out the wall paper in faded blue and red imperial roses. This photograph was also projected into the "real space" of the gallery. Through the doorway this huge projection appeared like a mirror image of the archive image, confirming the viewers' and my presence as part of the living history of the match workers in the present and again subverting "fixed," "official" history. The projection illuminated a far wall, papered with history book pages of written text, while I sat echoing the match woman's pose at a table. An-

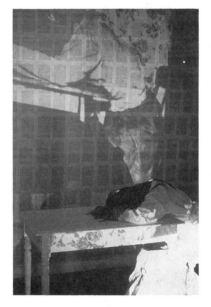

other projector hummed and clicked mechanical sounds as the names of Match Women were cast upon the hem of my skirt.

While I endured the pain of that posture, limbs aching, head and arms carrying my full weight, millions of thoughts rushed through my mind and emptied out into complete blankness—I lost track of time. Twice the painful nature of the pose caused me to look up, and, on confronting the gaze of the viewer, I subverted the photographic image of the woman as passive model. I hoped to challenge the spectators' role as voyeur and to create a new area of enquiry.[8]

The accompanying installation, "England's Glory," dominated the larger gallery space. I juxtaposed several suspended rolls of rose-printed wall paper against the archive postcard and enlargements, which I placed upon small shelves distributed across the entire length of the gallery to suggest and enhance a feeling of domestic space. Opposite, the Strike Register spread out in two panels, rose printed and cream toned, broken by a history book cover with ripped-out pages revealing a photograph of match workers' hands and the text: "Decisions over life and death, over

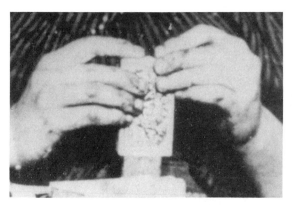

personal and national security are made at places where individuals have no control . . . The slaves of developed industrial civilisation are sublimated slaves, but they are slaves, for slavery is determined not only by obedience or by hardness of labour, but by the status of being a mere instrument, and the reduction of workers to the state of a thing. This is the pure form of servitude: to exist as an instrument, as a thing. The antagonistic relationship between the master and servant has been defused into mutual dependence."[9]

Wall Paper History/Reprinted Pages

The uprising of the match workers began on the day of the unveiling of a statue of Gladstone[10] on Bow Road (the workers wages were docked to pay for it).

Some of the women went to the ceremony armed with bricks and stones, and after the unveiling, they mobbed the statue. Shouting and screaming, yelling, they clung to it, beat it, twined their arms around it, and cut themselves so that their blood dripped on the stony plinth.[11]

Whilst the images of the home-working Match Women were the central large-scale focus of the previous installations, the postcard portrait of a group of match women now became a key image in large scale. Enlarged to seven square feet as a laser photocopy, the technical process of this media meant that it was constructed as a coordination of a series of pages. I filled otherwise blank areas of the print with hand-written names of Match Women to personalise the graphic machine-made image. I further collaged the image with rose bud wall paper fragments, map-like and stained with rising damp—a gritty image that undermined notions of nostalgia. Suspended from a household picture rail and against a wall of history book pages, the work again took on a monumental presence.

This installation was at the Tom Allen Centre, London, within walking distance of the Bryant & May match factory and near where many of the Match Women once lived. To coincide with this installation, I sited more than 150 fly posters on the street where the Match Women once lived and on the match factory walls.

At night I posted multiple laser enlargements from an image of match women around London's East End. In streets passing through wastelands, industrial estates, empty and lamp-lit, I walked. The pasted images, though creating a pathway which contrasted sharply with the surroundings, were somehow connected to this environment, alienated by time, but not nostalgic.

Some of the fly posters, especially those on the factory walls and developers' hoardings and those pasted on the Gladstone monument and bank cash tills, acted as graffiti, violating the surrounding location which had erased the women's past. Others, posted on run-down buildings and lamp posts, drew not only the physical surroundings into the project, but also the passers by who stopped to look and became interested.

Her face stared out, lamp light and headlights catching a face I could recognize as light among darkness. A face which was not individual but representative of years of smothered voices about to speak out.

Homes erased, a story forgotten, the factory transformed into luxury flats, fading into another monument once more reaffirming the class it has always represented.[12]

Wall Paper History/England's Glory

At 33 Arts Center in Luton, England, this installation was located in an art gallery that was formerly both a factory and living space. I covered the floor and walls with history book pages, projecting once more the image of the home worker. I also painted roses around the walls and scattered burnt traditional history books to

form a map of the U.K. An audio tape recalling the names of the Match Women echoed in the room, while projected names were cast across the fireplace where I stood in my live work at the installation preview. With my arms outstretched horizontally, I slowly and hypnotically burnt souvenir union jacks so that they melted into firey rain in the darkened space. Once the nylon flag fabrics had burnt, I held their sticks vertically so they set light like candles which I placed upright in the grate of the hearth. Then I slowly moved through the space to the chair to take up the Match Woman's pose only to find a woman from the audience sitting there with her child on her lap, as if in the pose of the other home worker. So I turned and carefully moved out of the installation space.[13]

The final installation/live work in the series took place at Central Space, London (26 February—16 March, 1989), which was formerly a Victorian School. The installation area was approximately 60 by 15 feet. I lined the far end of the long space with the pages of a traditional English history book (*The Making of Modern England*). Onto this surface, I projected the same postcard image I previously incorporated in "Wall Paper History/Reprinted Pages," along with a negative projection of rose wall paper enlarged from the home worker archive photograph.

In a further layer of projection, the names of the women from the strike register appeared and dissolved. Emanating from these projections and stretching out like a pathway was a landscape constructed from burnt British History/Financial Studies books. From the ashes of dominant history, the staring faces of the women shone out and across, as if raising voices previously silenced. These books were arranged in a manner reminiscent of the positions of roses on wall paper or the arrangement of school desks in a classroom. They appeared like dying leaves, huge black roses, charred rocks—branching images associated in the semi-dark space.

Nearer the entrance a sound tape played a monologue of the Re-Represented Text—the history of the Match Women's Strikes—accompanied by an echoing layer of sound built up as the names of Match Women were recited. On the opposite wall, another negative rose projection was cast across the original postcard image of Match Women, a contemporary Bryant & May matchbox—England's Glory—with 1888 written across it, and six pages of Re-Represented Historical Text. The Strike Register, printed with black roses, hung in the entrance in the harsh light of a bare light bulb.

Detail from "Wall Paper History/Eradicated Pages" Projection, Postcard, "Englands Glory" march box and re-represented historical text.

"Wall Paper History/Eradicated Pages" detail of source—postcard image as sited (with contempory Bryant & May) match box partly covered by smaller negative rose projection in the installation. By Alison Marchant 1989.

TRADITIONAL BRITISH HISTORY BOOKS MANAGERIAL/BUSINESS STUDIES BOOKS ROMANTIC NOVELS AND ONE BOOK ON THE ARTIFICIAL CULTIVATION OF WILD ROSES **HAVE BEEN BURNT IN THIS INSTALLATION**

Throughout the duration of the exhibition more history books were burnt and added to the floor piece. Pages became shrivelled, small fires kindled, permeating the air with an uncomfortable damp smoke.

At intervals I burnt the books with a gas torch, working my way from one end of the space to the next, until I met the wall. Stepping into the light of the projection and lining my face with that of the match woman, I could only breath the sinister toxicity of the acrid air. Moving before me, the image of the Match Women appeared on the smoky screen. It was as if the projectors became search lights in a dark landscape of distant shadowy figures moving around the edges of the space. I moved in and out of the image into the fragile area of burnt books, my shadow crossing the projections, appearing to weave in and out. At one moment I placed the burning stick I used as a poker into the projected hands of one of the Match Women. The other end of the stick touched a burnt book, physically relating the projection to the burnt books and drawing the two-dimensional image into three-dimensional space.[14]

Moving in and out of the work, as both subject and curator, my identity as Artist was deconstructed by creating an atmosphere conducive to the undermining of the specialisation the role presents. Viewers were also allowed access and moved across the projections into the space of burnt books, where they also burnt the books. This combination of reflection and activity—the reverberation of the historical subject matter—created a sense of fluidity around the work that denied any notion of the installation itself as a passive art object. The documents of the past recorded the history of the present in every changing arrangement. A living history was aimed at as a metaphor— attempting to intervene in the dominance of the gallery art involvement—as if to suggest a sense of actively contributing to the formation of their own history rather than inheriting the history of power.

The Match Women once lived in the East London areas of Whitechapel, Bethnal Green, Globe Town, Old Ford, Mile End, Stepney, Shadwell, Limehouse, Bow, Bromley, Canning Town and Stratford—London, England.

One or several fly posters were sited depending on how many Match Workers were registered as living in those streets.

Grace Street
Powis Road
Devas Street
Empson Street
Teviot Street
Ashton Street
Godbold Street
Star Lane
Bidder Street
Victoria Dock Road
Sabbarton Street
Nelson Street
St. Thomas Road
Fords Park Road
Livingstone Road
Union Street
Channelsea Road
Bridge Road
Hotham Street
West Street
Albert Square
Benton Street
Wendon Street
Maroon Street
Lambeth Street
Hancock Road
High Street, Bow
Glaucas Street
Reeves Road
Abbey Street
Abbey Lane
High Street, Stratford
Fairfield Road
Three Colts Corner

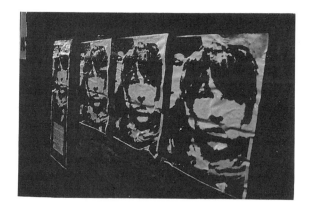

Lambeth Street
Redchurch Street
(Formerly Church
Street)
Three Colts Lane
Collingwood Street
Roman Road
Smart Street
Palm Street
Old Ford Road
Ford Road
St. Stephens Road
Lefevre Walk
Wendon Street
Parnell Road
Jupps Road
Longfellow Road
Ashford Road
Commodore Street
Ben Johnson Road
Latimer Street
Clarke Street
Ashton Street
Dupont Street
Conder Street
Sutton Street
Cable Street
Juniper Street
School House Lane
Turners Road
Gill Street
Gaselee Street
Arnold Street
Bow Common Lane
Joseph Street
Tidey Street
Whitehorn Street
Blackthorn Street
Gale Street
Barchester Street
Clutton Street
St. Leonards Road
Hancock Road
Franklin Street

NOTES

1. "Slumming" became a trend in the 1880s for the middle and upper classes, who regarded their visits to the East End as one of their "social duties." Patronising attitudes such as these continue today and are particularly evident in the history and practice of social documentary photography when the subject is working class and the photographer is middle class. The documenters, their experience worlds apart, can only take provisional solace for guilt feelings that replace any real conviction or experience of hardship. Our images, our representations, are literally "taken."

2. Prior to the 1888 strike, which is said to have been "led" by Fabian and Writer Annie Bessant, there was the 1882 uprising, and, though before 1888 the Match Women had not formed a Trade Union, they frequently discussed their grievances and stuck up for each other against the injustices of the factory conditions. In 1871 a strike took place; so too in 1885 because of the lowering of wages and the undermining of their health, particularly the loss of their teeth through the constant inhaling of phosphorous fumes. The Match Women were no strangers to strikes, yet Labourist history, with its focus on middle-class Annie Bessant and the 1888 strike, suggests that Bessant was "a mediator for the strikers who could hardly read and write." This notion is quickly undermined by the presence of Match Women's signatures in the original strike register, and the history of the earlier strikes which the Match Women led themselves.

Galsworthy and Dickens were two of the many writers who viewed the poverty of the Match Women. The words of one of the women Galsworthy interviewed reflected her sense of pride and refusal to succumb to the overwhelming burdens of her life. She also commented on those who "fuss" and "quarrel" over the poor as though they were artifacts to be dealt with as their "betters" saw fit.

The words of the Match Woman should be recognized as more poignant than the descriptions given by Dickens and Galsworthy. But her history is misplaced and her language misrepresented, so that her words take second place, despite her direct experience of the situation.

3. Transcript from medical papers, Hackney Archive, London.

4. Malcolm Dickson, "Wall Paper History," review of "Wall Paper History," by Alison Marchant, *Variant—Art & Ideas Magazine* 5 (1988).

5. *Artslink* (April/May, 1989).

6. Alison Marchant, "Wall Paper History," *The Medium and the Message Exhibition Catalogue*, Rochdale Art Gallery, England, 1988.

7. Review of "Wall Paper History," by Alison Marchant, *Spare Rib*, Issue 189 (April 1988).

8. Alison Marchant, artist's statement, *Women Artist Slide Library Journal*, Issue 26 (1988).

9. Herbert Marcuse, *One Dimensional Man* (London: Ark Paperbacks, 1964), pp. 32–33.

10. Gladstone was British Prime Minister in the late nineteenth century. His statue in East London stands on Bow Road today and was unveiled in 1884.

11. "Wall Paper History: Re-Represented Installation Text," compiled by Alison Marchant from sources in Hackney Archives and the Museum of Labour History, 1988.

12. Wall Paper History fly poster event description by Alison Marchant, 1989.

13. Alison Marchant, "Wall Paper History/England's Glory," exhibition publicity brochure, 33 Arts Centre, Luton, 1989.

14. Alison Marchant, "Wall Paper History/Eradicated Pages," *Journal of Art & Art Education*, Issue 20 (1989) and *Women Focusing*, Issue 4 (1989).

GERTRUDE M. JAMES GONZALEZ

Fading Prints of Childhood in St. Croix

the bath is over.

on this bed,
this edge,
i sit
wrapped
in pink and white-
a robe
long and laced.

on this edge,
i see no bruises,
only yesteryear scars
and they are fading.

look at my hands
so pale
. . . no daily sun caresses
no mending of soil nor
planting of flowers, fruits and vegetables.

❧

i,
see green veins,
through pale skin

no rinsing and wringing of clothes
on large tin basins
under overgrown shading trees.

my hands are soft and
        the scars are fading

they are no longer
sweeping, mopping, . . . pulling shrubs
from between concrete cracks
climbing mango and gooseberry trees,
hiding in tall grasses
next to inch worms and *gongolis,*
catching butterflies,
burying dead birds.

my hands are pale and soft now,
        and the scars are fading.

ॐ

the bottoms of my feet are smooth,
no walks on sharp coral shores,
no barefoot runs across the backyard,
encouraging the dogs to chase
urging my friends on a race.
no neighborly visits across dirt roads,
to deliver a phone message
asking for sugar, or saying hello.

the soles of my feet are soft.
        my skin is mapped with green veins
                and the scars are fading.
my skin has only scars
no *llagas,*
no torn dresses,
and bleeding backs
from barbed wire fences
and casha trees to look at

the new puppies Blackie just had.
no legs rubbed
against *pringamosa* to pick
the oranges and reds of mango.

     my skin is smooth.
         my skin is soft.
             i only have scars,
                 and they are fading.

LUCY R. LIPPARD

Anti-Amnesia

Amid the signage jungle of lower Manhattan, the metal plaques attached high on lampposts might first be taken as standard warnings from officialdom. But the imagery seems unlikely— a falling body, the photo of an open grave, portraits of a homeless man and a radical politician, a floating ladder and the noose. And the texts just don't have that bureaucratic thud. On closer scrutiny of the information offered, mutiny is apparent. The lively array of pictorial signs are, of course, art. But rather than "review" the products (most of which work really well in context), I want to explore the process of this exemplary public art project.

The goal was to repossess history. "Whose History Is Remembered? Who Will We Forget?" is the fundamental question asked by REPOhistory, a multiethnic collective of artists, writers, and educators whose Sign Project opened with panache and a parade in lower Manhattan in June (1992). The two-sided, 18 x 24", three-color photosilkscreen historical markers, thirty-nine of them in all, are clustered between Canal Street and the Battery, mostly south of City Hall Park. Although their projected life span is six months (through Jan. 1, 1993), some may last longer. It's kind of a miracle that they are there at all.

The project was conceived by experienced alumni of PADD (Political Art Documentation/Distribution), the activist art group (and Archive, now at the Museum of Modern Art) that almost survived the '80s. First called "The History Project," it began as a study group and developed by the fall of 1989 into a proposal "to retrieve and relocate absent historical narratives at specific locations in the New York City area through counter-monuments, actions and events." Because many of the members were working already to counteract the official Columbus Quincentennial events, it was suggested at early meetings that the theme of colonialism/ racism be adopted and the signs be scattered all over the city and Brooklyn, so that people could deal with their own neighborhoods and local education. One ambitious idea was to map the entire city and catalogue the historical sites in order to determine an overriding theme. Finally the group decided to focus for the time being on the lost history of lower Manhattan, where it all began, and where most events could indeed be categorized as colonialism and racism. (For instance, Tess Timoney's and Mark O'Brian's sign marking the site of the city's Meal and Slave Market from 1709–62, notes that "New York ranked second, behind Charleston, S.C., as an urban slave center.")

Various names were tossed around including Re-siting History, Repo-sites, Local '92, Second Story, Historical Society, and the contorted pun "History-city." Study of existing plaques, literature, walking tours, archives, and guides began; we raised issues about fundraising, public art guidelines, and where our energy would best be spent—gaining access to the Media or constructing alternate media? (The sign project does both.) The original plan was to do the whole project as guerrilla art, but it eventually became clear that too much work was going to be invested for a hit-and-run strategy.

The minutes record that we talked about historical layers, "the juxtaposition of oral history and more or less immediate history and 'untold' histories that exist beyond personal memories, histories told by different living generations posed against a presentation reaching much farther back." There were calls for a new historiography. We would emphasize "an understanding of history as something that is created and transmitted by people," along the lines of Howard Zinn's *A People's History of the United States.* We looked at the changed meanings of neighborhood symbols and sites; for example, Trinity Church: "Restore this 'innocent' and pretty detail in the cityscape to its original meaning as a monument to the everlasting presence of the new colonizers, its original position as dominant monument rising above the island."

Or we could "complement existing plaques at historical buildings and sites with our own signs dedicated to the same events but recounting them from a different perspective." A sign at the Museum of Modern Art (itself a monument to Rockefeller acquisitiveness) would "commemorate the Ludlow massacre and trace the origins of the Rockefellers' philanthropic interests back to a coal strike and successfully applied public relations methods."

Or we could make fictional narratives based on historic events—"make history without history." Because a number of theatre people were involved, it looked at one point as though performances might replace or augment signs. The issue of representation itself was at the core of many of the discussions. Someone suggested that "the human body could be a site of the political, experienced and manifested as the personal, through badges and wearable art." We talked about working on the site with students and/or community members, about the possibilities of actually disengaging from the "mediascape" and the culture industry, confronting the artist's paradoxical role therein.

In one early meeting we discussed different ways of looking at history: as monumental truth or as palimpsest, a labyrinth of memory; as documented facts or as oral and written narratives by participants; as a linear progression or a chaos of catastrophes; as simulacrum of the past or as runaway simulations, parodies; as mass spectacles for the passive viewer or as participatory ritual; as inevitable and "natural," or as an open text allowing for magic realism; as traditional documentary or as questions about the role of the maker.

The sign form was decided on in May 1990. But it was still to be a long process. What had seemed fairly simple—get a diverse bunch of artists together, pick sites and subjects, collectively discuss the projects, and put 'em up—took two more years. (Founding member Tom Klem kept a logbook on the whole project). Readings in radical and imaginative history continued. The meetings themselves were often lively history lessons as research began and people brought in possible sign subjects. Artists, writers, teachers joined and dropped out and others hung in and got serious and learned a lot about the historical enterprise as well as about working with other artists. (I'm still kicking myself that despite ongoing involvement with the group, I never got my sign together.) Sign prototypes were shown at the Marxist School in the summer of 1991 and the next year was devoted to construction, mapping, and endless fundraising—from individuals in the progressive art community, solicited by mail, from a lot of grant writing. There was a tremendous amount of bureaucratic and organizational work done by a hard-working core dedicated to the project's completion. The project finally cost about $10,000. It would have been a great deal more without the endless free labor.

Amazingly, there was little objection from the Community Board and other institutions about the radical content of the signs. Early on, there was a brief stir about the placement on Exchange Place, across the street from the J.P. Morgan corporate headquarters, of Greg Sholette's sign which identifies Morgan as a draft dodger, purchasing a "second" to take his place in the Civil War so he could keep on making money; it also comments on the ethnic and class makeup of America's armed forces. But when REPOhistory held firm, its opponents backed off. Later the Stock Exchange requested the removal of Jim Costanzo's "Advantages of an Unregulated Free Market Economy" (the image of a suicide); but again aesthetic justice prevailed.

After much negotiation, the lower Manhattan Cultural Council (LMCC) agreed to sponsor the Sign Project as their contribution to "Americas? A Borough-wide public art exhibition." Then the Municipal Art Society, the New York Historical Society came on board (as they say in the corporate navy). The Department of Transportation donated invaluable technical assistance, and eventually City Council President Andrew Stein proclaimed June 27, 1992, "REPOhistory Day," complete with a printed proclamation. The opening was a gala occasion on a lovely Saturday afternoon at Castle Clinton. A fullscale parade with papier mâché sculptures, a ship, tongues of flame ("Memories of Fire") stopped at each of ten nearby signs for content-specific storytelling/performances. (The liveliest was several African-American teenagers commemorating the visit of Nelson Mandela to lower New York.)

Popular history is an idea in the air, with its roots in community theatre. From the art angle, Jenny Holzer has used signage as an art form since the late '70s. In the '80s, Edgar Heap of Birds adapted it to resurrect Native history, while Martin Wong did a series of New York street signs featuring cryptic messages in American Sign Language, and REPOhistorian Ed Eisenberg's

"Groundworks" project informed communities about their exact distances from a planned nuclear port. More recently, other artists, especially Scott Parsons in South Dakota (commemorating massacres of Native people) and Gloria Bornstein in Seattle (original uses of the waterfront), have used deadpan public announcement form to commemorate lost and disturbing histories.

From where I stand at the moment (admittedly obsessed with history as the road of good intentions paved to a hellish present, a result of my own years of Columbus-bashing), this kind of activism is preeminently satisfying. Too "didactic," "agit-prop," or "preachy" for some tastes, it nevertheless offers the solid ground that so much progressive art appears to long for. Rejecting the museum/gallery system is no longer a real option as it gets harder and harder for any artist to survive the current economic depression. Most activist artists welcome the chance to exhibit their ideas while trying not to become too dependent on the system and continuing to seek out more encompassing, less compromising venues as well. The last decade has demonstrated that the latter is easier if one has acquired a modest reputation in the former. It has proved frustrating for those purists who have fully rejected (or been rejected by) even the mainstream fringes to see those who were willing to be politically eclectic in their exhibiting choices ("sellouts" to some) get the grants and invitations to do work in areas in which others have more experience.

Collective endeavours like REPOhistory—which has now evolved into a loose but ongoing group with several shows to its credit and several upcoming projects—heal some of these socially inflicted wounds. Some who worked on the Sign Project had shown a good deal more than others; many of the participating artists' names are recognized and respected within the "alternative" art world, if not exactly as coffee-table commodities. While many did their signs alone, fourteen were collaborative efforts, often cross-cultural and interdisciplinary.

REPOhistorian Lisa Maya Knauer observes that the signs took the current debates on history, multiculturalism, and school curriculum into the streets where everybody "can be confronted or provoked or challenged by the information." The audience consists of people living and working in the neighborhood, and the tourists who throng lower Manhattan. Understanding their movement and thought patterns, tying into their daily routines, was one of the challenges of the project. In mid-summer, the *New York Times* reported that Hilary Kliros's and Betty Beaumont's sign about how Maiden Lane got its name, which included the disembodied drawing of a hymen, had been found "disgusting" by a New Jersey secretary who felt it was "offensive to women" and had "caused a small furor" in the neighborhood. My own haphazard interviewing around the signs indicated that while some people didn't even notice them at all, those who took the time got involved in what they saw and enjoyed it.

The signs do not take the place of books; reciprocal, cross-cultural histories are too complex for such brief texts. But with their image hooks and brief texts, they are subversive picture-bites that can evoke far more than they can cover. At the very least they can elicit a "Hey, I never learned *that* in school" response. They can suggest for a moment the bones, the middens, the villages, the farmhouses, the theatres, and the gallows lying beneath the pavement. Accessible, democratic, the signs are neither intrusive nor condescending. They can make people want to know more. The idea was not just to evoke history, but to provide a critical view, to disrupt the ingrained and conditioned perceptions of history and, finally, of who the audience thinks they are.

Altogether the Sign Project's form provides an incredibly open frame within which to pursue personal agendas/obsessions, and I offer it here as a model for any community, large or small. Progressive feminists have long maintained that social change begins with self transformation. History offers information about the self that leads outward. (For example, in 1991 the families of eight African American school children filed a suit against New York City for failing to revise the public school's curricula to reflect their cultural heritage.) The ways in which the political is personal are at the heart of this project. REPOhistorians and their audiences find themselves understanding better their own lives and those of their families, their communities, their places, within the context of other lost histories.

The signs cover a vast amount of ground. The visuals range from slick professional graphics to poetic collage to colorful poster-like boldness. It seems worth listing some of the other subjects covered to give a sense of the scope not only of this project but of those you could be doing this or other ways in your own communities:

• Leisler's Rebellion, when working people occupied Fort James in 1689 in an attempt to construct a new and more just government in New York. The revolt was put down by merchants and landowners, but they could find no carpenter in town who would furnish a ladder to use at Leisler's execution (Stephen Duncombe's sign).

• The First All Women's strike in the US by the United Tailoresses' Society in 1825 (Stephanie Basch).

• The (alleged) Great Negro Plot of 1741, conspiracy hysteria that led to burning of thirteen enslaved people at the stake, to hanging seventeen more, and to deporting dozens (Mark O'Brien and Willie Birch).

• The former Army Induction Center on Whitehall Street, target of Vietnam war demonstrations in the 1960s (Betti Sue Hertz).

• The Negro Burial Ground (Lisa Knauer and Dan Wiley). This sign led to more activism as REPOhistory participated in the summer protests against the office buildings rising on the site; in a remarkable turnaround, a large area has been partially saved and there is a move underway to construct a museum of colonial African life there, a project after REPOhistory's heart.

And, in brief: Potter's Field/unwanted immigrants/Ellis Island (Jayne Pagnucco); Indian Giver, or When Will America be Discovered (Todd Ayoung); Bullet made from Statue of King George (Darin Wacs); Homelessness: Forgotten Histories (in Spanish and English, by Tom Klem); Origin of Pearl Street (Sabra Moore); Mandela's Visit to New York (Curlee Holton); Origin of the Word Indian (Gustavo Silva); Indian Settlement Sites (Tchin); India house (Leela Ramotar); False Democracy/Inequality of the U.S. Senate, on the site where Congress first met (Ed Eisenberg); Subway Fire (Sam Binkley); Insurance and National Health Care, related to slave insurance and AIDS (Carin Kuoni); Rose Schneiderman: Union Activist (Nanette Yanuzzi Maclas and Jeff Skoller); First Chinese Community in NYC (EPOXY, an Asian American collaborative); Jacob Astor & Native Americans (Alan

Michelson); The Story of the Waterfront (Dan Wiley); Madame Restell & Anthony Comstock (Lisa Maya Knaer and Janet Koenig); Office Workers Eat Their Lunch (Neill Bogan and Irene Ledwith); Gotham City (Lise Prown and Curt Belshe); Epidemics (Brian Goldfarb); Frances Wright: Racial and Sexual Equality (Josely Carvalho and Deborah Mesa-Pelly); Vito Marcantonio: Radical Congressmen (Gerald Meyer, author of a Marcantonio biography, and Marina Gutierrez); Civil Defense Drill Arrests 1950s (Jody Wright); Boxing and Exploitation (George Spencer and Cynthia Anderson); Forlorn Hope/Debtor's Jail (Laurie Ourlicht and Joe Ciment); The First Alms House (Anita Morse & Andy Musilli); Smith Act Trials (Keith Christensen).

There is a chance the signs will be permanently maintained. In any case, there are ways to keep this project moving. (The general print media has been good to the Sign Project, while the art press has for the most part ignored it). In an early meeting, children's history cards were suggested as an auxiliary; humorously disjunctive historical postcards and more general stickers questioning existing historical markers would also keep the spirit alive, as would video documentaries that students can watch and evaluate in relation to where they live and what they know. REPOhistory led walking tours, and these could be extended by an altered map of lower Manhattan to hand out to tourists. On a general level, other artists could remap their own towns, reframing and renaming what's already there. We can apply to art what Eduardo Galeano has said of literature: "Our effectiveness depends on our capacity to be audacious and astute, clear and appealing. I would hope that we can create a language more fearless and beautiful than that used by conformist writers to greet the twilight."

UPDATE: REPOhistory's latest project (May 1998) is *Civil Disturbances,* another sign project, chronicling some of the important legal struggles waged by public interest lawyers and activists over the past 30 years, and executed in conjunction with New York Lawyers for the Public Interest. Some of these controversial cases are still pending, no doubt a factor in Mayor Rudy Giuliani's refusal of permission to hang the signs, a few minutes before the press conference on the steps of the Senate Supreme Court, despite the city's full cooperation with REPOhistory's two previous sign projects. —L.R.L.

ADRIENNE RICH

Through Corralitos Under Rolls of Cloud

I

Through Corralitos under rolls of cloud
between winter-stiff, ranged apple-trees
each netted in transparent air,
thin sinking light, heartsick within and filmed
in heartsickness around you, gelatin cocoon
invisible yet impervious—to the hawk
steering against the cloudbank, to the clear
oranges burning at the rancher's gate
rosetree, agave, stiff beauties holding fast
with or without your passion,
the pruners freeing up the boughs
in the unsearched faith these strange stiff shapes will bear.

II

Showering after 'flu; stripping the bed;
running the shrouds of sickness through the wash;
airing the rooms; emptying the trash;
it's as if part of you had died in the house
sometime in that last low-lit afternoon
when your dreams ebbed salt-thick into the sheets
and now this other's left to wash the corpse,
burn eucalyptus, turn the mirrors over—
this other who herself barely came back,
whose breath was fog to your mist, whose stubborn shadow
covered you as you lay freezing, she survived
uncertain who she is or will be without you.

III

If you know who died in that bed, do you know
who has survived? If you say, *she was weaker,*
held life less dear, expected others
to fight for her if pride lets you name her
victim and the one who got up and threw
the windows open, stripped the bed, *survivor*
—what have you said, what do you know
of the survivor when you know her
only in opposition to the lost?
What does it mean to say *I have survived*
until you take the mirrors and turn them outward
and read your own face in their outraged light?

IV

That light of outrage is the light of history
springing upon us when we're least prepared,
thinking maybe a little glade of time
leaf-thick and with clear water
is ours, is promised us, for all we've hacked
and tracked our way through: to this:
What will it be? Your wish or mine? your
prayers or my wish then: that those we love
be well, whatever that means, to be well.
Outrage: who dare claim protection for their own
amid such unprotection? What kind of prayer
is that? To what kind of god? What kind of wish?

V

She who died on that bed sees it her way:
She who went under peers through the translucent shell
cupping her death and sees her other well,
through a long lens, in silvered outline, well
she sees her other and she cannot tell
why when the boom of surf struck at them both
she felt the undertow and heard the bell,
thought death would be their twinning, till the swell
smashed her against the reef, her other still
fighting the pull, struggling somewhere away
further and further, calling her all the while:
she who went under summons her other still.

1989-1990

Geographies

site   location   territory   colony   border   map
landings   ports of call   departures   arrivals   embarkations

᷎

The hearts are broken inside a string of cowry shells: medium of exchange. Buy and sell. Hearts for sale, the edges, little razor teeth. Open your mouth, girl. Let the gentleman see your choppers.

The brilliance of this white, hot sand astonishes; the heat stuns. The young white boys plunge into the ocean, emerging with heads sleek as seals. A wave tears at the strap of my bathing suit, rips it from my shoulder, exposes my right breast to the bright sun and the stares of young white boys. The air is hot and dries the salt on my body, leaving white streaks you cannot kiss or lick away.

I.

Will I leap into the water too, my fear of drowning
overcome by my fear
of rape,
of not knowing where this foul ship might land?
Will I fall into the waves like the others? Some even took
their babies with

them. Of course.
I am an inland girl. My feet love dusty paths, not this
unforgiving water,
not this water that swallows women and their babies.
Still, we are strung like beads, what makes us women,
now or becoming, the
slits an echo of the cowry shell,
stripped down to what essentials?
If only we were armed with teeth, *vagina dentata*, different
medium of
exchange, dividends to be collected later.
Who will buy me and never count the cost?

*Inside this hot, wet hole, the floor, the ground is never still. And we
cannot practice our sacred ceremonies in front of the men nor tend our
women's bodies without shame.*

*Sometimes the pale, shadow men descend into the hold; fear slithers through
like the smell of rotten meat. They squint and point, usually at a young
girl, though sometimes a boy or man, and herd them, up and away.
When they return, we never hear their stories. We only see their eyes, empty
and dead.*

*Foul water washes over us as we lie on these narrow wooden shelves. Foul
water and ourselves here in our own waste, with our own fear and
our own sourness, not knowing where we are going or when we will
arrive, not knowing, what then? Beneath the sickness in my belly and
the smell of skin rotting in the damp, my heart's ache is faint but
deeper than any pain I've ever known. My family is lost to me. I am
the only one left to honour our ancestors, to remember their names.
For that, I must stay alive. But my heart is broken. The woman who
came to my hut so many nights, the one who walks with the village
men, will return from her season of hunting and find me gone. I
will never repair that rip in my heart.*

Finally, we cut the strand,
and
like beads, the other women, me, their babies,
disappear over the sides of this ship,

shells around my heart, a tiny hand grasping at my ear.
We slip into the murk, joined at the throat of swallowed fear,
our lungs
fill and we do not float. Of course not.
The knowledge that the milk this baby's mouth seeks out
starts up and flows only at the shock of the ocean's frigid waves
washing us back to the middle,
between what was home and somewhere else,
a robbery I cannot bear,
though without a visible weapon, it appears a simple theft.
Once submerged, perhaps the tears, the milk combine.
As I offer this thin blend to the tiny lips,
the watery wall rushes up,
the cradle rocks us down and out to sea.
And I open my mouth to meet it.
Shore break: hearts pulverized, reduced to sand,
each grain, its stunning glitter, piece of the ancestral mirror
even infinite
patience cannot entirely restore. The reconstructed image will
always be a bit
out of focus.
We must learn to love the hybrids we will become.

Some mothers, of course, survive the passage, me beside them,
caught between home and somewhere else.
We wade in the waters of rivers as they thaw, or fly up, the
stories persist.
But some of us don't make it before the rivers freeze, and
those who remain,
we bring our dead with us, not leaving them behind,
that's a lie still making the rounds.
We set up camp on the river banks, our skin going ashy in
the cold.
We wait for spring.
After the thaw, the rivers run, and so do we.
Spreading out, the mothers cover the map,
not knowing into which port their daughters will disappear,
covering their nakedness with alluvial sand,
falling between my fingers like silk.

A tiny hand on my ear, searching for sound of a heart,
beating or breaking. The small pink tongue,
searching for food, finds only the salt that dried on my skin
in the quickness of the sun's heat.
My arms' reluctant cradle,
my heart's reluctant love,
the treachery is double-edged and life in between will
become the recognized
mark.

If they told you I didn't jump, they told you lies, but
understandable,
their knowledge is empty. As far as they can see, I stand on
the block before
them.
But beware of holographic Hottentots, consequences of the
bills of
sale, dividends to be paid off later,
at some point in the future
on which I keep my eyes firmly fixed.
The next gentleman who opens my mouth will reap the benefit
of all that stringing,
the cowry shells in a line, by the mouthful,
the tiny teeth vicious and sharp
but patient as bullets
spit out and sure of their aim,
particularly at pointblank range.
The choppers are ready, girl. Show him.

II.

Mitotic memory
Luggage: the inside pockets smell like home, between here
and someplace
else.
This point of skin
Lingual inscription   labial tran/scription
Mother tongue, lapping

Re-membering
  -inventing
This is not about lacking or making do, this is an original
reclamation;
we step through each other to the other side.
They say we do not exist
but then we come like thunder, whispering each other's names.
We become constructed reality,
their invented nightmare,
each other's remembered dreams.
We vanish like smoke, disappear like air, embracing their
lungs—breathe us
in or die.

Cellular luggage: I carry my own memory.
We are botanical sports.
The street outside is quiet. The juniper bushes beneath the
bedroom window
shiver, stroking the house's wooden skin.

Our imaginary lust fills the corners, our unreal voices escape,
leaving tongues hungry for what exists only in narcissistic
evidence. Will we self-destruct or come, arriving on the continent
of each other's lost horizons, found only by consulting out-
dated maps? But the geography remains unchanged, we
recognize the landmarks, have known them since knowledge
was invented.

We choose to traverse the face of non-existent mountains,
calculating distances from one side of imaginary canyons to
the other, algebraic bridges swaying in the interval.

The echo of you, coming, of me, coming,

again, like smoke, entwined with necessary elements, we
breathe it in, as if we were real and the confusion we create is
what they want to kill. Life's necessary food betrays them.

The edge has defined my skin—the ocean's shore, days lost
behind, I meet the intersection and sob with wonder and in

grief: the water wants me back. We float in dimensionless space. The cells rearrange themselves in order to comprehend that this now is real, these smells and sounds described by the shape of wooden slats, the shadows of ghostmen, blocking out the light. The transformation remains incomplete. We continue to find tendrils of Wild Yam between our teeth, encircling our necks. The Middle Passage is defined: the journey has not yet arrived.

It is the discovery that shame ceases to exist that is the power of my passion and desire. I come to you because your gaze insists on recognizing what I want. I become transparent, a self-reflecting mirror illustrating smoke. Pleasure's deepest hold lies in understanding we can only cup each other in simple solitude. We ask the impossible and are tender in our forgiving the failure to provide it perfectly; even amidst the most exquisite terror, rising from the nexus of pleasure and pain.

The original injuries cannot be retracted. But we kiss the wounds anyway and find comfort in the defiance—our lips were not meant to meet again. If we cannot heal the original pain, we honour it and risk our lives in order to do so. And we have no way of knowing if this is total truth. Our only evidence is the ferocity with which our non-existence is hunted down, roped and subdued, forced to don the captives' uniform. But we leak away beneath our clothes, breathe life into our holographic selves, and slip away,
again like smoke,
especially like smoke,
when we are burned or branded, to distinguish the owners of our various flesh.

We are contradictions with deadly intent, only this is not about intent. Surfacing on the binary plane, we are bored with references to either/or. And yet, like our holographic understudies, stand-ins,
body-doubles,
we appear, some of us, to embody, from uninformed or intuitive mimicry,

the phallic or the sheath
butch or femme.

Our desire occurs off-stage, the main event is our cover. Our
desire cannot be contained in scripted form. The balcony
scene goes on, fueled by a combination of sure-footedness
and stumbling—

Will I leap over, will you climb up?

We are inventing as we go along, pulling lines from certain
knowledge, grasping at the smoking tendrils that hover in the
vast space between balcony and ground. Gauge the distance,
the calculus' lifeline, our feet scramble for purchase only after
the receipts are destroyed: They have no proof of ownership.

We cannot escape duality, doomed to model ourselves in
pitiful imitation of the natural order of things

fingers slipped inside the glove

We lose what little sympathy they might offer,
evoke cool condescension because we are unaware of the
pathetic picture we present—they can't even give tickets away.

But what if none of it is true, imitation being the sincerest
form of flattery? But this is no imitation, the point is. Where
do you get off? At the niche hollowed out under your arm,
skin soft, laced, tendrilled with curls of hair.
Where do you get off?
At the small of your back, where it waits for my mouth.

Where do you get off?
Any place I can   (get to)
Every place you'll let me.

What if the lesbian body, the conceptual and literal lesbian
desire invents itself, innocent of reference, responsible for
its own continuum, enraptured with the invention of

self-contained desire, perpetuated by the gaze that recognizes
the original wound, the original lust and knows she will find
home in the same location each time she moves?

Tired of negotiating life along the continuum, submit to binary
seduction, the lure of the sirens' songs, sure and easy, warbling
from their opposite rocks, their clearly demarcated zones,
giving not a single thought to the country in between—
spectrum unconscious, there are no notes to compose these
spaces' anthems. Algebraic bridges continue to sway, coming
and going beneath our feet.

Dichotomous.

The middle ground, bereft of desire, instructions not to fall
prey to sexual objectification, throw out desire with oppression. WARNING: DON'T DRINK THE BABY'S BATH WATER!
Fearful of venturing too near the edge, either end, we stand
defiantly in the middle, guard boxes on either side of the
border, an ultimately mute statement that they've won,
again—we forget who we are and why. Our wanting drains
away, leaching. If you hurry, however, you might catch a last
glimpse of the tainted artifacts—a tie draped easily across the
bodice of a silky black slip, a dildo rammed into the throat of
a high-heeled shoe. We use the tools available. The point is.

Locus of desire,
excised, a metaphorised female circumcision and infibulation,
if you will, the conclusion a convenient repression, trading in
numbed sexuality, she then kills pieces of herself, a part of
the very humanity she seeks to reclaim. We ultimately do their
dirty work for them, implicit acceptance that what the
ghostmen perceive spins the truth like spiders' webs.
The beholder's eye.

The historical body, site of occupation and colony,
contours of the landscape defined by those who print the maps.

Wearing the mask, technique for survival,
a stand-in,

body double for psychic dislocation. The new job description is filed under
desire, reclamation of.

Collect the pieces of your divided self, binary calculations long since rendered irrelevant.

Until we remember, the ink continues to fade, bills of sale return to tree
pulp, dust,
shadow marks upon the paper, tracks of ghostmen blocking light, leaving
their marks like dust from the bodies of long-dead moths.

III.

Unchaste productions, but acceptable commodities,
stock the shelves of the slave market.
No lace-trimmed illusions of intrinsic worth.
Elephant chorus   singing hounds trudging
Maps of amber locations
monkeys behind curtains
roasting sweet potatoes as a way to stave off hunger.
There will be no Earl Grey tea today due to a strike in the kitchen. The wenches are calling for a sit-down and will use their sharp little teeth to subdue anyone who doesn't honour the picket line.

Extract the juice of Bitter Cassava, enough to kill the product and preserve the producer.

Zulu Love Letters: A Found Poem:

Green: I have become thin like the sweet cane in a damp field and green as the first shoots of trees because of my love for you.

Red: My heart bleeds and is full of love.

Black: I have turned pitch black as rafters of the hut because I miss you so.

Blue: If I were a dove I would fly to your home and pick food at your door.

There were many nights when she would come to my hut in my family's compound. After I cooked for her, she would sit on a stool, watching me from the shadows as I slowly painted my body, circles and lines drawn with the salty water into which I rhythmically dipped my fingers. When it dried, she licked away the salty designs; my skin, cooling in the night air, grew hot under her tongue. Now, she will return from the hunting season and
find
me
gone.

The look, the gaze, the lesbian gaze.
I am the femme, I am perhaps the purdahed woman, cloaked in robes, the cloth of denial, the place between home and someplace else.
My body, no part, visible: What you see is not what you get. What you don't see, in the absence of ownership's documents, the male gaze, the phallocentric obsession of who belongs to whom and we all belong to them, even those of us they refuse to claim, our skin wrong, our thighs wrong, our attitudes wrong, we cannot be allowed to free float, and we cannot belong to each other. Without patriarchal imprimatur, we are relegated to the status of whores. Have we forgotten, or is it that we refuse to remember that this naming should engender shame?

Open your mouth, girl. Let the gentleman see your choppers. On the streets, they are profligate with the coin of the realm—
Hey Mama!
Chica, chica!
Umm-umm,
I-want-summa-that-let-me-go-home-with-you-sweetmeat.

But the competition is without contest; the butches win
hands down,
hands
up
our
skirts,
hands on,
hands on our asses. You look at us and think all we need is a
good ... what?
But hey, look here,
sorry,
It's been done, boys, it's been done. And tonight, she'll do
me again. I'll know it when I feel it.

It is what I give her: My lesbian body.
Knowledge is compelling, power fully recognized,
that we go wet and limp,
full and eager, the erotic evoked in each other's eyes, the
mirror talking back, indifferent to Freudian interrogations,
(though Lacanian embraces are not precisely full-hearted)
or appropriating them for our own use.

Freud's daughter was still her father's child.

"Altruistic surrender." Didn't Anna know there is no such thing?
The pleasure embedded in the sacrifice. Surrender need not
be visible. Sometimes, it can only be detected in the psychic
shiver that races along my spine. Or in the clench my belly
muscles make, lazily heading in the pussy's direction.
She waits,
tail swishing
this way and that,
back and forth,
circling the perimeters,
waiting,
waiting,
waiting perhaps, to be lifted up by the scruff of her neck,
waiting,
waiting,
to be petted.

In my camouflage, from behind the veil, cloaked in denial,
the women I love,
the women I track from behind the veil of my passing, these
butch women
cannot escape. They may run but they cannot hide. But I can
look at
whatever I choose,
my gaze freely lingers, darts and sweeps the streets,
looking, looking for the hands down women.
In my camouflage, I am protected from the consequences of
my searches. I
look at the butch beauties,
from beneath lowered lids or full force, and if I choose, my
gaze grows
secret, I lock on and locate without her knowledge. Cloaked in
the uniform
that passes for reality,
I am free
to consume
what feeds my hunger, embrace the consequences only if I
allow them.
The robes in which I shelter, the veil from behind which I
look at her,
tailored from bolts of old cloth and assumptions of fixed
points, I wonder if
this is a joke. What is real? This body I inhabit, this lesbian
body, this
compelling want,
heating, igniting me from the inside—this is what I must have,
what I choose,
what I set my sights on, Kristevian declarations aside—surely
this is a joke,
this erasing of desire.
The sex men trumpet from their sidewalk perches, occurs as
easy, predictable events.
Oh yes, once, I did invite them in, and during that
time, I learned I was a
gracious but less than passionate hostess: Just because it fits,
doesn't mean

it needs to be there.
And I marvel: Julia, Julia,
I can't help but wonder,
is this a joke?

Still, my protection is ambivalent.
I can look, I can gaze.
But I am cloaked in a uniform announcing spurious ownership,
I can only safely desire her
because I am a woman passing.
I approximate,
I successfully imitate
the profile
of a woman
presumed to
want
men.
To want a woman, and to have her, does not figure into the
equation. No
one suspects, no one even thinks to think that such a thing is
possible.

Or it is constructed as a joke.
I am protected, though erased,
my desire refused entry.
And this is where they make critical errors: They think it is
the butch
against whom they must guard,
but then that's to be expected.
But we know,
here,
beneath our clothes,
we know who will destroy their peace of mind.
We undermine their presumptions of safety,
we appear to be just like them.
We appear,
on the streets,
in the sheets,
contiguous with the silhouette of a real woman.

And yet, we pay an extravagant price for this masquerade. We can miss each
other as we pass the men gazing from their sidewalk perches.
I recognize her
gait, the angle of her jaw, the way she holds the object of her gaze in
steady, piercing thrall. But how will she know me, confused in form with the
real women I move among?
I lose my signs:
How will she find me unless I announce my presence?
But once I've brought her to me, the phallic chatter dropping off into a dull hum.

Locus of desire,
excised, a metaphorised female circumcision and infibulation, if you will,
the conclusion a convenient repression, trading in numbed sexuality. She
then kills pieces of herself, a part of the very humanity she seeks to
reclaim. Implicit acceptance that what the ghostmen perceive spins the truth
like spiders' webs.   The beholder's eye.

But who is real? I do not toss my hair; it does not blow in the wind. The face
in the mirror of the sand's stunning glitter, is not delicately drawn.
Playing in chambers where the beating of hearts,
or the echo of lost voices trapped
behind the teeth of cowry shells is mistaken for music.

IV.

Swimming in a variety of oceans,
boneless, one-cell deep, my skin like the jellyfish, floating and drifting in

the tanks
of the Monterey Bay Aquarium.
Crowds jostle past these gelatinous captives,
elbows and knees cutting paths,
eager to see
these creatures without bones.
Boneless am I in the days of lusting love,
my legs like tendrils drifting
around your body,
pulling you close.
How close
can we come to obliterating the bone-stiff, engrammatic traces
of memories we'd rather forget but cannot remember how?
The sun's heat penetrates, warms the coldest spot on the
planet, the place
where ice freezes and frost is the warmest form of life you'll find.
Even here, the sun's heat seeps, but cannot bring a thermal,
not even
fractions,
to the place where memory hides.

In the wild, raging rivers that run through the back lot of the
movie set that is my life, I swallow pride in lieu of the food I
crave but would die not to need. It mingles in bowls of sand,
filling my mouth with its gritty wisdom. And I ache for the
water to wash the wounds left when they stole me away from
the pot of mush I was stirring. The rift is so deep, I cannot
see the bottom.

Outside my window, a sparrow, possessed with an unnatural
talent for irony, is singing like a mocking bird; it never stops
singing. And the fear is thick in my throat, and the welling up
of tears isn't enough to offer release. I want to scream to the
heavens like the *castrati*, their involuntary trade— voices like
angels in exchange for the luggage in which they carried
slumbering replications. In whose ear does my song sing
sweeter for the surgery performed? The altering of the cowry
shells' echoes, stitched imitations.

Where are my angels, saints, unreal images to whom I can
pray in times of genocidal warfare? Here, in the ancestors'
world, angels and saints are not ethereal. They do not drift,
boneless like jellyfish. Here, they are of a much sturdier stock.
Appearing in rivers and yam fields, they complain about the
heat, demanding cold drinks of water, which you are ordered
to fetch, from no matter how far. I admire their pragmatism,
their scratchiness. I also find no comfort there.

I long for the gentleness of cherubim, their bodies round and
chubby with innocence, their wings fanning the air like eager
children. It is not their blond curls I care about, or their pink
skin, or the inevitable blue of their eyes. It is the innocence
and softness I want, the wide-eyed, wise gaze they cast on all
they behold, from the ceilings of trendy restaurants, from the
corner of rooms. It is the sound of their name, angels.

I cannot conjure them in colours other than those on the
screen of my eyelids, permanently etched. There is a heart-
deep pain. I cannot associate my mirror image with comfort
and safe harbor, though I know the descendants of the
ghostmen found much comfort in the circle of arms the
colour of mine, or darker, or lighter, that held them close,
in boneless embraces, drifting between home and someplace
else, the route
crossing terrains of survival,
interrupted by unexpected signs of love.

V.

the race of sex   *the sex of race*
theory versus experience   *theory versus practice*

Phillis Wheatley, if alive today, would she be a revered member of the academy, staunch defender of the canon,
with her Greek and Latin, her gentlewoman's sensibilities?
Whose colours would she wear in the sex wars?

The historical body, site of occupation and colony,
contours of the landscape defined by those who print the maps.
But we still retain our toponymic secrets.

My fingers clamber across your skin, encounter the features,
recognize the climate, roam the expanses your body offers up
to me.
With sacred patience, I assemble my own relief map,
carefully naming each region.
We cross the boundaries freely, passports unchecked,
though terror
sometimes
captures our breath.

Wearing the mask, technique for survival,
embrace psychic dislocation.
Collect the pieces, bind up your divided self,
discover new computations,
remove the privileging of binary calculations. They are no
longer relevant.
Until we remember, the ink continues to fade, bills of sale
return to tree
pulp, dust,
shadow marks upon the paper,
tracks of ghostmen blocking light, leaving their marks like
trails constructed
from the bodies of long-dead moths.
File the new job description under desire, reclamation of.

Bones and Shadow

DEVIL THINGS
Ronald Gonzalez

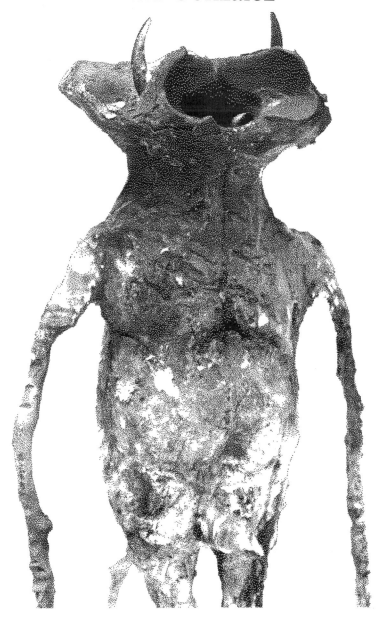

Nobody believes in the Devil,
nobody believes
in the Devil. Everybody thinks
the Devil
as bein'
with horns
and a tail and
that's the way
he looks
to people.
In fact,
when I was little
I used to think of
the Devil
with horns and
tails
and I never
really – really
knew
the Devil was
like a
power

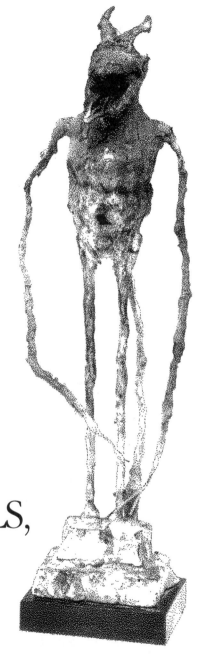

And we knew
the Devil was somethin',
but we didn't know what.
We would even have
nightmares thinkin'
the DEVIL'S
gonna get us,
ya know.
That's the way the kids
see it and even on
Halloween everybody
"dresses up" as DEVILS errr,
errr -- SKELETONS -- errr
whatever -- anything
that scares everybody
they think that
"Well, I'll be a DEVIL,"
ya know, but
THERE IS MANY DEVILS,
the Devil has a lot to do
with different evil.

And Satan isn't really the Devil.
He has many people workin' for him
and that's what you call
DEVILS,
ya know, but Satan has like a whole,
ahhuummm, like an
ARMY

And there's many Devils around,
and they're not dressed in uh, uh red outfits
with ah, ah tails.
The Devils are real.
They are spiritual beings; they never die.

THEY WILL NEVER DIE.

You can only cast them away --
you can pray them away sometimes.

Everybody has certain

fear,

Everybody's fears are different.
My fear is I used to have many animals.
I had my cats:
I loved my cats.
And I remember I loved my animals
and every place I went
I would see

dead cats on the highway

and the next day sometimes I would drive by
and there wasn't a dead cat at all.
There was just like

a cloth in the road.

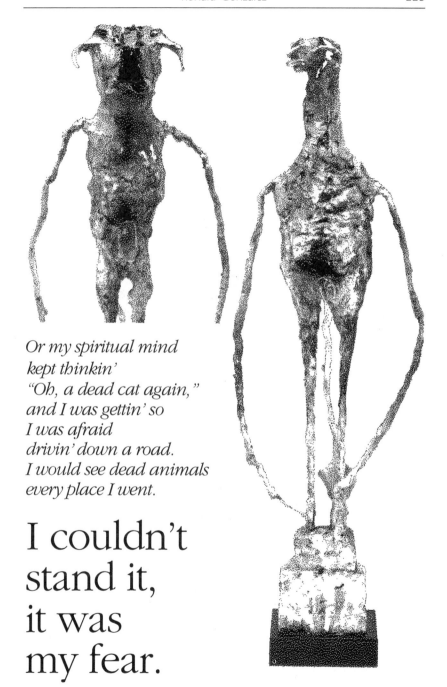

*Or my spiritual mind
kept thinkin'
"Oh, a dead cat again,"
and I was gettin' so
I was afraid
drivin' down a road.
I would see dead animals
every place I went.*

I couldn't
stand it,
it was
my fear.

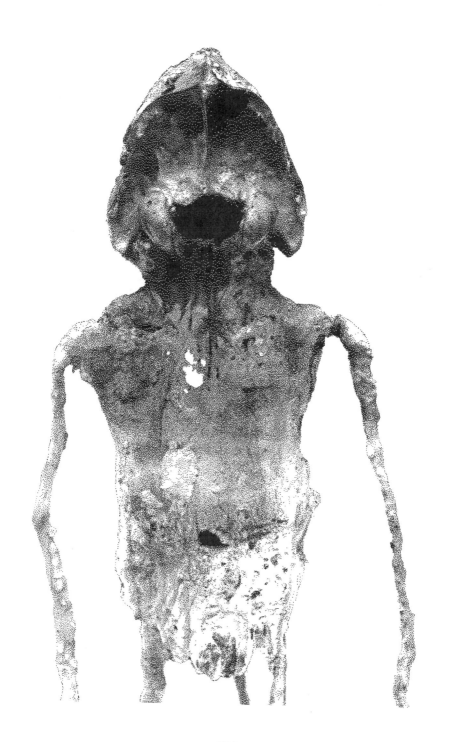

And then one day, one night I was watchin'
a religious program
and were praisin' God, it was sooo wonderful.
I comes home
and my favorite cat was out in the road annn,

the Devil
got even with me.

And not only that--

my cat wasn't dead.

I had to pick the cat up, bring her in the house.
And I prayed for God to take her immediately.
I put my hand on that cat
and she fell asleep right away.

But that cat was killed --

that Devil
killed that cat,

and everything,
because he know how much I loved her.

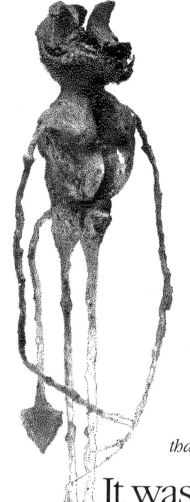

I could not understand

why God allowed that to happen.

You know that was my fear, that's what I had, that's what the Devil did with me.

It was a Devil thing.

(Excepted from interviews on the devil with the sculptor's mother, Lilia Gonzalez. Binghamton, NY. February 6, 1996.)

Catching the Devil

Into the idle hands of one
who can summon up a strange body
accustomed to memory and transformation
Take shape
as in the original fall of great despair
Animal
descending into oblivion
petrified tears no spirit will touch
Doomed figure
pitted against God and the human race
come close to the surface
of our deepest body
magic   punishment
loss of identity   emptiness
fear
We wanted wings
but were given bones and shadow

RG '96

MARTÍN ESPADA

The Hidalgo's Hat and a Hawk's Bell of Gold

Columbus hallucinated gold
wherever sunlight darted
from rock to water, spelled the word
slowly in his logbook
so that the Lord might see
and blow his ship
into a storm of gleaming dust.
When God would not puff his cheeks
for trade winds of gold, the Admiral flourished
a decree on parchment: a hawk's bell
full of gold from every Indio
where the rivers gilded the soil
of Española, 1495.

The Indios could only load the bells
with mirrored sunlight. For bells
without gold, the hands were pressed together
as if in prayer, gripped on the block,
then the knobs of wrists were splintered
by a bright and heavy sword.
Their stumps became torches
seething flames of blood,
the vowels of their language
lamentations flattening the tongue.

While the Admiral slept
in the exhaustion of dysentery,
or amused the Queen
with his zoo of shackled caciques,
the town he named Isabela
dissolved into the stones
like a rumor of gold, deserted swampground.
There is a spirit legend:
that the moans of men in rusting helmets
would radiate from the vine-matted walls,
starved with a mouthful of bark
or mad with a brain soaking in syphilis,
or digging an arrowhead from the eye
fired by an Indio with two hands.

Someone saw the hidalgos there, ghosts of noblemen
bowing in a row, a swirl of velvet cloaks.
As each swept off his feathered hat
in greeting, his head unscrewed
from the hollow between caped shoulders,
swinging in the hat
like a cannonball in a sack.

The Skull beneath the Skin of the Mango

—El Salvador, 1992

The woman spoke
with the tranquillity of shock:
the Army massacre was here.
But there were no peasant corpses,
no white crosses; even the houses
gone. Cameras chattered,
notebooks filled with rows of words.
Some muttered that slaughter
is only superstition
in a land of new treaties and ballot boxes.

Everyone gathered mangoes
before leaving. An American reporter,
arms crowded with fruit, could not see
what he kicked jutting from the ground.
He glanced down and found his sneaker
pressing against the forehead
of a human skull, yellow
like the flesh of a mango.

He wondered how many skulls
are crated with the mangoes
for sale at market, how many
grow yellow flesh and green skin
in the wooden boxes exported
to the States. This would explain,
he said to me,
why so many bodies
are found without heads
in El Salvador.

When Songs Become Water

—for *Diario Latino*, El Salvador, 1991

Where dubbed commercials
sell the tobacco and alcohol
of a far winter metropolis,
where the lungs of night
cough artillery shots
into the ears of sleep,
where strikers with howls
stiff on their faces
and warnings pinned to their shirts
are harvested from garbage heaps,
where olive uniforms keep watch
over the plaza
from a nest of rifle eyes and sandbags,
where the government party
campaigns chanting through loudspeakers
that this country
will be the common grave of the reds,
there the newsprint of mutiny
is as medicine
on the fingertips,
and the beat of the press printing mutiny
is like the pounding of tortillas in the hands.

When the beat of the press
is like the pounding of tortillas,
and the newsprint is medicine
on the fingertips,
come the men with faces
wiped away by the hood,
who smother the mouth of witness night,
shaking the gasoline can across the floor,
then scattering in a dark orange eruption
of windows,
leaving the paper to wrinkle gray in the heat.

Cuando los cantos se vuelven agua
—*Para Diario Latino,* El Salvador, 1991

Donde los anuncios doblados
venden el tabaco y el alcohol
de una metrópoli invernal lejana,
donde los pulmones de la noche
tosen tiros de artillería
en los oídos del sueño
donde huelguistas con aúllos
tiesos en sus caras
y amenazas prendidas a sus camisas
son cosechados de los basureros,
donde uniformes verde olivo
vigilan la plaza
desde un nido de ojos-fusil y sacos de arena,
donde el partido del gobierno
hace campaña coreando por altavoces
que este país
será la tumba de los rojos,
allí la tinta de imprenta amotinada
es como medicina
sobre las yemas de los dedos,
y el compás de la imprenta imprimiendo motín
es como el torteo de la masa entre las manos.

Cuando el compás de la imprenta
es como el torteo de la masa,
y la tinta de imprenta es medicina
sobre las yemas de los dedos,
vienen los hombres con caras
borradas por la capucha,
que ahogan la boca de la noche testigo,
sacudiendo la lata de gasolina por el piso,
luego esparciendose en una anaranjada erupción oscura
de ventanas,
dejando el papel para arrugarse gris en el calor.

Where the faces wiped away by the hood
are known by the breath of gasoline
on their clothes,
and paper wrinkles gray as the skin
of incarcerated talkers,
another Army helicopter plunges from the sky
with blades burning
like the wings of a gargoyle,
the tortilla and medicine words
are smuggled in shawls,
the newspapers are hoarded
like bundles of letters from the missing,
the poems become songs
and the songs become water
streaming through the arteries
of the earth, where others at the well
will cool the sweat in their hair
and begin to think.

Donde las caras borradas por la capucha
se conocen por el aliento de gasolina
en su ropa,
y el papel se arruga tan gris como la piel
de los habladores encarcelados,
otro helicóptero del ejército se desploma del cielo
con hélices quemándose
como las alas de una gárgola,
las palabras de tortilla y medicina
son contrabandeadas en rebozos,
los periódicos son acaparados
como bultos de cartas de los desaparecidos,
los poemas se vuelven cantos
y los cantos se vuelven agua
fluyendo por las arterias
de la tierra, donde otros alrededor del pozo
refrescarán el sudor de su pelo
y se pondrán a pensar.

—Translation: Camilo Pérez-Bustillo and the author

In the Life

Mother, do you know
I roam alone at night?
I wear colognes,
tight pants, and
chains of gold,
as I search
for men willing
to come back
to candlelight.

I'm not scared of these men
though some are killers
of sons like me. I learned
there is no tender mercy
for men of color,
for sons who love men
like me.

Do not feel shame for how I live.
I chose this tribe
of warriors and outlaws.
Do not feel you failed
some test of motherhood.
My life has borne fruit

no woman could have given me
anyway.

In one of these thick-lipped,
wet, black nights
while I'm out walking,
I find freedom in this village.
If I can take it with my tribe
I'll bring you here.
And you will never notice
the absence of rice
and bridesmaids.

Family Jewels

For Washington, D.C.

I live in a town
where pretense and bone structure
prevail as credentials
of status and beauty—
a town bewitched
by mirrors, horoscopes,
and corruption.

I intrude on this nightmare,
arm outstretched from curbside.
I'm not pointing to Zimbabwe.
I want a cab
to take me to Southeast
so I can visit my mother.
I am not ashamed to cross
the bridge that takes me there.

No matter where I live
or what I wear
the cabs speed by.
Or they suddenly brake
a few feet away
spewing fumes in my face
to serve a fair-skinned fare.

I live in a town
where everyone is afraid
of the dark.
I stand my ground unarmed
facing a mounting disrespect,
a diminishing patience,
a need for defense.

In passing headlights
I appear to be a criminal.

I'm a weird-looking
muthafucka.
Shaggy green hair sprouts all over me.
My shoulders hunch and bulge. I growl
as blood drips from my glinting fangs.

My mother's flowers are wilting
while I wait.
Our dinner
is cold by now.

I live in a town
where pretense and structure
are devices of cruelty—
a town bewitched
by mirrors, horoscopes,
and blood.

Pressing Flats

You wanna sleep on my chest?
You wanna listen to my heart beat
all through the night?
It's the only jazz station
with a twenty-four-hour signal,
if you wanna listen.

If you answer yes
I expect you to be able
to sleep in a pit of cobras.
You should be willing
to destroy your enemy
if it comes to that.
If you have a weapon.
If you know how to use your hands.

You should be able to distinguish
oppression from pleasure.
Some pleasure is oppression
but then, that isn't pleasure, is it?
Some drugs induce pleasure
but isn't that oppression?

If you're immobilized you're oppressed.
If you're killing yourself you're oppressed.
If you don't know who you are
you're pressed.

❦

A prayer candle won't always solve the confusion.
The go-go won't always take the mind off things.
Our lives don't get better with coke
they just—get away from us.

There doesn't have to be a bomb
if we make up our minds

243

we don't want to die that way.
We're told what's right from left.
We're told there is good and evil,
laws and punishment,
but no one speaks of the good in evil
or the evil in good.

You wanna sleep on my chest?
You wanna listen to my heart beat
all through the night?
It's the only jazz station
with a twenty-four-hour signal
if you wanna listen.
If you know what I mean.

NKIRU NZEGWU

may the bullet not find me:
Writing Memories, Writing Identity

This writing is about remembrances, about the elliptical cycle of remembering, and of gathering together experiences of former lives. The weaving process of remembering unravels and re-fashions an identity while the act of remembering re-members the splits and tears in the fabric of consciousness. Remembering unravels the thread of memory from one patch of the identity fabric and reuses it in a different area to form new patterns and designs in the new location. Out of old fabrics, new patterns and identities are created. I remember myself remembering; I re-member my restored self each time. The process of remembering engages earlier conflicts and dilemmas, resolves them, or heals the person by skillfully hiding traumatic experiences away until one is strong enough to confront them. In the interim, rough and grainy patches of patterns on immaturely woven iden-tity-cloth are smoothed out. This time, the refashioning of my identity involved visiting grainy patches of war experiences I had hidden away. It became a process for fusing together two differ-ent personality traits—the creative and the critical (the Uwechia and the Nzegwu)—which the binary framework of modernity underpinning the structures of academia had rent apart into two opposing voices. This memory-writing reconciles and repairs the split as a path towards self-recovery and understanding what it means to "know thyself."

I

Did you hear that Chris Okigbo is dead? You know, the poet?

Eewoo! Him too! Everyone is gone. Where did he die?

At Opi Junction. They said it was the last stand!

What happened?

Actually nobody saw him die, but they said he faced it boldly. They said he wouldn't move from the machine gun even when everyone was "falling back."

BBC! How do you know?

Oh you don't believe me!

I didn't say that, broadcaster. I just asked how you know.

Well I was there. I was there when Ifeajuna was telling my cousins. You know, he visits them whenever he is passing through. He said, he was told that Chris wouldn't move. Hm, Chris, *na mmuo ibe ya* (in his spirit identity), defiantly clung on to his machine gun and refused to leave. Can you imagine that, foolhardedly taunting death like that?

He's always been crazy!

He has to be mad!

Stark raving mad!

Yes mad!

Pity he's dead, though. I could have checked him out. There's something fascinating about anyone who would do that.

You mean, dumb!

I remember.
I remember those days
those dark fearful days
when the morrow seemed like yesterday
and the past was the child to come.
  Silence reigned supreme
  cautious silence
  deceptive silence
  innocently clad
  with arrows of death.
A cornered beast's
wary silence,

trapped by the wall
it cannot escape,
steely mustering reserves of strength
for the last fierce struggle
in a dice-cast war.
 Unpalatable silence
 deadly still,
 heavy as *otangele*[1]
 disrupting the normal flow of blood.
 Ominously still
 chillingly calm
 muscles taut in readiness
 for the final spring.

 —"Eye of a Storm," Uwechia, 11/74

Months earlier . . .

Report had reached my cousins of the death of their family friend at Opi junction. The bearer of the news Major Emma Ifeajuna had spoken of the frantic attempts to dissuade Okigbo from his course of action. They had tried to talk him out of the senselessness of his stand. "There are still many battles to fight in the future," they pleaded. "We need all the men we can find."

 Nkiti kpom kpom (silence knock knock)
 Sealed lips
 deadened ears
 stone walls of
 silence.
 Asi na onwu kolu igbu nwa nkita
 oda' anuzi isisi nsi.
 (It is said that when death is about to kill the dog,
 it stops it from smelling the appetizing aroma of shit.)

"Bush meat"!
What's that?
That's why he didn't mind dying in Nsukka. "Bush meat."
They say he loved "bush meat."
Well, he's become one now.

Oh you don't get it. Listen, Nsukka male students and dons have this ritual. Whenever they get tired of their books, they head out into the villages to reconnect with reality, as they say. They really get down on all fours. They look for the uninhibited village-maidens whom they bring back to Nsukka for trysts. There was this day when this don was really going, flying high, thinking he was scoring and giving this girl the time of her life. After a few seconds in the second round, the girl said to him barely concealing her irritation: "Place your feet on the wall; place them on the wall and push; the drum that Chineke (God) created never breaks."

I remember those nights
those dark fearful nights
when the dreaming began
the dream of shadows
of broken limbs
and broken lives
when the morrow moved to yesteryears
and the past was the child to come.

Life became spirit as the living passed through the doorway into spirit realm. Okigbo lives in spirit. His passage came from disobeying orders. Stubborn child. He cradled his machine gun and vowed to die to see mother Idoto. The last words they heard him shout over the exploding shells and crackling gunfire as they hastily beat a retreat were: "Upon this machine gun I'll stay. I won't move away from it." Yes, the lone sentinel stood steadfast. But he died at his post.

In timeless eternity,
they lay
in slumberlike sleep,
stiffened by
the contact-shock from
the shadow of life
relentlessly sweeping across thresholds
relieving burdened souls
burdening recalcitrant souls.

—"The Lull," Uwechia, 7/3/73

gom . . . gom . . . gom

Before you mother Idoto
naked I stand
before your watery gate
a prodigal . . .

—"Labyrinths," Okigbo

At heavensgate stood I
in prayer
willing the winds
to carry forth my message
to realms unknown
where mortals thread not
I wait in hope . . .

—"Heritage Transferred," Uwechia

The heroism of the last stand haunted my imagination. It burned like bush fire; wildly it burned. I was on fire. I became fire. I am fire. How is death experienced? What happens when one "sees" death? How do you face it? How do you enter into death? How do you do it fearlessly?

No one will return to tell, the cavernous echo replied. "Knowledge is in experiencing."

I visualized the front: exploding mortars, whizzing bullets, crawling bodies, thumps of urgently retreating boots, bloodied bodies, crashing bodies, thuds of falling bodies, thrashing bodies, frantic orders, shouts, urgent orders, more shouts, and a lone watchman calmly guarding the passage way intones:

Upon this machine gun here I'll stay
I won't move away from it
as coming danger threatens me
I'm here to save my motherland.
Over my dead body
will the enemy enter my fatherland
upon this machine gun here I'll die
no matter what type of death.

—"The Last Stand," Uwechia, 5/68

I wondered what I would have done in similar circumstances. Would I have stayed on? Why should I have stayed on? I really wanted to believe I would. But why? To show I can repel all earthly lures. So what? So that the past may more swiftly be born and the future recede to yesterday!

The more I tried to believe, the more my imagination took wind and flew. Lost in the power of inner conviction, I journeyed into the spirit and wrote . . . and wrote . . . and wrote . . . :

> While blood and mangled bodies lie
> we leap and twirl our supple frame,
> and the long weary trail
> in the never-ending race
> hears the stout-hearted voice
> dwell on morale-lifting feats.
>
> Bulging bellies on skeletal frames
> large hungry eyes
> with empty plates of food.
> A table creaks under heavy load
> of rarest delicacies for the chosen few.
>
> Stolen glances, loving smiles
> confetti like sprayed fivers[2] fall
> herald the arrival of the bird of prey.
> Flying wigs, floating veils
> one abandoned bridal shoe . . .
> but many abandoned human lives.
>
> Laughter and smiles at the bundle of life
> a joy and happiness to dry the tears.
> In dim glow of light
> we crouch around the box
> and listened intently to the voice of fate.

　—"War Panorama," Uwechia, 5/72

　　　　　　　　　　　　. . . exhausted I slept.

In my dream
I prayed,

may the bullet not find me.
O Lord
Uray, Ojedi, Otumoye
Forces of Appeal
may the shrapnel not find me.
Those were dark
fearful dreams
those despondent dreams
where tunnels seemed endless
and the morrow was still yesterday.
May the bullet not find me
I prayed
with kolanut in hand
and nzu smeared around the eyes
I prayed:
Olisaebuluwa
The known unknowable
Force of Final Arbitration
I salute you
Obinamili[3]
Olinri[4]
Ani Onicha[5]
Ojedi[6]
Uray ukwu[7]
I greet you
The day that is Eke
the day that is Oye
the day that is Afo
the day that is Nkwo[8]
I greet you.
I pray
that if evil is before
I shall be behind
that if it is behind
I will be in front
that if it is in front
and behind

and the two sides
I shall catapult out of danger
for my prayer is to hear
not to experience.
I shall hear
not experience
may the bullet not find me
I dreamily prayed
may the bullet not find me
I prayed.

War!!! Have you ever seen war? Do you know what it is?
Fiam!
a streak of lightening
the growl of thunder
a piercing scream
then a heart wrenching wail
Tears . . .
they fail to come
they hamper and hinder the nimble in flight
the fall of tears at the death of one
is a precious drop on a desert floor.
Fear!
a ghastly silence pervades the town
human-leaves[9] as in a violent storm
bloody scene, mangled bodies
in mute acceptance of oppressive fate.

—*"Air Raid," Uwechia, 3/2/73*

I was in form three (grade nine) when the Biafran war started in 1967. My secondary school was in Owerri, sixty-seven miles from my home in Onitsha. I was in boarding school, Owerri Girls' Secondary School. They called us "Ogimgbo," sometimes "Ogisco." We sometimes called ourselves that, too. We called them "Hogosco," not the Holy Ghost College mouthful the unimaginative Catholic priests had dreamt up. Hogosco was our brother school. Its students were our brothers. You know how it is: brothers, sisters, one large happy fraternizing

family. But a lot more went on than was brotherly or sisterly. A lot of what happened resembled the stolen sensuous glances, fugitive touches, bodily rubs that we observed occuring between the reverend sisters and the reverend fathers in the holy sacristy.
Alu (abomination)!
Nso (sinfulness)!
We were holy!

The udala falls into sacred ground
who will shrine desecrate
to pick the fruit?
The fish vanishes from the river main
who will Nkisi defy
to subdue hunger?
  Before our earthly church
  and our watery altar
  we faithfully stood in prayer.
  With pertinent fingers
  libations were poured,
  to remove adversities
  offerings were burnt,
  my ancestors' lives.
"Heresy! Heathens!"
croaked the white garbed ravens
feverishly clutching
their black bound book;
while
desperately struggling to retain
the handful of converts
steeped in tradition
they cannot cast off.
  Beneath my feet, a solid rock
  within my life, my faith
  but rootless as the wind
  that sweeps the earth bare
  from *ilo,* the village square
  your beliefs leave hollow

one, who without thought follows
your creed.

—"My Ancestors," Uwechia, 3/11/73

The white-child destroyed what it feared
to make us forget.
the white-child did not realise
that memories sing.
the white-child did not hear
the memories sing
and so my memories sang:
    the world is a river current
    threading cultures
    binding peoples.
    The water-thread cuts a path
    of unity
    the white-child
    cuts a path
    of desolation:
may the white-child's bullet not find me
I prayed
may the white-child's bullet not find me.

At that time in Eastern Nigeria, it was the common practice for kids to be packed off to boarding schools many miles
away from home, sometimes miles away from nowhere, at least
that's how we saw it. My family had always lived in Enugu:
Constitution Road, Bishop Onyeabo Crescent, and the last road
whose name is erased from memory. That was where father
died. Though Enugu was where I've lived most of my life, I
had always known I was not from Enugu. Enugu is and is not
my home. There were no two ways about it. In my mind's eye
and consciousness, home was Onitsha. Enugu was the home of
Ngwo people, not mine. Onitsha was where I can come into
myself and be, it was how Ngwo people perceived and would
relate to me.

    I knew with certitude what was my relationship to the place.
I was a stranger. I saw it through stranger's and resident's eyes.

Enugu is a scenic hilly resort, a nice place where father worked
while we waited for him to retire. Except that he didn't retire as
we thought; he died. And so we had to go home to Onitsha in
1965, much sooner than we'd expected, much much sooner.
That was when some dreaming began.
I was fourteen in 1968 when I flew into Okigbo's mind.
After an intense agonizing labour I gave birth to my first poem.
Exhausted, yet exhilirated, I knew I had broken through the
invisible barrier. I knew that in this spirit-space I could fly, and
soar; I could sing, and dream. I knew then that the past would
surely come, that it would be born. I knew that the spiral will coil
from the enclosing circle. Jubilant and buoyant, I let my imagination soar and poured out my soul in words.
I saw the coil of *ogbanje:*

Again she comes
again like the galloping waves
that break on the shore
recede . . .
and then again she comes once more.
She drives with the fury
of wall-battering rams,
with a will that drives
wild horses free.
Round, round and round
in a circle she goes,
no trace of a beginning
no hope of an end.

Her birth was like a funeral knell,
we recognize her that heartless tormentor,
those missing toes and scar traversing the face
are all signs of your former visits
to our humble abode.
To you they are nothing;
nothing but a mocking triumph
of all our futile work.
Hope has killed hope and spirit destroyed
by your ceaseless, selfish wandering.
You come by morn and go by night,
regardless of our pleas.

Stay, we implore you, stay
but once again you elude us with your smile.
    Again she comes,
    again like the galloping waves
    that break on the shore
    recede, . . .

    —"Ogbanje," Uwechia, 8–9/5/73

Dreaming was singing poems, writing was daydreaming.
Writing and dreaming was all I could safely do, and so I dreamed
on. I wrote myself into my memory, and traced out the line of my
identity:
    Uray Ukwu
    your height surpasses all
    the strength girding
    the loin of braves
    cannot attain that
    which carries your crown.
    Flow mighty spirit
    through all and in all
    the *ogwe*[10] that heedlessly dams the stream
    prepares the path of a deluge . . .
    Uray!
    my hands lift up in salute
    before your gate;
    I raise my *ofo*[11] to you
    in praise
    beseeching your blessings.
    In the dark labyrinths of seasons
    gone into the shadow of yesteryears;
    desolate thou village
    laid waste by war,
    haunted by starving ghosts
    whose ceremonies of dawn
    not yet performed
    continue their ceaseless wanderings
    in search of peace
    in search of rest;

while
you've stood firm
spreading your wings afar in watch,
without food
without rest
without grudge.

—"Sacred Grove," Uwechia, 15/11/73

Those days I dreamt. Those days I could dream, and I was
allowed to dream. We were in Biafra and schools were closed. Tele-
phones no longer rang, the televisions wore blank faces, and the
mail refused to move. The abnormal became real, and reality became unreal. There was nothing to do and nowhere to go. All the
boys had joined the Biafran Army. Girls, like myself, had to be
protected from the war, and so we stayed home. It wasn't quite clear
to me why it was only pubescent girls that had to be protected. Why
couldn't I be like Mary, Rose, and Joy? What could war do to a girl
like me? Mother-witch wouldn't let me find out. So I found myself
with lots of time on my hands. For company, I had pesky little
brothers and sisters to tax my patience. And so I dreamed:

Were I to choose
the tiniest nut in the spiky dome
of the fronded palm
I'd choose,
succulent with oil that had tasted
the sweetness of morning dew
and preserved its secrets,
I'd pluck
and lay beneath my head-rest
to impart its richness of life to me

Were I to choose
the secret of life
I'd take
and lay within the palm
of hands
chapped and roughened
from taming
the terrain.

Were I to choose
I'd fashion out a hill-like strength
and create a world
to stand a colossus;
that winds which blow
from north to south
and rays that spring
from east to west
may carry forth the tales
to centuries unborn;
that they who seek
that they may find
the footprints in the sands of time.
Yes,
were I to choose
I'd take from destiny's house
a seal
and leave the mark around.

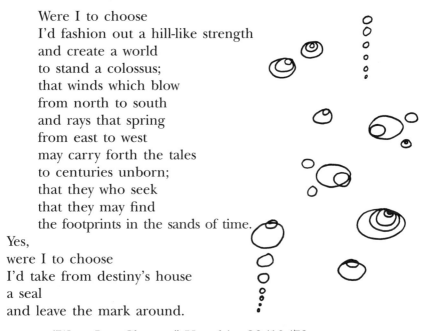

—"Were I to Choose," Uwechia, 26/10/73

With the closure of schools, I lost contact with most of my
friends. Like me, they too had returned to their respective homes
and villages to be with their families. Since I had spent most of
my childhood in Enugu, and the other remaining bit in a boarding school, I did not have many friends in Onitsha. True, I had
a large extended family of uncles, aunts, numerous cousins, and
countless relatives, whom I had to get to know pretty quickly.
Onitsha relatives get extremely cross when they are not instantly
recognized. You are lucky, very lucky to get away with just a
scolding.

With no homework to occupy my time, I gradually turned
my attention to drawing. Drawing was a hobby that had always
given me great joy. I sketched a lot. I had even won an art prize
at the Festival of Arts in Enugu when I was six years? Seven years?
Eight years? Oh, I can't quite remember right now.

I was saying . . .

Working from photographs in *Drum* magazine (Africa's foremost magazine, those days), I produced sketches of many of

Nigeria's political leaders. Looking back years later, it seems I was trying to find the reason for the country's ills in the faces of those politicians. What other explanation could there be for what seems to me to be an obsessive interest in the faces of scoundrels. Scoundrels, whom I had been taught to believe were honorable men, and who had unleashed the hounds.

The hounds are after
the scent of my blood
red blood, same,
but Igbo blood.

    Is there no mercy in the heart of humans
    have sorrowful memories not carved a niche
    in their soul?
    Why has *ebele* (pity)
    removed its presence
    from the feelings of my compeers?
Calumny has been heaped on me
as temper rides the crest of power.
My back's interlaced with a maze of strips
raked and peeled by the strokes of the hide.
What harm is there to be born an Igbo?
What harm is there to speak the tongue?
innocent I am,
what is the charge?
    Degradation in its truest form
    by man to man
    has been heaped on me.
    But the flicker of life
    is a persistent flame
    suppression will not stifle a group.

    —"Lament of the Detainee," Uwechia, 27/7/74

    It was just as well that I lost all those sketches during one of our hasty departures from one of our various wartime places of refuge. It was just as well they were lost.

I still remember.
I remember those days
those dark fearful days
when the morrow seemed like yesterday

and the past was the child to come.
I prayed then
I prayed now
I prayed
that the bullet may not find me.

After the fall of Onitsha in March 1968 a few days after my birthday, my family, that is my mother, grandmother, two brothers and two sisters, were moved to Asaba for safety. Asaba is just across the River Niger from Onitsha. At that time, Asaba seemed to offer better security than Onitsha which was still being bombarded by the recently dislodged Biafran troops. Major Yusuf, then Camp Commandant of 2nd Division of the Nigerian Army, oversaw our move. Late Gen. Muritala Muhammed, who was then a Colonel and the General Officer Commanding (GOC) 2nd Division, had entrusted our welfare to the Major after we surrendered to him.

We later learned that our surrender was highly significant for three reasons. First, the colonel had never captured a civilian in his entire military career, beginning from the 1960 Congo crises in which he participated to this war. (He was more accustomed to capturing soldiers or deserted towns.) Second, he was in a swiftly moving convoy under tight security when mother dramatically emerged to surrender and stopped beside his car. (Allah must be with her!) Last, he was highly rumored to be psychically shielded at the war front. Ringed by a circle of mallams, women were not allowed near his vicinity since *they* could destroy the power of the shield. (Yet one penetrated in the most unlikely circumstance as his high-speed convoy sped to his base. This must be the work of Allah.)[12]

Fortunately for us, the colonel saw the hand of Allah and viewed events favourably. However, it would be an understatement to say he was not taken aback by the whole event. Fortunately for us, as far as mother and grandmother were concerned, the unexpected outcome of our surrender guaranteed us the highest protection. It was the best thing that could have happened since it meant that their pubescent daughters and little sons would be spared those unmentionable vicissitudes of war.

Having entrusted us to the fatherly care of Major Yusuf, Muritala Mohammed went out of our lives the same way he came into it. Our welfare in the Camp became the responsibility of the Major. Reluctant to leave us in Onitsha while he went on a two-week pass to visit his family, Yusuf took us to Asaba where he hoped we would have greater security. We were given refuge by the late Chief Ogbolu. As fate would have it, our intended two-week stay in Asaba stretched into months. Major Yusuf had lost the contact address we had given him and was unable to locate us as he passed on to Onitsha at the end of his leave.

Three months into our stay, the Biafrans infiltrated into Asaba and some other neighbouring towns of the Mid-West region and the nightmare began.

those dark fearful nights
when the morrow seemed like yesteryears
and the past was the child to come.
We constantly prayed,
may the bullet not find us.
We loudly prayed,
may the bullet not find us
we prayed, nightly
may the bullet not find us.

This Biafran infiltration created panic in Nigerian military circles and large scale chaos in Asaba. The Nigerian soldiers forcibly evacuated people from their homes, and herded them into the makeshift refugee camp they had set up at St. Patrick's College. Nervous stormtroopers fanned out into the town to search for Biafrans. Armchair officers at the military Command Center reasoned that the Biafran infiltration was successful because Asaba civilians were "bloody collaborators and sympathizers." They launched their soldiers into every village, hamlet, home, and building to root out the enemy. As day became night, fear stalked life. Fearful and jittery, the soldiers fired erratically at anything that moved. They "confused" any adult Igbo-speaking male with a Biafran soldier, and shot them dead before asking questions. As a result, many Asaba men and boys lost their lives.

Too traumatized to wail, families huddled in groups to blot out the scene. Children wimpered in fear and in cold.

Back in the Command Centre, the military pronounced the counterattack as successful. Militarily speaking, the Nigerian response was swift and decisive. It had killed off as many of the "bloody Igbos" as they could find. From Lagos, Kaduna, and Benin, the media hailed it a victory. But for us on the scene, receiving the lesson of bewilderment, it was a living hell; an incalculable tragedy, an unmitigated disaster. Many have lost a son, a husband, or both.

Silent women raged in spirit
silent cries shattered the stillness of sound
they cried today
for the morrow
and all preceding scenes.
Their *oja* (flutes) lay broken
beside the road . . .
their *oja* lay broken
on muddy paths . . .

Our flight from our place of refuge began with the arrival of armed fiery-eyed soldiers searching for infiltrators. Firing erratically into the air they herded us outside and instructed us to pack out in five minutes. At the expiration of the time, we were informed, the soldiers would shoot their way into the house. And so we learned that a house was not a safe abode, or refuge. It was the unsafest place to be.

Gripped by fear, the urgency of the eviction order, and the wild appearance of the soldiers, my prized sketches were the last thing on my mind as we fought to meet the deadline. Many things were forgotten in our hurried state; only the very essentials were remembered. Huddling together for safety and comfort, we began the long, endless journey through the uncharted, dangerous zone of stray, uncensored, bullets.

We fearfully intoned:
may the bullet not find us . . .
may the bullet not find us . . .
may the bullet not find us . . .
I looked around
and I saw nothing.
Nothing but blood and the dead
blood gushing from newly cut arteries,
coagulating, but still sluggishly flowing
determined to find its way out
from the clayey moulds, the lifeless casts.

Again I saw the dead
and death in its most imperfect image.
The skull of one, dead,
with a bloody gaping hole
had its entire contents scooped out
and plastered on the face of the next.
Bulging eyeballs dropping from sockets
saw the glassy end of all.
The mouth of another, plugged with blood
revealed jarred teeth
adorned with specks of blood.
The heart of another
was a hollow black mass,
and the guts of a friend
wrenched from its rightful place
was resting caressingly
on the brow of his friend.
Headless and limbless bodies lay
carelessly thrown where the fatal impact
of the bullet had dumped them.
The sky darkens
as winged creatures appear
scavengers of the earth
they're called;
I looked
I saw them peck out juicy eyeballs
filling gut, a heaven trail formed;
brains of men, a rare delicacy
such a feast at the folly of men.
I shudder with revulsion
but I lay not my blame on them
for they must feed.
I can only find it in my heart
to lay my curse
on Men's Folly.
Now I listened
and I heard nothing
Nothing but groans, moans and cries
of those who have had their bitter taste

crying out in frenzied agony
knowing they are beyond recall
but waiting impatiently
for their only friend, death.
I listened again,
closely,
and I knew that a neighbour has had it.
    I pictured
    for I cannot look:
back arched in pain
limbs drumming the bare dusty earth
       in a rhythmless, tuneless sound;
       face disfigured with pain

       fiery eyes wide and roving
       but seeing naught;
            nostrils stretched taut
            and labouring under heavy breathing.
       I saw the sweat pores open
       and sweat
            trickling out in little rivulets
            bathe his flaming dirty brow
            (and there were no caring hands
            to sooth and comfort).
He calls
and I cannot ignore
I turn
    but with a sharp gasp, for
    he was in a far worse condition
    a revolting state
    and in intense pain.
    I offered my help
but what help?
My heart became charged with
bitterness
    bitterness for the war
    a destructive war
    that took the toll of unfledged lives.
He managed a ghost of a smile
and said:

"Don't worry, I know I'm gone.
I ... only ... "
  he stopped to cough
  and coughed out a safe supply of blood.
"I only called to say farewell, neighbour
may God protect you
so you may give my message to mankind."
My eyes filled with tears
  at my helplessness
    I knew I was no use
      nor better than he
        I gazed on with sorrow
          in my soul and wondered,
          why should he die a useless death
        a worthless death, and an unknown man
      Why was he used as a mere tool
    to further the vanities of ambitious men?
As I thought
  I saw the brief flicker of life
    rustle as it sought to leave
      then he smiled, and faintly said:
      "*oja n'a kom*"
        (the flute is calling me)
      oja Nnoli
    Nnoli's flute
  I'm going, *kemesia*."[13]
A great peace settled on him
as he breathed out
  his troubled last
  I was a mere spectator
    as the law of nature ran its course.
    I wondered what flute my neighbour heard:
  the whizzing of bullets?
  the groans of the dying?
    the explosions of shells?
    or a soul stirring sound?
  Which ever it was,
  the sound brought comfort and peace
to my neighbour, and rest
to a troubled man.

His closing chapter of life ends here
       of mine, I know not where
              I do not know
                     what destiny has in store for me
                            Will I end like him?
                            Will I live to see the end of the war?
                     Whatever it is to be
       I only echo my neighbour's message to all
"War is evil!"

       —"The Front," Uwechia

NOTES

1. *Otangele* is graphite, used as eye liner by Igbo women.

2. "Sprayed fivers" is an idiomatic expression for pasting money (which in this case happens to be a five pound note denomination) on the forehead of a good performer. The practice is a typical Nigerian way of honoring artists or dancers for an excellent show. At the time the poem was written the Nigerian currency had not been changed to the current value of naira.

3. Female ruler Force of the water.

4. Force of the passage way.

5. Force of our land, Onitsha.

6. Guardian force of mother's kin-group.

7. Guardian force of father's kin-group.

8. Eke, Oye, Afo, and Nkwo are the four weekdays of the lunar cycle.

9. "Human-leaves" is a simile that draws a parallel between people's spasmatic response in a state of fear or shock to the shaking leaves on a tree during a storm.

10. Outsize objects or materials that dam a stream or river.

11. Ofo is a spiritual staff of office.

12. It is interesting that this was also how he was killed, in 1975. As the Head of State, his well-fortified convoy ran into a thicket of coup-plotters, on his way back from the mosque.

13. Goodbye.

ELIZABETH CLARE

Battle Rock

I.

We were landed at Port Orford on the morning of the 9th of June, 1851. We found the Indians, who made their appearance when we first landed, to be somewhat friendly, manifesting a disposition to trade with us.[*]

When I was three, the surf at low tide could knock me over. Driftwood lined the cliffs, bone white and rough, a jungle gym of logs.

June, 1851: nine white men landed in the port, put it on their maps, summer wind bellowing from the north. And now even on the calmest days, Main Street past Pitch's Tavern down to the cannery whistles and creaks. The fishermen tie their boats tight.

Age twelve, I swung bull kelp over my head, the strands pulled ten feet long against my arm. Gulls circled all day, beggars and outlaws waiting for the fishing boats to return.

---

*The italicized passages come from the personal letters of Captain J. M. Kirkpatrick, one of the white explorers who "discovered" Port Orford, Oregon.

Town whitewashed and ragged, wind blows mean through the
gaps. June, 1851: the Tunis gathered their weapons. Smallpox
and alcohol already littered the beaches.

At seventeen, I ran the two miles to Rocky Point and back
every day for a summer. High tide ocean drummed at the
rocks, then receded: rock dripped water, sea anemones closed
up, green purple orange starfish held to the crevices.

*This did not last longer than the steamer lay in the bay. As soon as she
left, the Indians grew saucy and ordered us off. We took possession of a
small island or rock. We had a four-pounder cannon, which we
brought from the steamer. This we planted in front of our encampment.*

II.

Fourth of July in Port Orford: the mounted posse leads the
parade through town. Playground smells of charcoal, beer,
and barbecued salmon. I wait through the dingy boat races,
sand castle contest, quilt raffle, horse games, impatient for the
fireworks. Wander the swarming town: Mr. Black falling down
drunk, Mrs. Marsh selling oatmeal cookies and brownies, Coot
turning the salmon on long hot grills, flags flapping on every
street corner.

*In the morning the Indians began to gather on the beach in consider-
able numbers. I noticed that they were better armed than when we first
landed. There were about forty of them on the ground.*

Before dusk we settle on the bluffs, air full of smoke bombs
and dust. White boys dressed as Indians leap around a bon-
fire, I want to scuffle in the surf with them, half-naked, face
and chest painted red blue yellow. Down the beach white men
dressed as themselves climb Battle Rock, dragging a cannon
behind them, rifles loaded. They fire blanks into the air and
wait for the "Indians" to come scrambling up the path.

I wheedle money for one last cotton candy, whistle and clap
as the boys crowd toward the Rock, fall one by one to the

cannon's boom. Faces to the sand, they play dead. Mr. Peterson, born-again preacher, newspaper editor, declares victory for the white men over the public address system, leads a cheer for the founding of Port Orford.

At sunrise they built several fires and went through with a regular war-dance. They were joined by others who came over the hills, and shortly after by twelve others with a chief, who came in a large canoe. By this time, there were about sixty of them.

And then it's dark. Fireworks spread across the sky; bursts of light, colors twirl against the stars, sound of honking horns, surf, sizzle of rockets. I am convinced that each burst will land in my lap. Later I follow my parents home, half-asleep, confused by the cars, headlights, streams of people.

III.

As soon as the chief landed, they began to come up the island. We met them and made signs that we would shoot if they did not go back. This had no effect on them, and they still came on.

Savages, rogues, natives, redskins: what did you call yourselves in the centuries before those nine white men arrived, sick with goldrush fever? They abandoned a sluice box to the south side of Battle Rock. It rusted away, ready to slide into the ocean. I had vague notions of gold hunting and mountain men.

You built sturdy red cedar houses half underground, collected and traded beads, shells, acorns, measured your plenty in obsidian. Burnt grass every year as an offering to the salmon. This is a half-vision.

We then retired to the top of the island, where we had our guns stationed. Then they made a rush to pitch into camp among us, the chief leading the way. The great crowd of them were within six feet of the mouth of the cannon. I jerked up a firebrand and discharged the cannon among them, killing some six or eight dead.

Again and again I climbed that rock, parents warning against
poison oak. Now on my wall a photograph, black and white
silhouette, rock against ocean.

Guns, felling axes, negotiated lies. You fought desperate
battles, learned the art of ambush and blood. Carried your
dead into the hills, arms growing tired under their weight.
Resistance turned round and hard as cobbles knocking one
against another at high tide.

Or did you burn your dead on driftwood pyres, let the tide
carry the ashes away like so many pieces of shell? You joined
the Takelmas and Latgawas, waged a war that lasted many
months.

*The fight lasted about fifteen minutes, when the Indians broke and
ran, leaving thirteen dead on the ground. They fled to the hills and
rocks, and continued to shoot their arrows at us for some time. There
were a great many of them wounded.*

IV.

They rounded you up, a long forced migration north and east
over the mountains, another bitter trail. Grand Ronde, Siletz,
Warm Springs.

*During the afternoon, the chief came up the beach, and made signs
that he wanted to come into camp. He threw his arms down on the
sand. He made signs that he wanted to take away the dead. This we
let him do.*

That reservation at the end, you began your lives again,
middle of sagebrush country: no ocean, no rain, no huckle-
berries, salal, Sitka spruce. And every year we dressed ourselves in mockery, my most familiar beach.

How to Talk to a New Lover
about Cerebral Palsy

Tell her: *Complete strangers*
have patted my head, kissed
my cheek, called me courageous.

Tell this story more than once, ask
her to hold you, rock you
against her body, breast to back,

her arms curving round, only
you flinch unchosen, right arm trembles.
Don't use the word *spastic.*

> In Europe after centuries
> of death by exposure
> and drowning,
> they banished us
> to the streets.

Let her feel the tension burn down your arms,
tremors jump. Take it slow: when she asks
about the difference between CP and MS,

refrain from handing her an encyclopedia.
If you leave, know that you will ache.
Resist the urge to ignore your body. Tell her:

They taunted me retard, cripple,
defect. *The words sank into my body.*
The rocks and fists left bruises.

> Gimps and crips, caps
> in hand, we still
> wander the streets but now
> the options abound: telethons,
> nursing homes, and welfare lines.

Try not to be ashamed as you flinch and tremble
under her warm hands. Think of the stories
you haven't told yet. Tension grips fierce.

Ask her what she thinks as your hands shake
along her body, sleep curled against her,
and remember to listen: she might surprise you.

JO WHITEHORSE COCHRAN

A Bone's Story

We never knew the desert would be
    like this—as we went in.
Nothing was ever without shade—
Nothing was ever without water—
    water in the ground
    water in the air
    water vapor, water on the knee,
    water on the lips, water
    cascading from river, stream, creek.
Nothing was ever without rain
                without green
        without grass
        without the scent of fir needles
without humidity—without.
At first, all we noticed was what
    there was not . . . what we
    were without. Absence.
Even, the wind sang in a strange voice,
not even the drummers could find the beat.
But we knew we would be here
    noticing what was lost to us.
We never imagined that the Great Spirit
    had imagined this too for us,
that this too would be on the way home.

We never imagined the mountain of mud
        that had become our lives—
that would become this arid plateau
        would turn to dust dervishes
        would leave sand in our bread—
        grit in every orifice of our bodies.

But where else would we have come to—
to find the desolation of the Soul—
but on this road, in this place,
in the desert, where bones
splinter and flake gray—
        as the flesh, the water, the life
of whatever animal that moved
        in this place has long been
stripped away, piece by piece.

Now only the bones, this last physical proof
        dissolves as the wind again becomes
        our lover, our Mother.
We did not listen, did not believe
        that this would be how
        we gave up our bodies—the desert wind would be the
                tongue,
that we would dissolve, vanish
        before our eyes.

Trickster's Song

Tricksters are always the magical peoples,
the bag people, crazy Indians,
those who see visions,
those who mumble to themselves,
those who sing at any moon,
those who wear or do not wear socks,
those rolled in dirt,
those rolled in their own sight of God,
their own sight of aliens,
their own sight of the Mother Mary,
their own sight of Coyote,
their own sight of time,
their own chant to call on our souls,
their own chant to call out our dimes and quarters,
their own chant to call out our lies,
their own chant to call out our disbelief—
in the Great Spirit, the unseen, the seen,
by who, by who.

But what about the Trickster who creates
other disguises, other guises?
What about the Trickster in the business suit?
What about the Trickster who is a yuppie?
What about the Trickster at the computer?
What about the Trickster, who can read your lips?
What about Trickster, who has money and uses it to make you?
What about Trickster with a video camera,
                with a pen,
                with a quiet glint in the eye—
always a step ahead of you,
                invisible until the trap springs
and your ankle is crushed in the vise.

This is the Trickster you can walk by
            without averting your eyes,
            without scenting the dark reek of human,
            without feeling there must be a place for these people.

This Trickster may be fullblood,
                                mixed blood
                                        any racial stew.

This Trickster has the heart and eyes of the Lynx.
The secret keeper, the silent watcher,
quick—so deadly, you will never hear
her approach across the snow.
This Trickster is ancient—is certain of God,
                                                of her own sight,
                                his own song,
                                her own vision,
                                his own chant,
                                her own soul.
                Seen, unseen, seen, not heard.

End of the Rainbow

for Rob Roy Mac Veigh

Gaunt visage,
teeth seeming to rattle in a mouth
where cheeks have become scooped in.
Dark spaces between these teeth,
eyes seem larger. I look at
the mantle of the fireplace,
to photos just six months before
and as my Mother would say,
"there's flesh over those bones."

Now, I'd give anything for round,
fatty, dimpled flesh over his bones.
Over the bones of many of my friends.
In the last months, they've all come
to look like the milagros skeletons.
Clothing draped over them.
But I will not wait for them—dance
to celebrate the dead.

These days of the dead,
draw into weeks and months, where
we come to speak of how we were
as children, how we were in our twenties,
when dressing up in goblin,
or vampire, or mummy costumes
in March or June. And then going on the city bus
in costume was fun, a game, camp.
We always went to the expensive,
high class places on Friday nights
and waited for a table in our masquerade.
We always laughed as they carded us.
We were free to be anyone.
Free to do anything outrageous or wild.
Soon we were pointing back,
at our onlookers and laughing at them.

Mocking their dreariness,
their common lives. We were giddy
and gay in those costumes of the night.

Now the night rests on his body,
and will not wipe off with cold cream.
Will not go away if I close my eyes,
and wish for Kansas.
I have watched this waning away
in others. It has planted anger
between my bones like pus,
it has bred doubt when the words,
"HIV positive," are uttered.

It is difficult to not start
the mourning that day.
The skeleton's grip,
searched for day to week to month.
Until even the softest touch
becomes too much, too painful,
between lovers, between friends.
How do we keep company with death?
How do we keep company with life?

The eternal optimist or pessimist,
which glass do I really look
into, hold onto, to survive this journey?

And I do survive, to mark
these years in my mid-thirties.
The names of loved ones,
whose skeletal remains walked the planet—
David, Ron, Steve, T.J., Michael,—
and too soon—Rob Roy.
There are other names,
I dare not utter in this company.
I utter them only in my prayers
for their lives.

Every night,
I light candles in the cathedral
of a God of miracles, a God of life.
Every night, I pray,
"there is no place like home,
God let my loved ones find you there."

CAROLYN FORCHÉ

Book Codes: I

We must know *whether*
And if not: then what is the task
very much on the surface
by means of finite signs
when one is frightened of the truth
"Are there simple things?"
  What depends on my life?
would be possible for me to write
like the film on deep water
over too wide chasms of thought
the world does not change
the visual field has not a form like this
so many graces of fate
the boundary (not a part) of the world
mirrored in its use
nothing except what can be said

a field tunneled by mice the same thought continually
like two hands indissolubly clasped to begin
as if in a coffin and can therefore think of nothing else
how incomplete a moment is human life

fragments together into a story before the shape of the whole
like a madman—time and again torn from my mouth
out of a nearby chimney each child's hand was taken
though this is not a fairy tale explained in advance

the sign of the cross on an invisible face with the calm of a butcher
as if it bore witness to some truth
with whom every connection had been severed
as if in a coffin and can therefore think of nothing else

an afternoon swallowing down whole years its every hour
troops marching by in the snow until they are transparent
from the woods through tall firs a wood with no apparent end
cathedrals at the tip of our tongues with countries not yet seen

whoever can cry should come here

stories no more substantial than the clouds or what had been
   his face
the view, the wind, the light disposing of the bodies
who walked in the realm of dreams but like everything else

for our having tried to cross the river caught between walls
one could hear a voice "Bear the unbearable"
and the broadcast was at an end

you might relay the message the rivers and mountains remained
the unseen figure of the enemy entirely covered
the central portion of their visual fields this blindness for names

the bone became black with flies again hatching in ruins
here were the black, burnt ceilings and boxes of flags
the walls covered with soot like a kitchen

smaller clouds spread out a golden screen
given the task of painting wounds
through the darkened town as though it had been light

at the moment of the birth of this cloud

The angel handed me a book, saying, "It contains everything that you could possibly wish to know." And he disappeared.

So I opened the book, which was not particularly fat.

It was written in an unknown character.

Scholars translated it, but they produced altogether different versions.

They differed even about the very senses of their own readings, agreeing upon neither the tops nor the bottoms of them, nor upon the beginnings of them nor the ends.

Toward the close of this vision it seemed to me that the book melted, until it could no longer be distinguished from this world that is about us.

—Paul Valéry

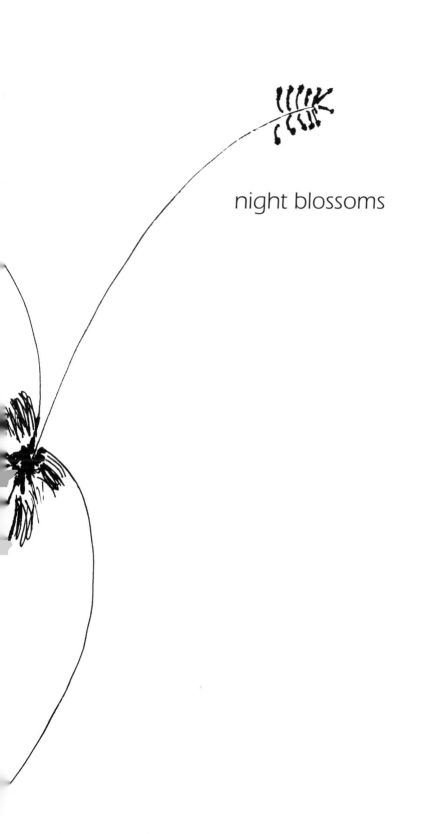

night blossoms

JEFFNER ALLEN

tea on the beach at midnight

sound of the thighbone flute that carries her from land to
land   sound that can avert hailstorms   sound of the
thighbone flute carved bone of she who has died violently
   sound that can shake crumble a mountain   sound that
carries her to and from

your leg   you i   open your leg again   lift away gluteus
maximus gluteus medius periformis   move across gemellus
obturator internus quadratus femoris   lift away and move
across until   you i   femur in countless pieces   arranging
pieces   drop in a metal bar   pat bone nerves blood vessels
   around bar   close   leg closed   your leg closed on a
jewel box gold with mirrors and angels   jewel box wood
   with dried spring flowers   while she who listens   she
who has been listening   lets out a scream and tears for what
is

you i she her   intimate chattings   near across what still
is happening   unstable junctions of midnight and morning
not only feathers but string not only sea grass but rocks sand
a bouncing moon and two trees running sweet cakes a
blanket a thermos of hot tea a feeling of instability before
dawn

there are some lands of beautiful noise terrible noise
   around the bay sun sparkling   eucalyptus pines hills
brown with drought roll down to the ocean   sea lions
early afternoon beginning of summer in california
driving south on highway ①

crash metal glass again crash how to keep alive at the
edge of life?   yes all things are connected   but please not
now and my friends?   crash metal glass again crash
my body this body at the edge of life thin thin as
cellophane body of luminous colors and light   crash
metal glass again crash glass i spit out glass and blood
spitting out glass more glass and blood

not to discard persistent disturbance   to resist continuous
prunings that would mark the random as not functional and
breed it out   her she you i invoked by wayside markers
that obscure

tones shapes gestures textures myriad streams through
which energies pass   touched by their power to move
molecules atoms you i arms shoulders hands thicker
denser now   reach into her navel and pull out a crocus

running downhill over soft pine needles slowly   not raw
fear which has blown away which has passed   but a
vortex pushing driving red that flies up and out over your
shoulder that whirls away   and in the tall grasses
rhinestones   pink blue lilac   swirl loop flip over and come
down   light rains of early spring

sonic shadows   echoes in a valley as unfinished
conversations touch   interferences inconveniences in each
sound produced where sound image event vary by
movement of the wind   if you i make time so that
shadows are heard   taking six different names in a lifetime
  two names for today when i am with you

tide going out i skip from rock to rock two eyes in the
rocks i put my finger through the two eyes and up comes
eyes wide and long across   mouth open grey stone
cheekbones cheeks chin holes through mouth and left eye
    shells embedded in neck unmistakably a face or not a
face at all

lost the car keys twice in two days keys to engine and keys
to gas tank   out of gas and can't unlock the gas cap to add
more   you tell me on the phone that you wanted to make
a change   a change of direction and are going west to the
green growing things

a sea of microtones   ambiguous tones of differing intervals
and unexpected effects   that color the heart of you i she her
    that vary according to time of day season mood

life arising here and going away there gathering dispersing
ageing emerging according to environment and relations
among beings   microtonal spins

response improvisations microtonal readings combine
and recombine landscapes   drift along across nearby on the
edges of

the mouth as point of particularity and individuality   the
mouth dissolves

a tree on the beach a tree of mouths eyes at the peak of
upper lips golden flashing eyes   hollow eyes at juncture
of lower and upper lips   a pink mouth   a peach mouth a
buff mouth brown mouths red pink red purple mouths
green glowing mouths   salmon mouths

a page of mouths a book of mouths   you i she her
vibrating intervals neither fused not entirely distinct
   mouths labial fleshy folds muscles   mouths labile open
to change adaptable undergoing chemical alteration
unstable forgetful wandering liable to slip mouths
slipping across deaths lives

an afterbirth with blood clots the size of tennis balls color
of the brown pot over there   and pieces of the cosmic eggs
minutes before rolling by you i her in trance   dream
incubation tonight visiting lands where a loosening of
jaws   pouring rose water over jaws   whiskers metal
whiskers growing around jaws   whiskers long and so
heavy then drop off   melt into the ground   metal and
spitting out glass   metal and glass over heart pouring rose
water over jaws as the debris comes out   look about
   there is so much of it

turning cartwheels two bodies make one body or three or
four bodies arms legs flying long shadows on the beach
how to do again what has been done   what is done but
with a love   a ritual of healing?

absolute dividing line before and after forever lost and
never to be two halves that cannot be pasted together
pushed together fused

how to love when there may be nothing in common?   this
today and (not) that tomorrow as the line gallops plunges
   prances bucks scatters   over distance   scenes
disentangling tangling   simultaneously cyclically
youyoush eiiheri iher sheyo ui green star turquoise red
small pencil floats out of leg   intervals in diffusion
confusion   hammer chisel sit pause

so glad you called   yes she was to have graduated from high school this year   summer had arrived after a long winter and snow into the spring driving with her two friends to a picnic at the inlet the meadow had just turned green and the woodlands were dotted with purple irises   and then it happened noontime at the intersection by your house where the dirt roads cross next to the train tracks

if only i could take her place she was my only daughter   if only it might have been me instead

her best friend was taken to the hospital and that night was found wandering around the morgue looking for her

near the end of june just one day after i had
arrived here in california
he was driving drunk at full speed in the wrong
direction on highway ⚐1⚐

you said that you wanted to get back your body to
get back your life
i'm feeling lots better now   i spend most of
my time stretching strengthening doing physical
therapy pilates cybex nautilus i hope to walk
again

of course i'll be glad to look after your house while
you're away   thanks i'll be thinking of you

it is rumored that folk in the fairy-world have power to
charm the souls of such as are inclined to them forth from
their bodies in sleep and take them ajourneying in strange
lands

ella young, "book of opal," *triptych*

scent of pink beach roses or   tall green reeds by the stream
she and she hands in the water   hands huge ovals full of
   water pass to you and you on the bank a small round
shape with a sun on it a sun rising

the sunrise makes my shirt a little brighter
won't you come with me?   this field is dark and
chill our breath is white   she carries her dead
one dear one on her back blossoming
knowledge   earth roaring sound

connective tissues muscles webbing   once flexible elastic
resilient now intervals bunched together undifferentiated
glued

looking at the leg   touching the leg   hands on left leg right
   leg rub one hour daily for four months   notice where
kneecap is stuck and adjust hand pressure accordingly   and
your leg my leg may bend   tissues memories lift separate
slowly release spin out

some say that she and her could light fires by singing certain
songs or bring rain melt stones cause flowers to bloom
draw birds and animals around a peaceful circle of singing
musicians

in compassionate celebration   happiness my sorrow is
sorrow you are nearby my happiness how to say your
   sorrow is my sorrow your happiness is my happiness?

you i she her sound of mountains colliding ocean sound
sound of the thighbone flute   and then a moment later
they were gone

BECKY BIRTHA

Mythology

You read us the words
you have written about
Demeter, Hecate, Diana.
When we no longer want to listen
you say—
But your people have myths of their own.
Why don't you find them out?
Why don't you write them down?
Why don't you bring them
for us to read?

Yes, we know that
our great great grandmothers
remembered many truths.
We also know
how those ancestors were
separated and sold
severed by the middle passage
disease, death
and design
so no two
women who spoke the same language
came to the same place.

To talk in the old tongues
was forbidden.

To learn to write
forbidden.
To sing the old stories
forbidden,
forbidden even
to speak secrets in
the sacred voice of the drum.

We live out our lives
in languages with no names
for the Goddesses
of our great grandmothers,
no characters in which to inscribe
their wisdom,
no verbs that encompass
their power,
no constructions that can contain
their rage.

Yes, we will find them out.
As we uncover and claim those words
we may never choose to write them down.
We will not be bringing them
to you.

Doors

The carpenter came
this week.
She finished the two small jobs
we had asked of her.
She told me the solid wooden door
I had found on the street
for my room
would fit just fine—
and it did.

Downstairs
she took the back door
from its hinges
planed the edges and
aligned it right,
hung it plumb
so the bolts slide
into the strike plate,
flush.
Now the lock turns
easily.

I can go out to the garden, now.
Sweet smelling curls of wood
have fallen among the purple violets.
I can close the door to my room
lie in the patch of east sun
that laps across the floor.

And I wonder,
that I never thought how all the while
what I needed was so simply
this:
a door, to the outside
that opens
a door, to the inside
that shuts.

My Vision of a Women's Community

I call my friend to find out if she owns
a round cake pan
deep dish
"the kind with the hole in the middle?"

Yes—but she's on her way out the door.
She'll leave it on the porch.
the four blocks between our houses
vibrate with color from every garden
all blossoms wide open
so early in the day.

Up the stairs, on the porch
the cake pan waits in a corner.
The downstairs neighbor's mother
who speaks no English
nods and smiles at me.

I bake a cake with cinnamon and sour cream
from a recipe passed on to me,
invert it on my prettiest plate
to take to the potluck.

My friend is there, too
with chips and pasta salad.
I've remembered to bring her cake pan
but she says I can keep it—

she hardly ever makes that kind of
cake any more
but if she wants to
she can always borrow it back.

"Anytime—"
She already has the keys to my house.
Like everyone else, she loves the cake

and probably will never know
that in this simple back and forth
this day-long thread of gifts
I've been given
something I've wanted all my life.

The Way I Want to Be Friends

*(with thanks to Susan Windle for her
"Work Poem" which inspired this)*

Can we touch each other more, please?
Can we each have our fill of hugs every day,
fill each other's arms again and again

Can we let our bare arms brush against each other's
and or knees bump, with no apologies
squeeze close together in small spaces
can we tickle and tumble and remember play
giggle and stop with a head plopped in an open lap

Can we braid each other's hair
sprinkle each other's feet
spread each other's backs with pungent oils
slip the rings from finger to finger
fasten the clasp at the neck's nape
wrap each other's heads in wide, woven bands

Can we spend the day together
laugh and lean against one another
catch hands in the sunlight and leave them linked
and swinging in the rhythm of our matching stride

Can we spend the night together
and not end up ex-lovers
can we cuddle close on a blanket under stars
and tell each other stories, sing each other songs
lie long in one another's arms
holding, holding through the dark

Can we touch each other more please
can we fill each other's lives
can we fill each other
again and again and again?

ANNE J. M. MAMARY

Performance Art

FANTASIES I

Heterosexual fantasies about a lesbian life demand that I put my own life on hold, utterly—both the tasks I must accomplish and the ways in which I invent myself alone and with other lesbians.

I have no husband—but why would I want to live with moldy sinks?

I have no children—but why would I want to live entirely on peanut butter?

Your spirited kindness, earnest friendship, warm me. Your family brings me laughter, conversation, connection.

No small living thing will perish if I do not watch constantly—but does this mean you and your children have unlimited access to my attention?

I go to the store in the middle of the night, acting out my frustration, acting out my life. I know I need to nourish my own life, even if husband and wife do not. A small cart holding lentils, milk, lettuce, peppers, pasta, crackers, mushrooms and ice cream, cat food, green tea, bread, beans, oil, fruit. Defiantly, lovingly, I gather my life, assorted fruits as allies, close to my chest.

I am glad she values my friendship and I enjoy giggly, squirming, cuddly children. I also have other friends, straight friends, gay friends, bi friends, lesbian friends, with and without children— a rich and full life. Can she imagine it?

Daddy has to go to work—his work is long and difficult, some- times uncertain. It is true, when the work calls he must go—to feed himself, to feed her, to feed the children.

Mommy teaches and cooks and dances and watches over three children, a cat, a dog, a house. It is true, she is constantly inter- rupted.

They see my work as neatly contained, flexible. It is not enough that I visit sometimes. Now I am expected, pushed. I often work at 5:00 in the morning, cradle tomatoes in the middle of the night.

My students think sexuality ought to be private. Husband, wife, children (I sneak my life in around the demands of heterosexual- ity). I am often tired and sometimes cry in despair—I can't bear to see another wedding band, hear one more academic presenta- tion about the copula or pretend to smile at the omnipresent heterosexual ritual in the high school performance of *Oklahoma!* my friend has choreographed. With two of her children on my lap, I wonder how she might see the movements of my own life, dancing sometimes with hers and sometimes not. I wonder what it would take for her to attend to me seriously, seriously.

FANTASIES II

I came out in 1982, when I was a freshwym (as we called our- selves) in college. I was almost 18, and I came out listening to Holly Near, Faith Nolan, Ferron, and Alix Dobkin and was totally in love with "square," separatist, "flaky" lesbians.[1]

Some of those women, ones I knew and ones whose writings I read and whose music I devoured, were breathtakingly beautiful to me for their wicked senses of humor, their flexible lesbian imaginations, their sometimes scary toughness and their over-whelming tenderness. I didn't remember feeling any pressure to be sex-radical or prude. There was plenty of sex, some of which went on without any physical touch for months, as we saw each other and made each other mad in the most exciting of ways—in dorms, in chemistry labs, at our lifeguard and dining hall and library jobs.

And there was the map that could show you how every dyke at the place had either been lovers with a Miss J.C. or with someone who had been. The excitement was not only in flirting right under the nose of the closeted college president or in the class-room of the 35-year-old math teacher who thought he was so hot any 18-year-old girl would swoon with his masculine attention. I didn't see myself as a "sexual minority"—not a "queer" or "sex outlaw" or part of an alliance with gay men. I came out as a lesbian separatist, with sex, perhaps, decentered, as Joyce Trebilcot suggests. The excitement was in the creativity, the stories, the realization that we didn't need men for anything and that we could invent lesbian realities in all sorts of ways, some of which included passionate kisses and some of which melted in red-hot exchanges over tea and a difficult book or in a late-night plan-ning meeting over a particular political action.

A friend told me her story: When she was 19, my friend met B, a then 26-year-old dyke. B was beautiful and smart and manipu-lative and controlling. My friend didn't understand monogamy or rough sex. B told her that no one else in the world thought that way. This may have been true (although my friend and I doubted it), but in B's mind it was an indication that there was something wrong with my friend. After nearly a year of being controlled and belittled, my friend said she was so used to being kept from her work and her family that she sometimes couldn't name the controlling or say outloud, even to herself, that it was a problem, even though she felt terribly alone. She says, looking back over nearly 15 years' distance, that what she thought was love at the time was part of the cage she was in.

My friend told me that, in her isolation, she sometimes felt as though her desires for freedom and attention which was not jealous and which was passionately gentle were weird, strange, impossible. B often made my friend miss an event she very much wanted to attend (and my friend would tell me stories at the time about her life and relationship that left me uneasy, even though she worked very hard to appear "fine". How many ways have I failed in my attention to friends?) or keep her from studying so she would feel thoroughly panicked or be jealous of her friends and activities and meetings so she would feel guilty whenever she was not with B.

Sex: B said my friend was not loud enough, rough enough, interested enough. If she let B tie her hands with ribbons because she pleaded long enough, she ended up in tears. B said my friend was a prude and just needed more practice and, god knows, more trust.

My friend was often depressed without knowing why. And then, because she didn't confide in anyone until years later, she would end up in B's arms for comfort. And, with time, this pattern became more and more eroticized. Was my friend consenting? At the time, she says, she would have sworn that she was, partly because her mother was trying to undermine the relationship only somewhat out of concern for my friend's well-being and largely out of lesbian hating, manipulation and control. Looking back, my friend says she was often powerless to consent or not consent. What she thought were her desires then terrify her now or flood her with a deep sorrow. She says she was not being a prude; she was trying to hang on to her fantasies—fantasies which were being torn from her heart and soul in jagged tears of flesh.

My dearest friend: I fantasize about gentleness. I don't mean the kind of gentleness that keeps women from having ourselves, remembering our own lives. I fantasize about the kind of serious attention women might give each other, even if we each have different memories, desires, feelings. I don't think my friend is a prude. I am not a prude, when I want with every fiber of who I am to be carefully attended to, to have my attention be nourishing.

I fantasize about gentleness, try to live it and often fail. It can be hard work, serious fun, intensely political, no matter who tries to deny it.

My words, her smile, my dances, her imagination, my hips, her breasts, my hair, her heart . . . Gentleness is so rare. Your voice in the middle of the night across a live wire—"I will be your light and you know I can do. And I can sing in the night, when you think your light is almost fading. Out of sight, in the night I will call. . . ."[2]

Cami, Amy, Jenny, Tracy, Sharon, Ann, Debbie, Mary Ann, Geneva, Vivion, Renee, Sharon, Angela, Elisabeth, Hideko, Karin, Martha, Farar, Bernadette, Myra

GENTLENESS

Monday

After work, after school, sweet time with friends. At home the answering machine blinks out a message from Madison. Are you still interested in this job? A job, I should be thrilled, but I choke back tears. I have always expected to leave this town where I've lived most of my life. And now it calls me out into the night to read her words, to trace familiar paths and to be held by the new spring air which comforts me, because it also holds her and her, holds him, holds my life in this place. My life—precious, fragile, tenacious connections—fills me more deeply than circling philosophies. Volumes of answers cannot solve the mystery of the trees.[3]

Tuesday

Last fall I walked these same streets and said goodnight to nodding trees. And now I touch their soft pink buds and admire tiny green hands uncurling by sunlight and streetlight. Memory is touched by a landscape and the words I practiced in the evening of winter melt into this springtime.

Wednesday

Read me a poem, my mother asked this afternoon. As we whiz down the highway, she eats the biggest cone of soft ice cream I have ever seen, and I recite Mary Oliver's "Answers." My grandmother died when my mother was eight years old. She, in my mother's memory, urged my mother's education and music lessons while "she poured confusion out and cooled and labelled all the wild sauces"[4] of her brief life. The poem made my mother cry. She, too, encourages my lessons and work, but I like to hear her tell the story about my grandfather welcoming with wide-eyed delight the green shoots of new corn year after year. He didn't have much use for god and didn't believe anyone ever went to the moon, but the young corn lifted his heart, heavy with losses.

Thursday

She calls me to say she may follow her husband to Georgia where he has a job interview next week. Last fall they moved from this town, where she has friends and family and newly budding connections, to Philadelphia. He is an alcoholic and last month she was coming home alone. Now he's sobered up and everything is fine (again). She is alone. I miss her. Sometimes her sister and I meet her half way for dinner in remote Clarks Summit to giggle and gossip and remind each other we are still together, no matter where she goes after a husband who is different now or I go after a job which will expect me to sort through piles of answers and think of the secrets of the trees with disdain.

Friday

She drew a picture of the soul, which looked suspiciously like a dill pickle to me. When I had a cyst removed, it was covered with bumps. He wryly suggested I'd had my soul removed and replaced with a tea bag, citing the strings poking from my navel as evidence. It would be just my luck to have sleepy time tea for a soul instead of a cranky green pickle.

๑฿๏

I am so glad you are home this Friday night. I am tired of hearing "not political" when I try to describe how there are many ways of being in relation to the academy and that putting all of one's soul on the table for discussion is only one way. I find that relationship dangerous; it looks too much like her life with a man who wants to know what she's doing every minute and who demands she can never really be with her friends without him— even if he's miles away, he's given her guilt which reminds her, reminds us, all the time of his presence.

I don't know if my words are heard at all when I try to explain to her how you have negotiated through skilled determination, pried open with your bare hands, held on tight to spaces here for dykes and women to breathe, spaces which would be penetrated if everyone had to engage everyone else all the time. Sometimes I feel like I will drown, and your voice, your words, your presence, restores my soul.

ॐ

My grandmother's presence. The fact of her existence. To be, to take up space. "Orphaned early, she was a woman who'd ask/ almost everyone to her table. It's her/touch I want to bring to the drum,/playing steady past the erratic/heartbeat that could not sustain her/body."[5] To insist on one's life among the sweet and wild mysteries of friends' presences and concern, in the memory of grandmothers' presences, seems, to me, an intensely political stance in a world which demands attention, demands guilt, demands, demands, demands everyone have the same memories, the same hopes, the same desires.

Saturday

Hanging on, he says his soul is wounded, full of holes. I take her a sunflower and her a stem of purple fresia. We invoke the found goddesses Getuffa, Laboria (who offers strength to women who do demoralizing work for not enough money) and Hillaria to boost our spirits.[6] I give him a pickle wrapped in deli-paper and hope it has restorative powers.

Sunday

I call her to see how her surgery went. I'm glad to hear she is healing quickly. We compare notes and news clips. It's bad, it's getting worse. Compulsory Christianity in Mississippi, which just

ratified the 13th amendment last week. In Montana, lesbians and
gay men required to register, along with rapists and child molest-
ers, with the police as sex criminals. We hear on the news reports
blaming young unmarried mothers for nearly everything. The
destruction of the public university system in New York State. A
student, a young Black man, tells our class how he is routinely
trailed in stores. His existence signalling "criminal," he and his
white woman friend fantasize fighting back. She will walk around
the store lifting whatever the two of them want while "security"
is occupied with their surveillance of him.

She says she is reminded of the Weimar Republic. An American-
born Jew tells her she is a pessimist. A Russian-born Jew, she, I
believe, knows a rat when she hears it scratching. I ask what we
will all do for each other. She says she is sure people will hide
me. Will you wear a yellow star with the King of Denmark? a pink
triangle, a black triangle? Will I have the courage to hide her, to
hide her, to hide him, to hide you? Last week, I bought a jar of
dill pickles, and I wonder, will I be strong? Will I be a "shelter in
a storm? Your willow, a willow?"[7] I will try to keep these words in
my mind, this melody in my blood. I will try to remember, when
answers are many and mysteries too few.

Maria, Yevgenia, Jeffner, Lauren, Peter, Hannah, Janet, Anne
Marie, Wendy, Gertrude, Carol, Pearl, Roberta, Jo, Eli, Tonya

PERFORMANCE ART

What a babe! Michelle in a black silk blouse unbuttoned down to her—well, unbuttoned far enough. She remembers vaguely how to walk in high heels and I'm at her side, hair french braided, black stockings accenting long slender legs all the way up to my—well, the black velveteen dress is short.

We go to the opening of the student art show. Some of her students have pieces in the show; other faculty are there. Michelle and I pay attention to the art, she shows me what she likes best. Michelle and I pay attention to each other, to the women students, to the women faculty.

Where did you two meet, the president of the union wants to know. Michelle and I smile at each other; the president sees longing. We know we've got her.

One of the men in my department just two days ago told me one of my white male students was raving about my class. The student said it was the best course he'd taken in college and that I'd really made him think. My colleague then launched into a reverie about sexual attraction between students and professors, or directed at professors from students. What was he trying to tell me? I wished he'd been at the opening to see Michelle and me, all decked out, paying attention to each other. No access point in this fantasy!

My colleague wasn't at the opening, but another professor invoked his presence. Michelle and I smile at each other; the professor sees longing. We know the man from my department will hear the rumors.

After the show, Michelle makes me dinner; I bring her peanut butter chocolate chip cookies. She shows me the album from her wedding. We roar over the picture of Michelle, the bride, with Joanne, the maid of honor. Eleven years later, Michelle and Joanne have been lovers for seven years and the husband is—well, who knows where—and Michelle and Joanne are still best friends.

The next morning the man in my department can almost not look at me. Michelle calls to tell me about the vague questions her colleagues have asked after the show. One man said she looked very nice last night (but he couldn't quite mention me on her arm). The students' pieces are still in the gallery, but Michelle and I are getting around. I laugh, she laughs. Performance art. What a babe!

NOTES

1. See *Her Tongue on My Theory* (Toronto: Press Gang, 1994).

2. Cris Williamson, "Live Wire," on *The Best of Cris Williamson* (Oakland: Olivia, 1990).

3. Mary Oliver, "Answers," in *New and Selected Poems* (Boston: Beacon, 1992), 235.

4. Oliver, 235.

5. David Williams, "My Grandmother and the Dirbakeh," in *Traveling Mercies* (Cambridge: Alice James Books, 1993), 7.

6. Morgan Grey, *Found Goddesses* (Norwich, Vt.: New Victoria Publishers, 1988).

7. Joan Armatrading, "Willow," on *Boys On the Side: Original Soundtrack* (New York: Ariota, 1995).

TAMAI KOBAYASHI

Duet in which the beloved remains silent

to all of our homelands
and homecomings

I come back to you
across
what could only be called
a chasm
or a river
the rising mountains
of somewhere lost

returning to you
who began this journey

returning to you
even as you turn away
as fleetingly
as the wind
chasing swallows
in flight

and here
in a landscape drawn with tears
pale blue skies and endlessness
where the autumn sheds
into winter falling

as a silent imprint of leaves

strange
how we have never talked of this
this silence binding us
to pathways
worn with memory
the threading stream
to the mountain

yet you have always turned away
eyes averted

and how i have dreamt chasms
and how i have dreamt streams
even as you turn away
the light darkening in your eyes
pathways lost to time
memory of this
the nature of memory
in these prisons of hope
labyrinths of desire

and how
if I could sing to you
singing of birds
melodies sweeter
than lullabies in dreams,
longings of such strength
and such power
desire becoming flesh
becoming

remember me as one who could have been
and you
who turn
yet in turning remain unchanged
this
the nature of memory

the light rustling
through your silken hair
like the wind
or a hand
stroked by shadows

I come back to you
remembering
the fields green with thunder
the hills
lush with want

even here
you could have been
your hands crafting animals
unimagined
but for you
this stitch of canvas
this stretch of light
remembering
turtles
basking in the sun
carps beneath the bridges
the schoolgirls
in their yellow hats
and the shaven heads
of boys

remembering trains
the endlessness of stations
history of lives in transit
the collision of wars
and other unnatural disasters

yet
even here
the children play
by the shrine of martyrs

kannon by the water

I come back to you
in this landscape drawn with tears
the watercolour frailness
of parchment and paper

with this
as fragile
as promises of spring
your hand
reaching out
held fiercely
in what could only be called

desire

beginning with the landscape of your eyes

time etched
blueprint of this
the misshapen scars
the rope-bitten callous
hand over hand
across the mountain of tears
rock bed
and wind
even here
can weep with distant voices

THOMAS GLAVE

Baychester: A Memory

As we step from the car out onto the ground that is still muddy from last night's gentle rain, feeling its sucking at our feet as we imprint our soles on it, a light breath of spring blows the first scents of wildflowers to us: shovel in hand, I close my eyes and breathe in, deeply. Queen Anne's lace and honeysuckle, I tell my father, above me at my side; already preoccupied with our coming tasks, he smiles at my youthful enthusiasm but does not reply. These thicker morning fragrances, which never find their way as easily into dreams as do those of night, are soon replaced by the briny smell of Eastchester Bay, just off to our right; as we also become aware of the oddly delightful aroma of what we've come for: horse manure, to be dug at the Italian-owned Pelham Bay stables, directly ahead, for my parents' garden. With luck, we'll return home with several large garbage bags full, to empty them out later on the soft, loamy beds my father has spent the week preparing at our home in Baychester, a few miles north of here. There, they'll lay spread upon the ground, drying in the sun that each day now lasts a little longer, until we're ready to plant the seedlings which in adulthood will bear the vegetables my parents love: eggplant, summer and winter squash, onions, red cabbage, romaine and iceberg lettuce, and corn; allowing a little here and there for our still-straggly strawberries, the grape vines already clambering over the white-painted arbor beneath the front-lawn apple tree; some for the mulberry tree (whose berries have no taste) that nods heavy shade over our rabbit hutches; and—how can we forget?—some also for the seven fig trees which each spring emerge naked and groggy from the tar paper, plastic, and cardboard we've wrapped them in for the winter. The flowering cherry trees will get some, as will the apricots, pear, and plums. "You mean you have all this in the *Bronx*? On so little land?"—so a million passers-by will ask, have asked, on their way to or from the elevated subway, to or from the nearby apartment towers of Co-op City. (And in a *Black* neighborhood, too?, their question seems to imply, although almost all of those who will ask are Black). They will ask us this throughout the season, until the arrival of those long heavy burning days of summer when the early crops yield. My father— Daddy, as I always call him—will respond with a Jamaican-of-few-words musically-accented simple "Yes"—lowering his gaze as if ashamed for the speaker at the obvious silliness of such a question.

We continue on, stepping carefully along the downward path from the car to the stables, aware now of the whinnying of horses—something of a miracle in a place which has already become more well-known for nightly siren discordances and gunshots than for the honks of geese, which we also hear. In migration to points farther north, several pairs flutter down this morning to fuss and rest on the Bay. Perhaps a few of them will decide to summer here; the marshy ground on this side of the Bay and to the north offers plenty of good nesting sites, out of reach of would-be pests and assassins. Walking on, a screen of fragile spring foliage above our heads shimmers with each breeze off the water: a pale green life network along stems which bend but don't quite break beneath our fingertips' incautious curiosity. The time is eighteen years ago, a Saturday morning pulled from my memory, in this moment beyond fear, before any knowledge I will someday have of death and survival and the usefulness, cultural and otherwise, of masks. I am fourteen. Knobby-kneed, ashy-legged, I follow Daddy on the path. Today and every day, for as long as I can remember, he—only he—is master of the world.

This recounting serves by way of explanation in this present as to how I came to be in that other time and place. But in the moment, the actual moment of *being* and *feeling*, none of this explanation—this logic—matters. The backdrop tapestry of the day and its sight-wonders serves merely as an excuse for my coming along on this trip. I'm really here to watch trains, pretending all the while that I'm with Daddy doing something important—something adults will call "useful." The year is 1975, four years after Amtrak's acquiring the rights-of-way and passenger-service rolling stock of the nation's major railroads; we're lucky enough to live in what Amtrak calls the "Northeast Corridor" section of the country, near the former New Haven Railroad's trackage to Boston, which runs right past the Pelham Bay stables, out over the low Bay truss bridge (over which I've walked many an afternoon and early evening, daring death or simply not understanding its actual possibility), and on, obscured by woods, past the golf course, paralleling the New England Thruway to New Rochelle and Connecticut. As we press our spades into the rich, dark, earthworm-filled manure, I'm uneasy and alert, constantly turning back to face the tracks, afraid I might miss something of vital importance. Daddy begins to whistle, an old Jamaican song from his childhood, words I barely remember but attach to summer nights spent beneath banana trees in my great-grandmother's house as three headless roosters hopped about in dying frenzy outside and sea-wind lilted into the house to leave a trace of Caribbean salt spray on our lips.

Daddy loves this work. You can tell that just by watching him. He loves the breeze ruffling his hair, the free feeling of being out in the open near water (one of his unrealized dreams was to own a tall-masted schooner and sail the seas forever with shark-colored dolphins slicing the waters at his heels), away from a city he hates (the people are "unmannerly", the pace too fast); he loves the rich horseshit that he knows will produce the wine-dark eggplants he adores and the fat tomatoes my enterprising mother sells. This year he is fifty-nine, three years away from the diabetic onslaught that will sharply diminish his gardening days until it finally kills him twelve years later at the age of seventy-two. As I labor beside him, I think of all he doesn't know, or all I think he doesn't know: how I am slowly, painstakingly discovering a world very far from his own, through a medium he revered in his other, younger life as a journalist—books—but in this case

none of which he has read. C.A. Tripp's *The Homosexual Matrix,*
for one. For me, in my furtive readings of it on the subway each
day on my way to school in Manhattan, it has begun to clear a
way through a fog which still terrifies even as it exhilarates. By
now I've learned well of the shrieking violence the "H" word
(now the "G" word) produces—not so much from my parents as
from the boys my age and older who, at school and in our neighborhood, carry a wicked pugnacity in their necks and fists about
the subject. Hatred has come to them early via the killing cruelty
of a long line of harsh expletives which only begin with the word
"faggot." The feeling of that received hatred—the daily slam-
ming of its fists into my face and the taste of my own blood
drawn by the most vicious of these boys—is already steadily steering me away from what I'm learning can be, in this context, the
danger of direct, ambiguous eye contact with other young Black
men, young men outwardly just like me, who hit first and ask
questions later—as their parents probably did with them. I still
carry this fear, along with the constant furious rage and shame
that I've ever been afraid, am still afraid, have ever *had* to feel
afraid, at all; remembering with that fury and shame that to this
day I'm still extremely wary and skeptical of those Black men
who in convenient circumstances glibly call themselves "brothers," as I'm still wary and skeptical of those Black women who
capriciously call themselves "sisters"—both of whom then in their
own peculiar type of fear, loathing, and/or hypocrisy often inflict
violence on Black gay men and lesbians whenever we are found
either not to be useful or—far worse—too close to home. (The
word "faggot" itself is to me as nasty a form of violence as the
perennial spit-nastiness in that classic American word "nigger.")
I've never seen or sensed this type of violence in Daddy—as
proud of his image of his son (something I can't quite yet understand) as I will someday be of him (something he'll never completely know). Through texts such as Andrew Holleran's *Dancer
From the Dance* (of which in this time I understand neither its "in"
jokes and encoded language nor its not-so-subtle racism, and will
not until I re-read it fifteen years later), *The Church and the Homosexual*—I'm still something of a "good" Catholic, entranced by
incense and the Mysteries and the beautiful red ceremonial robes
of bishops—and *Gay* [white] *American History,* I feel myself evolv-

ing into something forged in a half-darkness of conscious longing and unself-conscious naivete, unbeknownst to Daddy; soon,
to my horror and later sadness, to grow away from him in his
coming illness as, fleeing the possibility of his leaving forever, I
take refuge in charting my own self-discovery. Becoming. To return
someday, fully armored, to the depthless riches of my father's
garden.

Today, however, digging, I know nothing of any of this. An
express train bound for Boston, silver-sided, hauling nine cars
which don't yet bear the Amtrak blue and red chevron logo,
comes clacking up the tracks toward us. The overhead electrical
wires hiss as, disturbed, the waterfowl roosting on the bridge rise
up into startled raised-eyebrow patterns. The horses, off feeding
in the distance, barely move. We turn slowly to watch the train.

"Look at the *pan*tograph," I shout, pulling on his arm, "—
that's the thing on top of the engine that connects to the overhead wires. Know what the wires are called? The *cate*nary." This
is enough to make me dance for the rest of the day—both having
seen a train, and such a dramatic one, and having been able to
share this knowledge carefully culled from too many model-rail-
road magazines. (Are there trains like this in Jamaica, I wonder?
But no!—I remember that time visiting the town in Clarendon
parish where Daddy was born and raised, learning in the midst
of all that headiness and excitement that Jamaica National Rail-
ways *does not use* electric trains.) I'm already in Boston with this
train as it hurtles northward on over the dark, low, rusty bridge,
on its way to the affluent Connecticut shore. The catenary is
high out of our reach, magical, something which neither the
subways nor the Long Island Rail Road, in their adherence to
boring regular old third-rail power, utilize. Daddy's brief nod, so
like my mother's stern glances, signals me to return to work.

What do I know today that he doesn't? Almost everything,
I dare to think, eyeing those squiggling earthworms at my shovel's
end with distaste; but not much, I finally hope. Except for this:
that, with the lengthening of these days, men who have already
learned the power and seduction of music-in-hips, slinky men
who fold shapely muscle and sinew into tight jeans and boots
that click out their own city rhythms, have begun to interest me.
I've already begun to leave the North Bronx, the trains to Bos-

ton, and the loud neighborhood bracelet-jangling teen-age girls (who laugh at my abashed fearful silence in the face of their bold how-can-you-resist-us flirts) for the streets of the West Village in lower Manhattan, where I'll watch these men in awed and sometimes skittish fascination: their slinks, their confident sashays past those like me whom they generally will ignore—we're too young still for most of them, and can make little sense of their complex ritualistic signals. This summer, I will also learn of a problem which won't make sense to me until years later: that is, that most of these men seem to be white. They, the most visible ones, whose teeth gleam from billboards and magazine covers and—unless the call is for HUGE (and probably "dangerous") penises—from sex ads. Mustached and plaid-shirted in the style of the day, flicking disdain in their wrists and what comes across as a self-protective outer disdain in their shoulders—what I think Eudora Welty signifies in her story "No Place For You, My Love" when she describes "human imperviousness": what many people call, simply, attitude—what so many of us receive so willingly from those who hate us and dole out so brutally to those who don't; that infuriating thing which hoods eyes and carves haughtiness in chins. Naturally by now I've been warned implicitly and explicitly numerous times by family members, friends, and general experience and observation not to trust white people, ever; not to let them ever get too close; if they do, the warnings tell me, I must keep something, many things, the most essential, precious, private part of the spirit-self, the gentleness, the personhood, out of their reach, protected and safe from the recklessness and inevitably destroying touch they've perfected— what my entire stateside family learned quickly through their own dehumanizing experiences as Black Caribbean immigrants to the United States, and before that in their daily lives under British West Indian colonialism; the general lesson Black children and adults in this country learn early on, without too much pain, if we're lucky. What will these new worlds teach me that my parents and grandparents and aunts and uncles, in their love and anxiety, will never be able to protect me from? To my unaccustomed eyes and ears raised on a street where the comfortable scents of rice and peas and curry goat and bammi breathe from houses along with the wails of O-you-got-me Ernie Smith, these new, mostly white people of the Village, who will live through the years before a ravaging epidemic whose horrors will claim many of our lives of every color and sexuality, will be the ones who spend summer weekends on that place called *fireisland*, out of sight and mind; who attend the opera and speak of *Tosca* (who? what? is she? he?); who sit in Village sidewalk cafes holding hands in the new enthrallments of romance and attraction (how I envy them!—their assurance, their ostensible imperturbability), sipping something called *cappuccino*, as they eye each other in ignorance of the fact that, intuitively, with a deep, creeping disappointment, I'm already anxiously eyeing them for someone who looks like me but whom I almost never find—or, when I do, he almost never sees what looks like *him*, nor apparently does he wish to—he having become an elegant, expensive black drape wrapped about the neck and arms of one of them. Like many white people before them, a number of these gay white men seem to have no problem expressing contempt and derision for what they've been raised to view as contemptible—Blackness, and other ethnicities—as at times, between moments of warmth and generosity, some of them will express another sort of contempt for each other, in the coldest of glances. A contempt for the gay brother or sister, a contempt for the self. (As, too often, we as Black gay men, lesbians, and others have learned to do to ourselves and other people of difference, having learned well from our former and sometimes contemporary masters.) They will continue to display an awesome capacity for this sort of contempt well into the future, to this very day; with such practiced skill and societal approval they will surely continue on long afterwards. Thus, to me, in their hands, in that way, some of those few now-and-then glimpsed Black men willingly evolve into new, bastardized creations formed out of the dregs of an old consciousness—they become the "it" of Gwendolyn Brooks's "Bronzeville Woman in a Red Hat," desired and feared and finally brought to heel, in a way, beneath the possessive-benignant paw of an owner: an it-thing to be fondled, stroked, assessed for the largesse of its thighs and presumed ferocity curled in its crotch. In this time and place, my teen-ager's eyes have trouble understanding exactly why he (or It) so frequently doesn't seem to mind his role as such a pet; my adult eyes will feel the fury that will tell me

more than I can ever make sense out of at fourteen—indeed,
more than I can stand to know, sometimes, when I begin to make
sense out of it as an adult. It is 1975, eleven years before Joseph
Beam (thank God for him!) will edit and publish *In the Life: A
Black Gay Anthology*; six years before Isaac Jackson will found the
Blackheart Collective which will publish the writings of Black gay
men, and sixteen more years before I will discover it; fourteen
years before I and others will experience the silencing chill of
Essex Hemphill's furious recital of "Now We Think" ["... as we
fuck"] in Marlon Riggs's award-winning film *Tongues Untied*, whose
title is taken from a British-published mini-anthology of five Black
gay poets; sixteen years before Hemphill will also edit and publish *Brother to Brother: New Writings by Black Gay Men*, the Beam-
conceived follow-up anthology to *In the Life*; sixteen years before
Assotto Saint,[1] another stalwart maverick in a time of great ones,
will edit and publish *The Road Before Us: 100 Gay Black Poets* (*one
hundred* gay Black poets? How far we've come! Who would have
bought/thought of/dreamt of such a book in 1975? Yet who *was*
dreaming of it then, in silence, in tongue-tied abject loneliness?);
and how many years before I meet Barbara Smith and cherish
her *Home Girls* anthology, discovering there the voices of Audre
Lorde, Pat Parker, June Jordan, and so many other powerful
Black lesbian writers; and how much more time before the founding of Other Countries, the New York-based Black gay men's
writing collective; and how many years, months, days, before what
else? How many?

   In the midst of all of this I think: where are the gay Jamaican voices? Where are the dark men who walk along those roads
to Constant Spring market or Saint Catherine market or along
the streets of Port Royal at sunset with Irish potatoes and bread-
fruit in their burlap bags and a pair of heavy dark eyes awaiting
them at home? Will this century's history leave us only Claude
McKay, one of the foremost voices of the Harlem Renaissance
but who—understandably for his time—never was able to come
out as of Jamaican descent *and* gay? Where are the gay—*openly*,
proudly gay—equivalents of John Hearne, A.L. Hendricks, Roy
Henry, Mervyn Morris, Roger Mais, Stuart Hall, and John
Figueroa?—to name only a few.[2] Where are the Jamaican openly
lesbian counterparts to Olive Senior, Lorna Goodison, Louise

Bennett, Velma Pollard, Christine Craig, Erna Brodber, and Opal Palmer Adisa—once again, to name only a few?

In this regard, amidst the silences and the voices of more than a few contemporary popular Jamaican singers screaming that we should be killed on sight, so far I know of only one challenging voice: that of the highly gifted writer Michelle Cliff. Lyrical, angry, haunting Michelle Cliff. A large personal voice. Prose that is poetry, lifesongs and threnodies. My nationhood-sister, like me an outsider both there and here. Her bravery and willingness to speak out as a lesbian privilege all of us and enable me, in particular, to do the same from the District of Look Behind, where we can't safely live, or up north, where, at least in the larger cities, we would like to think we can, and often don't. But where are the others? In a land where water and trees are never silent and ghosts speak nightly from mountaintops, who has enforced and colluded with this conspiratorial hush?

Still, in 1993 (what we consider "modern times"), what we have available in print by African-American lesbians and gay men are Bibles to me. Their works are severe speaking mirrors into which I look, now, and see several hundred lonely, laughing, desperate, silly, enraged, loving versions of myself and the men I dream to love. 1975—what feels like a century before these scattered eyes will look out and see signs that tell each other Yes, we exist. Here. Surviving amidst the terrible hushes and amidst the violence which daily threatens our lives. Safe only as long as we stand together—something we *must* do, and learn to do better, no matter how much the roaring mouth of that violence frightens us.

That *we*—the all-important We. Writing these words, I think of them—all of them whom I know now, whom I have known, whom I first met in the harsh enclosed spaces between silences and nervous laughter, behind shuttered eyelids, even as in seeking escape from bullies and bullets I've become something of a wanderer—as have so many of us. As I think of my father's body decaying these years in his grave, yet walking with me, *seeing* with me as surely as in those lonely discovering days I sought so many beyond the infuriating sheen of cold blue eyes that were so sure they had the power to make me disappear they even had me convinced. *Vanish*, that coldness said, "Vanish"—and I did, partly unmindful of injustice; always preferring life among the invisible, particularly if they're my own. I remember: becoming. Making my way from the North Bronx downtown to that unremarkable Harlem street where, in a building across from a littered, tattered excuse for a park, high, *high* above it all yet *in* it, I learned of love between nights of pink Champale and cheap reefer joked out from the singing, beer-chugging (and often loudly anti-gay) Puerto Rican boys on the corner. The young Black men who—restless, dreaming, agonized, wandering—also walked those searing streets of summer: walked, in that time, not yet clad in the 1990s high 'hood fashion of pants purposely-casually slung low on hips, so that you could still see quite clearly beneath their jeans and shorts the shapes and curves of their firm, high, beautiful be-hinds; as, inevitably, you recognized the pain and outrage in their eyes as something also completely yours—another common-ality beneath and beyond the skin, another responsibility beyond yet deep within and privy to the fear: the determination to sur-vive the ravages of that outrage and to do everything in your power to ensure that they too survived it if possible; no matter how fiercely it insisted, spurred on by those who had made it and named it, that you die. *For no, we would not die.* And still say No. Surviving the moment, continuing on. Seeing: up high, looking out: the roach-filled kitchen where a Siamese cat with the same smoky eyes as those I came to love drowsed to winter fatness in a corner, uncaring, unseeing, stretching out claws to somnolence as two Black men unashamedly, between awkward giggles, kissed. As we knew then and know now that even now those other worlds we know outside of our selves and sometimes within our selves will not make easy room for the (to some) threatening sum of this equation. Recalling: that long tree-lined street of brownstones and broad-windowed buildings where long brown eyelashes drooped over checkerboards and feisty old Black people mis-trustful of our youth turned up their (often light-skinned and proud of it) noses at two young Black men who entwined smooth dancer-limbs by day and went apartment-hunting by night, sway-ing that curious swing in the hips the old folks hadn't seen since they'd left behind the pine hills of North Carolina, the red earth of Georgia, the verdant Florida flatlands—and segregation and the fiery cross. Becoming. As my father still walked with me there and I learned the meaning of slow music-in-hips. And nights of

barbecued ribs on the fire escape, the thick greasy bodies of
scurrying scavenger rats far below, awaiting our bones. . . .

But no—I'm still here, still working beside Daddy on that
spring morning of trains and geese and horseshit. Already becoming a wanderer who will eventually return to a past beyond
complete recapturing in this North Bronx land that raised me,
I'll continue to work beside him, through all the years, slinging
horseshit into our plastic garbage bags as we dream, separately,
of what we both still have a chance to become amidst the en-
croachments of so many discrete personal confusions. Remembering all, making more sense out of this becoming process as we
drive up to Maine (*past* Boston!) to move me into my first year
of college there, where I'll study that new austere foreign landscape of cold sea and lobster shacks and pines in order to make
it a true part of my memory; celebrating the chance that will
later come for winter evening walks over gently arched bridges in
what will still be, in 1982, Leningrad (where, in that too-cold air,
I'll imagine myself in Paris, wondering if the coldness in white
people's and other strangers' eyes, and the occasional unexpected
kindness, is any different there or elsewhere from what I see in
the cold Russian-Soviet city, or on the North Bronx's largely Italian Allerton Avenue). In this urban mélange of ice and czarist
cake-architecture, the train-lover's eyes glide toward the blue sky-
sparks of electric trolleys on Nevsky Prospekt, as they also seek
out the dark wooden-seated *electrichka* that from Finlandsky Voksal
speeds with comfortable train-noise through snow-covered woods
to the *dacha* village of Olgino and farther northern points on the
Gulf of Finland; a place where I think of home, reminded of the
Throgs Neck Bridge lights we see from Baychester Avenue, as I
watch those other city lights across the freezing Gulf water green
their way into Leningrad evening life.

The process of connection and remembrance continues: as
I walk through six sultry Southern Hemisphere summer nights
in Buenos Aires, two *porteños*, fascinated by my dreadlocks, will
chase me down one of those wide cafe-lined avenues with their
cameras, shouting "Bob *Marley*! Bob *Marley*!" in not-so-innocent
and obnoxiously playful ignorance—what the Black traveler in
Latin America, particularly one who looks like me, comes to
know as unavoidable. (Later, amidst recollections of annoyance

at such foolishness, I'll learn easily enough to laugh at this—
recognizing that it must be an honor, surely, for anyone, and
particularly for a border-crossing Jamaican-American in transit
between notion-terrains of nationhood and cultural discovery, to
be called out as Bob Marley, anywhere.) To my outsider eyes, and
to their young ones, perhaps, we are far from *la guerra sucia*, far
from *The Official Story*, far from those drowning tragedies the
mothers of the Plaza de Mayo, thank God, will still not let us
forget. (I remember: today is Thursday. At three o'clock the
mothers march, and I am there, recording.) But there is warmth
here, too, often framed by deep sadness: apart from the ubiqui-
tous poverty which rings so many Latin American cities like swol-
len neck sores—a poverty which in this region of open veins
ringworms its way into the scalps of still too many Jamaican and
developing-nation children everywhere, as it encrusts their bare
feet and dusts over the mottled faces of their dead siblings—I
remember the light of longing in a Cuzco *indígena*'s face when,
admiring her llama, I tell her that I've just traveled by bus from
Chile up to this part of Peru, and, yes, I live in the States, and,
no, I'm not rich, haven't got a swimming pool, haven't got a
house with two cars, haven't got a beautiful blonde *gringa* girlfriend; her light vanishes. There will be the warm coffee-scented
Come, tell us how you live conversations with northern Argentines
in a public park in San Miguel de Tucumán, and the moments
of tears shared over cups of *tinto* with a woman in a small house
in a city high in the Andes, when we talk about the recent deaths
of people close to us: her husband, my sister. We still haven't
recovered, and still tell each other so. I take notes: on what I
remember, who and what I see, who I aim to be, and who I
continue to become. Recalling: in Colombia, walking chilly
Bogota's Carrera Septima beneath those dark-green Andes—what
Bogotanos locally call "los cerros," the hills, which flank the city's
eastern side from south to north—thinking of García Márquez
and his *costeño* world to the north, a world I'll come to know in
some small part during Holy Week; yet remembering—how can
any of us forget?—the eight-year-old Bogota prostitute whose
clients pay her five hundred pesos more—less than one U.S.
dollar at current exchange rates—if she will *not* insist they use a
condom; the ragged twelve-year-old boy missing two fingers and

an eye, at two o'clock A.M. selling cheap candies to weary unsmiling adults on a city bus; visions of Bogota's (and Lima's, and Santiago's) well-appointed, wealthy sections, where some residents employ doormen and guards to protect them from possible robberies and kidnappings by guerrilla groups (this protection usually works most forcefully against what occurs most frequently—the arrival of people begging at the door for food. In 1992, during city- and nationwide electricity rationings that cloak Bogota in dangerous darkness for four or more hours each day and night, the power is turned on here first); but also, in Bogota and the other cities, visions of poorer living areas, where people live practically *in* the dirt, often without water and electricity and even without walls—what our homeless in the United States share with those we dare to look down upon; and—perhaps most terrifying—the five or so Bogota drag queens mowed down by (army? police? "cleaning squad" terrorists'?) machine-gun fire early one morning, apparently because they simply existed, dared to exist. Neither *El Tiempo* nor *El Espectador*, Colombia's two major (and conservative) dailies, will carry any reportage on the murders. These nameless victims, along with so many impoverished children and countless others who wind up in mass graveyards of the anonymous unwanted, are called by many simply, coldly, "*desechables*"—disposables.

Remembering: that as a Black male who is also gay, I and my brothers and our Black lesbian sisters are considered "disposables" throughout the world, throughout time past and present, in our own Black communities and in white ones. This is clearly the case in Jamaica and most other Caribbean nations, and is certainly true in the supposedly more "progressive" United States. What will the force of this virulent hatred mean for our futures, and who will decide once again which of us is disposable?

And: will we stand together when the time comes for *us* to face that machine-gun fire? All of us? Beyond our prejudices?

(Remembering: the August 16, 1993 issue of *Stonewall News*, a New York gay weekly, features an article entitled "Amnesty International Denounces Treatment of Mexican Activists"; the article opens: "Amnesty International has expressed 'deep concern' over the arrest and ill-treatment of two gay activists by Mexican authorities. Other sources report that in 1992 *at least 23 gay men were murdered throughout Mexico by conservative death squads associated with the military or the police.*" [My italics] Such anti-gay/ lesbian violence persists as I write, in this moment, throughout most industrialized and developing nations of the world;[3] in many, with the increasingly prideful visibility and organizational effort-struggles of lesbians and gay men, it shows an unconscionably marked increase—so we learn from those lucky enough to survive the tortures to report them, or from those who grieve over lovers, family, and friends lost to disappearances, strategically repressive violence, and summary executions. We know, or ought to know by now, that the real-life dramas haven't changed. Neither have the characters. Will we be so smug, irresponsible, and selfish as to say "It's their problem"—and leave it at that? What will *this* mean for our futures?)

There will be evenings of racing dolphins (my father's dream) in the frigid South Pacific waters off the island of Chiloe, Chile, bringing to mind the wonderful works of Isabel Allende, whose magical writings, along with those of García Márquez and others, are so related to the magical writings and beliefs of peoples of African descent. The scent of mango and guava rising off the pages of *One Hundred Years of Solitude* or Rosario Ferré's *The Youngest Doll* instantly reminds me of another family garden in Norbrook, Jamaica, where not Barrabás but Marcus Garvey's voice comes to us by sea. When I return to Baychester, it will be with another type of knowledge of the richness of those ingrained textures, sounds, and sights: in those musical Jamaican accents and in our harsher Bronx cadences, in the smells of curry goat and sorrel and memories of ashy legs and cold cream and some of the small-town ways in which we live here—far from perfection but with spaces of occasional clarity between the relentless redness and confusion—everything of Toni Morrison's Ohio towns exists; everything even of Faulkner's far-off Yoknapatawpha County, and Flannery O'Connor's stark tree-edged Georgia fields—something of what the Jamaican writer Vic Reid wrote about so powerfully in *The Leopard* and *The Jamaicans*. With these realizations, an immeasurable solitude becomes clearer in you still out there, my exact and imprecise reflection, larger than myself and in your particular solitude owner of a darker knowledge than I acknowledge yet—or in some other life, some other moment of being, both owner and essence of something I've already carried and acknowledged. As Daddy discovered who I was in my new worlds simply by my one day telling him what he'd always known and had never hated, so now have I learned of *place*—that is, that these places are mine to return to and always will be: the North Bronx of my memory or that green blue-mountained island of my parents; the firm hand of a man in my own joined by the lasting power of my father's living spirit-grasp, guiding. Whichever, or all, if I choose; recognizing these places' pernicious dangers and hatreds of who I am—who *we* are—as I attempt to live as I *have* to live, telling the truth, as my parents raised me to do. In this, I hope that I'll neither fail along the way nor be killed for aiming to live my own truth, *our* truth, as I—we—refuse to be silenced. There will be time for all that and more. And time, too, for me to tell my father how much, how very much, I love him—how much I love the sweat on his neck as he hoists bags of horseshit into the car, the sweat shining on his face as he strains over those tender seedlings that tremble in his hands; how I love and mourn the glance of useless dreams in his beautiful cloudy-clear eyes, the soft gray hair on his head, and his always-formal courtliness—things I won't be able to say to him until shortly before he dies, yet still things which have never left me. Today, eighteen years ago or right now in the present, our *we* still exists in our acknowledged differences and strengths woven into the dream of a shared continuing history, the dream of so many still-silent and silenced voices throughout the world that are part of this We, inseparable from it. We can never let it be erased. *It will never be erased.* Today we carry the horseshit home, as yet another train passes through this memory, as yet another someone of this we—you, or him—walks here. I close my eyes and breathe in, deeply: the new long season breathes out its beginning. Deep in the blood, beating. Discovering. Becoming. Yes.

NOTES

1. Assotto Saint (Yves Lubin) died of AIDS-related illness on June 29th, 1994. For his long struggle against death, for his unequalled heralding and support of so many Black gay writers, and—most of all, never to be forgotten—for his nurturing and guidance of my work and vision, and for the love and privilege of his friendship—this essay is dedicated to his memory. My teacher. My brother.

2. As this essay goes to press, the news arrives that a prominent Jamaican writer has recently come out as gay. Because this news could not be satisfactorily substantiated, that writer will not be named as gay here. Yet, in one way or another, surely, we are beginning; in this way and others will we reinvent that which has long been circumscribed by the ruthlessness of paranoid and myopic limitation. To paraphrase George Lamming at the end of *Natives of My Person*, we will indeed become a future to be learned.

3. For further insights into and documentation of international human-rights abuses committed against lesbians and gay men—a topic still far too few nations, organizations, and individuals are willing to discuss, much less act on—Amnesty International's recent publication *Breaking the Silence: Human Rights Violations Based on Sexual Orientation* (1994) is recommended. This slim pamphlet, while somewhat abbreviated, offers at least a fairly adequate preliminary overview of some of the hateful consequences suffered by lesbians and gay men worldwide simply for the purported crime of being themselves. While Amnesty itself has only recently begun to work on behalf of persecuted lesbians and gay men, after years of lobbying efforts by gay-rights groups demanding that it do so, this booklet, to the organization's credit, is something of a proper beginning. Others must follow.

DAVID WILLIAMS

Made in Mexico

Seen from the air they're dark leaves
scattered before the wind

but no one lives on air

and the scattering forces are neither
random nor natural.

൦ᢩᢩ൦

She says again don't use her
name, don't take her
picture. But tell their story
on the other side of the border.

We could lose everything
for meeting like this,
women from all these maquiladoras
trying to make something better.

൦ᢩᢩ൦

All day her eyes follow
small dark plastic pellets

melted, extruded, molded
into sunglasses that say glamour,

mystery, leisure, protection—
nothing she can afford.

                    ☙

She lives close enough to walk.

The hardpack here can't save the rain.
She gathers it in an old chemical drum
scavenged from *maquila* trash.

No roots keep the bank from collapsing.
Old tires are stacked in its side,
stabbed, blown out, worn bald

with all the distances of Mexico
crossed, hitching, walking, scrimping
busfare, just to reach

this squatters' camp.

                    ☙

Her husband went home for a *cargo*—
weeding the churchyard, burning *copal*,
preparing rituals in the village
so their family will still belong.

This is no place. Besides he can't get
a *maquila* job. God gave women
the small hands and patience ideal
for assembly work.

                    ☙

She pauses descending the steps on the bank—
half-buried tires, wheels, cinderblocks—

and takes it all in, her standing there

a self-portrait, her naming of castoffs
part of a sacrament making the world.

Palo Santo

What does it look like, *palo santo*
—*lignum vitae*—tree of life
guitarmakers wander the hills
of Andalusia to find?
It gives medicine
and the dark sounds
gypsies love.

Here it grows scrubby and tough
both sides of the border.
Between coyotes and *la migra*
Jorge's friends had nowhere to cross
but Piedras Negras, where the Rio Grande
goes crazy,
                    and were lost.

Light in the Highlands

My daughter's shiny, straight black hair
catches sun—think of living water—
and gathers it in a ring, a common
crown, human, broken, whole.

☙❦☙

To bear the beams of love, Blake said.
Give birth to them? Endure them?
Or muscle them up, squared hearts of trees
to frame the sky, take the roof's weight?

☙❦☙

From her earliest steps she trusted
pine-dark slopes like a fragrant memory
while I wondered how far I could carry her
if need be.

☙❦☙

In the highlands, beams of light and mist
bare themselves between cornrows and trees.
No roof for the families afraid that even
a cookfire will draw back the army.

☙❦☙

Hungry, they stay alive, won't give in, run
clinging to the youngest, who cling to them,
the children's dusty, rain-tangled hair
crowned in secret with forest light.

(remembering Guatemala, and other places)

Getting Through

We call for days
to get a phone line through,
strain across the crackle
of borders and undersea
cables to read

voices, remember
how they put things there,

get straight
who's been killed,
who hasn't been seen
in weeks, who's walking
the roads tonight
a refugee
God knows where.

Or maybe the line's tapped
and all we can do
is make smalltalk,
so much feeling
dammed behind it,
clues
to who's still alive.

⊙⊹⊙

I walk around safe,
make smalltalk,
talk politics,
afraid
if I cried out
you might turn away
or answer in some brutally
innocent manner of speaking.

⊙⊹⊙

Distortions, explanations—
I want us to live
joined by nerve understanding

spreading inland
from coves and riverbanks
like the first green tendrils
over the earth.

Otherwise the dead stay dead
though their hearts go on
like the grieving sea.

So what if I outsmarted a fish
I found beautiful and didn't need to eat?
The pickerel's mouth was around the hook—
one more instant he'd bite and be torn.
I jiggled a warning down the line,
and he backed off quick and smooth.

Across the pond a woman came down,
waded in so far and stopped,
but kept throwing out a stick
for her dog to return
while light off the water
dappled up her thighs.

She thought she was alone
so I turned away.

I remember how my father always entered the water
shyly, carefully wetting his skin
like a shepherd smearing an orphaned lamb
with another ewe's blood so she'd claim it.
Once he swam out so far alone, he didn't
know the way back when dark surprised him.
Then someone on shore he never met,
thinking of something else,
flicked on a light and he didn't drown.

PJ McGANN

On the Transformation of Theory into Poetry and Praxis

What Audre was doing there I could not (at first) fathom.

I met her on a sticky summer's day traveling with a sweet Midwestern white boy in a van back to Minnesota. He introduced us in a mechanic's back lot while we—he and I—awaited a rebuilt carburetor (having spent the previous night sleeping alongside a river after his van collapsed and died—as it would do again another six times in the next thirty-six hours). I was sunning atop a pile of used tires, lounging sweating amidst dirt, asphalt and grime as the rubber rotted into destiny, eager to resume our/my journey, when he brought Audre to me.

She said, "I am standing here as a Black lesbian poet."[1] "What?" I started to ask, "How is that relevant? How does it and how do you speak to me? How—"

"Audre speaks to me," my friend interrupted earnestly, this straight man oozing the upper midwestern naivete and trust I had discarded. "You don't know her? *Sister Outsider?*" he asked incredulously, blinking in the sun.

"We've never met," I shrugged. "I guess we will now. Nothing else to do but wait."

❖

It was my first homecoming, the first return for my emerging scholarly self. I was fresh from my first two years of grad school, flush with the excitement of accomplishment, the knowledge that I had "made it"—or was about to. Proud that aside from the broken van I would be unrecognizable in my return. My path out of manual labor into the mind, begun in a small city junior college, converged now with an elite east coast Ph.D. program and a private audience with a world-renowned male European intellectual. I read and conversed fluently the works of dead men whose names only a year before I could not pronounce, whose importance I could not see, due not to their irrelevance for my life, but to my ignorance. I soon enough learned to conceal my rough, ignorant ways. I sipped tea, ate foods I'd never dreamed of. I learned of liberal arts educations, European travels and travails. I stopped talking of ball fields, trailer parks, hand-me-downs, assembly lines. I soon enough bracketed my shocked vulnerability by forgetting my surprise at $100 skirts, my nausea at $200 shirts, my cyclone of confusion that first day when on a bend in the path I stepped face to face with the teeth of a Jaguar. And then a Mercedes. And a Saab. A BMW....

Such beasts I had never seen before, let alone touched.

The distance I travelled those two years—it was a long, long way from my gravel driveway to Brandeis—proved to me the irrelevance of background and body. For I too, born of public schools and vocational technical training, could learn the European classics, could earn the highest degree in the land, could make myself over and become one of them. I thus began the re-making of myself in my understanding of their image. And so I wrote of Science and Reason and Epistemology, of Capitalism and Revolution and Social Change, of Phenomenology and Hermeneutics and Critical Theory. And so I started to learn German (and then French?) to avoid my thoughts being dependent upon the translations of others (and also so as to no longer feel ashamed of my background?). And so I studied Classical Social Thought, "American" Pragmatism, The Sociology of Knowledge, Philosophy of Science. And so, too, I wrote of ideology and the existentiality[2] of thought, of the self, all the while submerging any "contaminating" traces of myself, my body, my former connections to/with the world. (I did not write then of gender, of sexuality, of class, of bodies.)

It was then that Audre so rudely interrupted: "Because I am woman, because I am Black, because I am lesbian, because I am myself—a Black woman warrior poet doing my work—come to ask you, are you doing yours?"[3]

"Come to ask me, am I doing mine?" Her question leapt from the pages at me, sat squarely on my white skin soon to grow red in the fiery sun, demanding an answer.

I pondered.

She was insistent: " . . . come to ask you, are you doing yours?" But of course I was. I *must* be. I was theorizing macro structural change. Dialectics. I was the star pupil of a star. I was on the fast track. . . . Who was this woman, this Black lesbian poet, this mother of a son and a daughter? What was she asking me? What was she writing about so intimately, so passionately, so eloquently, that I could neither understand nor turn away? How could I learn from her, she so different from me?

The cadence of her words captured me, captivated me. The intensity of her theorizing outside the bounds of theory both frightened and attracted me. Blood, bodies, colors, sex, passion: all the irrelevant things. For another year I kept silent about our association, our growing familiarity, my sneaking suspicion that Audre was telling me something vital though I could not imagine what, whilst I wrestled free of Sociology.

It turns out I had to leave so that I could return. It turns out I had to first remember that I, too, had been a poet—until that night he wrenched my word songs from me, distorted them, lashed me with their honesty meant only for me. Later, when he was gone, I set them afire, held the silvery embers of my paper soul as the flames singed my skin. That night, and many nights after, I confused the pain of his treachery with my daring "sin" of embodied honesty. And I vowed not to be seduced again by the poet's risky call but to wrap myself instead in the safety of scientific fact. That I later recognized this error is due, in part, to my chance meeting with Audre and her subsequent gifts to me.[4]

❧

I am standing here as/in my white, female, queer, disabled, strong, weak, disciplined, lustful, falling in love (?), well-trained, yearning-to-be-free body—as a scholar, as *myself*—come to tell you I *am* doing my work. (Are you doing yours?)

As you may have guessed, it was not always the case that I would, or even could, say this. In part this is because some of these dimensions were not integrated parts of my identity (disabled, for example). But more than this, it is because the longer I was in graduate school, the closer I came to being an intellectual, the more dis-embodied I became. And the more disembodied, the more alienated, until the body I was no longer "in" swelled with pain. But then, a recalled whisper on a page: "I feel, therefore I can be free."[5] The juxtaposition of the classic Western dualism intrigued me. But what was it, exactly, that I felt?

Audre's insistence that I confront her feelings, her body, made it easier for me to confront my own. I came, eventually, to see that my confusion, my tension, my mis/fit were due not to personal inadequacy and difference, but were reflections of problems within the oppressively homogenizing scene of higher learning itself: a scene that presumes (and rewards) a privileged upper-middle-class upbringing and education and that overlooks (and punishes) "deviations" from that presumption. I tried then not to push the pain of my mis/fit away, hoping instead, that Audre was right: " . . . our feelings, and the honest exploration of them become sanctuaries and spawning grounds for the most radical and daring of ideas."[6]

The more I dared return to my body the more I discovered my power, my knowledge, and my feelings of confusion slid toward critique. The more I embraced the pain of my mis/fit the more ground I had to stand upon, and the more ground I had the more stable I was. Still, recognizing, and what's more, making visible, my "difference" was daunting: "we fear the visibility without which we cannot truly live. . . . And that visibility which makes us most vulnerable is that which is also the source of our greatest strength."[7] First in private, then in the company of other misfits, my marginality became my power. As I claimed my "outsider within,"[8] I felt the healing illuminating power of analytic self-narrative. I started to analyze my biography in the context of structure and history. In so doing I grew to see general patterns revealed in the particular. I saw that what I took for private troubles were, or should be, public issues.[9] Thus in my silence within I named the classism, the sexism, the homophobia, the racism that divided me from myself, from others, from Theory. And I began to trust the power of my own knowing.

Still, I could not write. Still, I dared not talk back. "What are the words you do not yet have? What do you need to say? What are the tyrannies you swallow day by day and attempt to make your own until you sicken and die of them, still in silence?"[10] Could it be? Could it be that it was not the rapes nor the harassment nor the homelessness nor the bashing nor the death of a friend from AIDS that was sickening me but the *denial* of these things? Could it be? Could it be that it was the erasure, the disappearance of these events as "relevant" in/for the theories I so treasured that was strangling me? Could it be?

But if I spoke these words, if I recounted these truths, would I not be told that they were irrelevant? Would I not then be out in the cold again? And now, having sustained a permanent bodily injury I could not return to manual labor. How would I survive? Audre interrupted again: "Your silence will not protect you."[11] "We have been socialized to respect fear more than our own needs for language and definition, and while we wait for that final luxury of fearlessness, the weight of that silence will choke us."[12]

My silence did not protect me when they followed me in the night. And my silence did not protect me when the nightmares returned. And my silence did not protect me when I was too queer for the job. And my silence did not protect me when I could not then buy food. And my silence did not protect me when they painted the swastika in my yard. But when I broke the silence I found relief. When I broke the silence I found dignity. When I broke the silence I found connection to others seemingly so different from me. And when I found relief and dignity and connection I found protection too. It was then that Black spoke to white, lesbian to bi, poet to theorist. It was then that the things most unfamiliar about Audre became familiar, and in that familiarity, insight: ". . . *survival is not an academic skill.* It is learning how to stand alone, unpopular and sometimes reviled, and how to make common cause with those others identified as outside the structures in order to define and seek a world in which we can all flourish. It is learning how to take our differences and make them strengths. *For the master's tools will never dismantle the master's house.*"[13]

The more I embraced difference within and across, the more clearly I saw it was not the differences that separate us, "it is rather our refusal to recognize those differences, and to examine the distortions which result from our misnaming them and their effect upon human behavior and expectation."[14] The more I examined these distortions the more I recognized the master's *adversarial* tools: division rather than connection, fear of difference rather than embrace, power over rather than power with. The more I broke my silence, the easier it became to leap across the polarities of difference, finding power and comfort in the space where our differences overlap.

"The master's tools will never dismantle the master's house." My rallying cry. For me this means adversarialism—as built into our social structure, as built into our consciousness—is the premiere tool of the master. I have thus committed myself to adversarialism's opposite: mutuality.[15] Because the master's tools will never dismantle the master's house, I take seriously that we cannot wait for the revolution; we must live it. We cannot strive for the ends through questionable means, because the means are the ends. Because the master's tools will never dismantle the master's house I work from the inside out, believing that personal and social change must occur simultaneously.

Thus I struggle not to deny but to sit with and *know* "that piece of the oppressor which is planted deep within."[16] On a personal level this putting down of the master's tools means addressing, owning up to, and ultimately rescinding my own racism, classism, ablism, sexism, homophobia. It means coming to see my place in the weblike matrix of domination where I am oppressed—but also where I am oppressor. This means educating myself about my oppressive acts, rooting out my internalized patterns of domination, setting down my privileges, taking up my responsibilities. This means breaking the silence, no matter how difficult and no matter the personal cost, when I witness racist, classist, ablist, sexist, homophobic manifestations of the larger adversarial tool.

This means teaching others the lessons I have learned. This teaching entails serious, attentive study of history, social structure, theory—but also the embrace of embodied subjectivities, the insights bursting forth in poetries. This teaching entails serious, reflexive attention to the details of my being in the world. "It is necessary to *teach by living* and speaking those truths which we believe and know beyond understanding."[17] If adversarialism is the glue of the master's tool kit, the transformation of silence must be done respectfully, if not lovingly, without recourse to personal attack or injury—for are these not other incarnations of the master's tools? If we wish to create a world where unity does not mean homogeneity, where difference is not only tolerated but "seen as a fund of necessary polarities between which our creativity can spark like a dialectic," we must make our interdependency unthreatening.[18] We must then, quite literally, disarm ourselves. We must, then, disarm also our rhetorics and relinquish the illusory defense of adversarial textual Mastery. We must, instead, speak our poetics.

Learning, truly deep learning of the sort I am trying to accomplish, means change. And "Change means growth, and growth can be painful."[19] In the midst of pain, the heart often constricts in defense. But this response can be shortcircuited, perhaps even unlearned—if all parties are vulnerable together in the absence of attack. Can I ask for honesty if I am not honest myself? Can I ask for vulnerability if I am not vulnerable myself? Thus in teaching I open my heart to my students. I reveal my vulnerability by letting them see my errors (in hopes that they will then be safe to see their own), by living the imagined future now (by treating them with kindness and respect whether they agree with me or not).

This openness, this vulnerability, requires a tremendous amount of energy. I find "my fullest concentration of energy is available to me only when I integrate all the parts of who I am, openly, allowing power from particular sources of my living to flow back and forth freely through all my different selves."[20]. And so in the classroom I am no longer the voice of Authority, but *a* voice more widely read and more systematically trained (perhaps). The more I subvert my own Authority in this way, the more legitimate I become—and also the more whole. This insistence on being whole, this refusal to disappear, this opening into mutuality is sometimes terrifying. It carries with it the threats of bruising, of misunderstanding. But this opening is also a source of tremendous joy, a joy I reveal in hopes others will join in. Soon enough, some do. "The sharing of joy, whether physical, emotional, psychic, or intellectual, forms a bridge between the

sharers which can be the basis for understanding much of what
is not shared between them, and lessens the threat of their difference."[21]

I believe this sharing of joy ultimately to be subversive. Thus
I teach not to the lowest common denominator but to the higher
self, to that which I hope we can all become. Thus I teach to and
with feelings: anger and joy. In being fully myself in this way I live
the interrogation of the master's false dichotomies—feeling "versus" reason, subjectivity "versus" objectivity, poetry "versus"
theory—through poetic theories and theoretical poetry. In so
doing I seek to bring the students back into themselves, into
their bodies, into their poetic visions of everyday life, by starting
with lived experience—theirs, mine, others'—then moving up
and out and eventually back. Doing so they, and I too, often feel
deeply. Doing so we uncover and recover flashes of insight long
silenced. We reconnect to power long disguised, and become less
tolerant of disempowerment and doubt. "Once we begin to feel
deeply all the aspects of our lives, we begin to demand from
ourselves and from our life-pursuits that they feel in accordance
with that joy which we know ourselves to be capable of."[22] And so
I find it necessary to teach history and theory *and* poetry, to
teach *and live*, mutualistically, non-violently. Thus I find it necessary to be brash, confrontational, challenging, insistent, meticu-
lous, but also respectful, open, disarmed, playful, silly, messy.
And I find it necessary, too, not only to interrogate the structures
of our oppression, but to take the hands of the oppressors and
invite them instead to dance.

NOTES

1. Audre Lorde, *Sister Outsider* (Freedom, Cal.: The Crossing Press,
1984), 40.

2. Karl Mannheim, *Ideology and Utopia* (New York: Harcourt Brace
Jovanovich, 1936).

3. Lorde, 41–42.

4. It is also due to the context and peculiarities of the Brandeis
Sociology department, a tradition linking a transmuted version of clas-

sic Chicago School Sociology (Reinharz 1995), European social and critical theory, radicalism, praxis, and feminism (Thorne 1987). Brandeis often makes possible close and loving associations between students. Its largely interdisciplinarily-trained faculty trusts students to combine seemingly disparate thought models (such as Buddhism and classical social theory, poetry, and grounded empiricism) in innovative and humanizing ways. While this spirit infuses the department, it was given to me most directly by my teachers, Gordie Fellman, Morrie Schwarz, and Irv Zola. It is to them I dedicate this essay.

5. Lorde, 38.

6. Lorde, 37.

7. Lorde, 42.

8. Patricia Hill-Collins, *Black Feminist Thought* (New York: Routledge, 1991).

9. C. Wright Mills, *The Sociological Imagination* (London: Oxford University Press, 1959).

10. Lorde, 41.

11. Lorde, 41.

12. Lorde, 44.

13. Lorde, 112.

14. Lorde, 115.

15. See Gordon Fellman, "Peace in the World or the World in Pieces," *Policy Studies 34* (September) (Jerusalem: The Leonard Davis Institute for International Relations, The Hebrew University of Jerusalem, 1989).

16. Lorde, 123.

17. Lorde, 43. Emphasis added.

18. Lorde, 111.

19. Lorde, 123.

20. Lorde, 120–121.

21. Lorde, 56.

22. Lorde, 57.

AUDRE LORDE

Echoes

There is a timbre of voice
that comes from not being heard
and knowing   you are not being
heard   noticed only
by others   not heard
for the same reason.

The flavor of midnight fruit   tongue
calling your body through dark light
piercing the allure of safety
ripping the glitter of silence
around you
     dazzle me with color
     and perhaps I won't notice
till after you're gone
your hot grain smell tattooed
into each new poem   resonant
beyond escape   I am listening
in that fine space
between desire and always
the grave stillness
before choice.

As my tongue unravels
in what pitch

will the scream hang unsung
or shiver like lace on the borders
of never recording
which dreams heal which
dream can kill
stabbing a man and burning his body
for cover being caught
making love to a woman
I do not know.

The Politics of Addiction

17 luxury condominiums
electronically protected
from criminal hunger   the homeless
seeking a night's warmth
across from the soup kitchen
St. Vincent's Hospital
razor wire covering the hot air grates.
Disrobed need
shrieks through the nearby streets.

Some no longer beg.
a brown sloe-eyed boy
picks blotches from his face
eyes my purse shivering
white dust a holy fire
in his blood
at the corner   fantasy
parodies desire   replaces longing
Green light.   The boy turns back
to the steaming grates.

Down the street in a show-window
camera   Havana
the well-shaped woman smiles
waves her plump arm along
half-filled market shelves
excess expectation
dusts across her words
"Si hubieran capitalismo
hubiesen tomates aquí!"
"If we had capitalism
tomatoes would be here now."

The Night-Blooming Jasmine

Lady of the Night   star-breathed
blooms along the searoad
between my house and the tasks before me
calls down a flute
carved from the legbone of a gull.

Through the core of me
a fine rigged wire
upon which pain will not falter
nor predict
I was no stranger to this arena
at high noon
beyond was not an enemy
to be avoided
but a challenge
against which my neck grew strong
against which my metal struck
and I rang like fire in the sun.

I still patrol that line
sword drawn
lighting red-glazed candles of petition
along the scar
the surest way of knowing
death is a fractured border
through the center of my days.

Bees seek their need
until flowers beckon
beyond the limit of their wings
then they drop where they fly
pollen baskets laden
the sweet work done.

They do not know the Lady of the Night
blossoms
between my house and the searoad
calling down a flute
carved from the legbone of a gull
your rich voice
riding the shadows of conquering air.

November 1990-May 1992

Contributors

Marcus Akinlana graduated from *the Art Institute of Chicago* and went on to join *Chicago Public Art Group* and execute numerous public and collaborative community-based projects. He has fabricated public art in Denver, Atlanta, New Orleans, Washington D.C., Milan (Italy), and Liverpool (England). He operates **Positive Creations**, his fine art company which retails originals, prints, and cards.

Jeffner Allen is Professor of Philosophy and Women's Studies at the State University of New York at Binghamton. She is the author of *SINUOSITIES, Lesbian Poetic Politics* (Indiana University Press, 1995), *reveberations across the shimmering CASCADAS* (SUNY Press, 1994), and *Lesbian Philosophy: Explorations* (Institute of Lesbian Studies, 1986), editor of *Lesbian Philosophies and Cultures* (SUNY Press, 1991), and co-editor of *The Thinking Muse: Feminism and Recent French Thought* (Indiana University Press, 1989).

James Baldwin was born in 1924 and educated in New York. He is the author of more than twenty works of fiction and nonfiction, including *Go Tell It on the Mountain, Notes of a Native Son, Giovanni's Room, The Fire Next Time, Blues for Mister Charlie, Going to Meet the Man, If Beale Street Could Talk, The Evidence of Things Not Seen,* and *The Price of the Ticket.* Among the Awards he received are a Eugene F. Saxon Memorial Trust Award, a Rosenwald Fellowship, a Guggenheim Fellowship, a *Partisan Review* Fellowship, and a Ford foundation grant. He was made a Commander of the Legion of Honor in 1986. He died in 1987.

Becky Birtha is the author of two collections of short stories, *For Nights Like This One: Stories of Loving Women* (Frog in the Well) and *Lovers' Choice* (Seal Press), and a poetry collection entitled *The Forbidden Poems* (Seal Press). She has received fellowships from the NEA and the Pennsylvania Council on the Arts. She lives in Philadelphia.

Regie Cabico is the winner of the 1993 New York Poetry Slam, a road poet on Lollapalooza, and the opening act of MTV's Free Your Mind Spoken Word Tour, for which he stars in a 30-second poetry video on MTV. His poetry and criticism appears in *Ikon, The Saint Mark's Poetry Project, Red Brick Review, Aloud: Voices from the Nuyorican Poet's Cafe,* and *The Name of Love,* among others.

Elizabeth Clare is a poet, essayist, and activist living in Michigan, transplanted from Oregon. She has an M.F.A. in Creative Writing from Goddard College. Her poems and essays have been published in various anthologies and periodicals, including *Sojourner, Sinister Wisdom, The Disability Rag, Hanging Loose,* and *The Arc of Love: An Anthology of Lesbian Love Poems.* Her first book, a collection of essays and poems, is to be published by South End Press in the spring of 1999.

Jo Whitehorse Cochran is a Lakota/Norwegian who holds an MFA in Creative Writing from the University of Washington. She currently lives in Ashland, Oregon, where she will be establishing a small press. Over the last few decades, Jo has been active in feminist lesbian and gay and Native American rights movements.

Britt Alice Coles has written for broadcasting, print, the theatre, and the World Wide Web. Her work is influenced by queries around multiple identities crossing the borderlines of gender, race, ethnicity, and sexual identities. "Drawing on Myself" is dedicated to her mother, Ing-Britt, and her mentor, Don.

Cathy Daley is a visual artist who lives in Toronto and has exhibited her work across Canada and internationally since 1980. Her recent drawings focus on the female body and its representation. She teaches drawing and painting at the Ontario College of Art and is represented by Paul Petro Contemporary Art.

Marcia Douglas is a Ph.D. candidate in the English Department at Binghamton University of the State University of New York where her work has focused on women writers from the African Diaspora. In 1993 she received an MFA in Creative writing from Ohio State University. She writes both poetry and fiction, and is currently at work on her first novel. Her work has been published in *Puerto del Sol, Sun Dog: Southeast Review,* and *A Place to Enter: Contemporary Fiction by Emerging Writers of African Descent.*

Martín Espada is the author of five poetry collections, most recently *Imagine the Angels of Bread* and *City of Coughing and Dead Radiators* (both W.W. Norton). He is also the editor of *Poetry Like Bread: Poets of the Political Imagination from Curbstone Press.* His awards include two NEA Fellowships and the PEN/Revson Fellowship. Espada teaches at the University of Massachusetts-Amherst.

Carolyn Forché's first poetry collection, *Gathering the Tribes* (Yale University Press, 1976) won the Yale Series of Younger Poets Award from the Yale University Press. In 1977, she received a John Simon Guggenheim Foundation Fellowship, which enabled her to live in El Salvador for almost two years, where she worked as a human rights activist. Her experiences there informed her second book, *The Country Between Us* (Harper and Row, 1982). Forché has worked as a correspondent in Beirut, Lebanon, for National Public Radio's "All Things Considered" and as a human rights Liaison in South Africa. She now teaches in the Fine Arts Program in Poetry at George Mason University in Virginia.

Living in Greece in the 1960s inspired **Ellen Frye** to research Greek Folklore and write fiction based upon Greek myths. Her works include her folk song collection, *The Marble Threshing Floor*

(University of Texas Press, 1972), and her novels, *The Other Sappho* (Firebrand, 1989) and *Amazon Story Bones* (Spinsters Ink, 1994).

Thomas Glave, a 1997 O. Henry Award winner, is a Graduate Teaching Assistant in the MFA Creative Writing Program at Brown University. His work has appeared in numerous journals and anthologies, among them *Callaloo, The Kenyon Review,* and *Children of the Night: The Best Short Stories by Black Writers, 1967-present* (Little Brown). He has recently completed his first story collection.

Gertrude M. James Gonzalez is a Ph.D. candidate in the Philosophy, Interpretation and Culture Program at Binghamton University of the State University of New York. Her work focuses on aesthetics, identity, and colonialism.

Sculptor **Ronald Gonzalez** was born in Johnson City, N.Y., in 1952 and received his BFA from the State University of New York at Binghamton. His work has appeared in numerous solo and group exhibitions, including at the Roberson Museum in Binghamton, at the Hanes Art Center at the University of North Carolina at Chapel Hill, at the Everson Museum of Art in Syracuse, at the *Neuberger Museum of Art Biennial Exhibition of Public Art* at SUNY Purchase and at the *Spoleto Festival U.S.A., Human/Nature: Art and Landscape in Charleston and the Low Country* in Charleston, S.C. He has been artist in residence at Cornell University, SUNY Binghamton, and at The University of North Carolina at Chapel Hill. He lives in Binghamton, N.Y.

Olivia Gude is an artist, organizer, and educator based in Chicago. She is currently an assistant professor and Coordinator of Art Education for the University of Illinois Chicago and is an active member of the Chicago Public Art Group. Gude has worked in the field of community art for twenty years and has created many large-scale mural and mosaic projects, working with intergenerational groups, teens, elders, and children.

Susanne de Lotbinière-Harwood is a feminist translator whose practice is centered in *Quebecoises* and Canadian feminists' writing and the Montréal visual arts milieu. Her own writing, in

French and in English, has been widely published. Winner of two literary translation awards, she teaches at Concordia University.

Essex Hemphill is a writer, poet, and cultural activist. He is well known through his participation in the Black gay films *Looking for Langston, Out of the Shadows,* and *Tongues Untied,* which aired on PBS in the summer of 1991. He is the editor of *Brother to Brother: New Writings by Black Gay Men,* the author of the collections of poetry, *Earth Life* and *Conditions,* and of *Ceremonies,* a book of prose and poetry.

Joanna Kadi is a writer, poet, and musician. She edited *Food For Our Grandmothers: Writings by Arab-American and Arab-Canadian Feminists,* which was published by South End Press in 1994. Her second book, *Thinking Class: Sketches from a Cultural Worker,* came out from South End in 1996.

Pauline Kaldas immigrated from Egypt to the United States at the age of eight in 1969. Her poetry has appeared in *Lift, Michigan Quarterly Review, International Quarterly,* and *Food for Our Grandmothers,* an anthology of Arab-American feminist writing. She is currently working on her Ph.D. in English at Binghamton University.

Tamai Kobayashi was born in Japan and raised in Canada. Nocturnal and solitary by nature, she has been known to hibernate for months at a time. She is one of the founding members of Asian Lesbians of Toronto. Her work has been published in "Awakening Thunder: Asian Canadian Women," Issue 30 of *Fireweed, Piece of My Heart: A Lesbian of Colour Anthology* (Sister Vision), and *Getting Wet: Tales of Lesbian Seduction* (Women's Press). She is co-author, with Mona Oikawa, of *All Names Spoken* (Sister Vision).

Lucy R. Lippard is a cultural activist based in New Mexico, author of seventeen books, including *Mixed Blessings: New Art in a Multicultural America, Partial Recall: Photographs of Native North Americans, The Pink Glass Swan: Selected Essays on Feminist Art,* and (forthcoming) *The Lure of the Local: Place in a Multicentered Society.*

Audre Lorde published ten volumes of poetry and five works of prose. She was a recipient of many distinguished honors and awards including honorary doctorates from Hunter, Oberlin, and Haverford colleges, and was named New York State Poet (1991– 1993).

Myra Love has a Ph.D in German from the University of California, Berkeley. She taught German language and literature for several years, first at Purdue, then at Bryn Mawr College. She published a book and several articles on Christa Wolf and East German literature. She now lives in Jamaica Plain, Mass., with her partner Martha, where she writes fiction. She is studying voice with the world's greatest teacher and working as a full-time carrot delivery system for her pet rabbit Kahlua, who proofreads all her manuscripts, which is why she hasn't yet published her first novel.

Anne J. Manbeck Mamary is Assistant Professor of Philosophy and Gender Studies at St. Lawrence University and has her Ph.D. from the Philosophy, Interpretation and Culture (PIC) program at the State University of New York at Binghamton. She lives in a nineteenth-century house in Canton, N.Y., with Java, one great cat, and loves the backyard gardening world she shares with her neighbors. She has been bitten by the Morris dancing bug and dances with the B.F. Harridans, based in Binghamton, NY.

Alison Marchant is an installation artist and researcher. She has exhibited nationally across Britain, and at Franklin Furnace, New York (1988); W139 Gallery, Amsterdam (1992); The Metropolitan Museum of Art, Tokyo (1992); & Tatranski Gallery, Slovakia (1994). She is currently Senior Lecturer in Contemporary Arts, Nottingham Trent University, England.

PJ McGann's expertise includes gender/sexuality, ethnography, social psychology, medicalization and the body, mountain biking, in-line skating, rock napping, snow sports, and all manner of binary transgressions. Her upcoming book, *The Ballfields of Our Hearts* (Temple), concerns tomboy identity and its legacies, gendered social control, and "feminine" bias in studies of women (stk).

D. H. Melhem is the author of four books of poetry, a novel, *Blight,* over fifty essays, and two critical works: *Gwendolyn Brooks* and *Heroism in the New Black Poetry,* which won an American Book Award. Her *Country: An Organic Poem* was published in 1998 by Cross-Cultural Communications. Among works in progress: co-editing *RAWI Sampler,* an Arab American anthology.

Beatriz Santiago Muñoz is a videomaker, muralist, and writer currently living in Chicago.

Nkiru Nzegwu, artist, curator, and poet, is an Associate Professor in the Departments of Philosophy and Art History at Binghamton University. She has a number of publications in philosophy, feminist issues, and African, African-American and African-Canadian art. She has curated major shows on African art, Nigerian art, African-Canadian art, and an international exhibition of African and Diaspora art. Her works have been exhibited in Canada, Nigeria, and the United States.

Pat Parker was born in Houston, Texas, on January 20, 1944. In her writing, as in her life, she insisted on all her voices: Black, female, gay, mother of two adopted children, softball player and coach, medical administrator, lover of women. She died on June 17, 1989, of breast cancer.

Charles Peterson is a native of Gary, Indiana. At present, he is working on his Ph.D. in Philosophy at Binghamton University (but is looking for a way out of this). He is the co-editor of an upcoming anthology of poetry by black men entitled *Sons of Lovers.*

Adrienne Rich was born in Baltimore in 1929. She is the author of many books of poetry and prose, including *Time's Power, Blood, Bread and Poetry, A Wild Patience Has Taken Me This Far, On Lies, Secrets, and Silence, The Dream of a Common Language, Of Woman Born: Motherhood as Experience and Institution, An Atlas of the Difficult World,* and *What is Found There: Notebooks on Poetry and Politics.* She has received numerous awards for her work, including two Guggenheim Fellowships, the Fellowship of the Academy of American Poets, the Common Wealth Award in Literature, the

Lambda Book Award, and the Frost Silver Medal of the Poetry Society of America. She has lived in California since 1984.

Paula Ross, a former television news reporter and ongoing femme, decided at almost fifty to return to the groves of "the academy," in pursuit of digital knowledge, computer music composition, and other elements of the well-rounded multimedia practitioner. Currently living in a 1952 Palace trailer in Orange County, she expects to receive her M.F.A. in studio art in 1998, and a certificate in the Graduate Feminist Emphasis in 1999, from UC Irvine.

Carlos J. Serrano is the winner of numerous playwriting awards which include the Irwin Shaw Award in Playwriting, and the Ottillie Grabanier Award. He received his BFA in Playwriting at Brooklyn College, and is currently the Artistic Director of the theatre company he founded, *Vaso De Leche Productions*. His playwriting works include *Alter Ego, The Blues of Daisy Pena,* and the upcoming *Not Just Another Puerto Rican Love Story.* Carlos is also a play director and a poet, and will soon work on his first film script.

Chihambuane is a native of Tennessee, a graduate of Morehouse College, and an assistant professor of philosophy at the University of Kentucky.

David Williams is the author of *Traveling Mercies* (Alice James Books, 1993), a collection of poetry, and has recently completed a novel, *Coyote Wells.* His work is discussed at length in *Memory and Cultural Politics,* ed. Amritjit Singh, Richard Singh et al. (Northeastern University Press, 1996). All of his grandparents came from Lebanon, and many of his poems reflect Middle Eastern concerns as well as his work with Central American refugees.